RACHAEL LINDSAY

Rachael
Woman of the Night

KWELA BOOKS

This is a true story. However, to protect identities, names have been changed.

The author wishes to acknowledge that snippets of the following songs have been used in the novel:

"I Believe In Music", written by M. Davis and sung by Liza Minelli, on p.19; "Private Dancer", written by Mark Knopfler and sung by Tina Turner, on p.29; "What you get is what you see", written by T. Britten and G. Lyle and sung by Tina Turner, on p. 41; "Nah Neh Nah", written by D. Schoufs and D. Klein and sung by Vaya Con Dios, on p.126; "You Can Leave Your Hat On", written by Randy Newman and sung by Joe Cocker, on p.156; "Cabaret", written by F. Ebb and J. Kander and sung by Liza Minelli, on p.192; "Rose Garden", written by Joe South and sung by Lynn Anderson, on p.197; "Cleaning Windows", written and sung by Van Morrison, on p.199; "I Am . . . I Said", written and sung by Neil Diamond, on p. 201; "Three Little Birds", written and sung by Bob Marley, on p. 214; "You needed me", written by Andy Goodrum and sung by Lynn Anderson, on p. 227; "I Wanna Dance With Somebody (Who Loves Me)", written by D. Merrill and S. Rubicam and sung by Whitney Houston, on p. 235; "Another One Bites the Dust", written by John Deacon and sung by Queen, on p.239; "Hair", written by Gerome Ragni and James Rado and sung by the Cowsills, on p.240, and "Imagine", written and sung by John Lennon, on p.245.

Kwela Books
40 Heerengracht, Cape Town 8001;
P.O. Box 6525, Roggebaai 8012
kwela@kwela.com

Cover photograph by Fred Jeffrey.
Cover design and typography by Nazli Jacobs
Set in Berkeley
Printed and bound by Paarl Print
Oosterland Street, Paarl, South Africa

First edition, first printing 2003

ISBN 0-7957-0170-5

A Dedication in Two Parts

Firstly, to:
The girls. The ones I've known personally. And to the ones I don't know.
Oh, that my written voice could soften thy plight.
Alas, I am but a mere whisper for your cause,
Forever hopeful of positive changes in society to ease your road.
Simple gratitude, respect and admiration must remain, for now, my only
contentment.
I wish for you to soar one day, whole and free, with dignity – like the eagle.
May the Keeper of your inner sanctuary bestow upon you
The gentleness of true peace in our world.

And secondly, to:
Me, Margaret.
My own memoir of therapies.
For that part of me
Which will always be
Rachael.

Chapter One
The Birth of Rachael

$\mathcal{T}$he Adult Entertainment section of the Argus newspaper was crucial. It was the afternoon of the 25th of January 1996, and the end of the month was only six days away. Sitting in my car, pen in hand, I scanned the classified section, found the column – and yes, there it was. The typeface loomed before me; my heart pounded.

"New Agency – adult female staff required," the advert read, followed by the telephone number. Quick money was what I needed, and the ad implied exactly that.

I had a responsibility to the ones I loved and cared about. My son, eighteen-year-old Bert, had just started in his first job up-country at a meagre salary – he'd need my financial help till he was on his feet. There was my daughter Mary-Lou, turning fourteen in March and in her first year of high school, and Matthew, our eighteen-year-old live-in lodger-cum-friend. They all needed to be provided for.

Then there were our animals: my faithful two-year-old Yorkshire terrier named General, Bert's two-month-old Jack Russell puppy, christened Bart, and our two cats – Chocolate, an adult female tortoiseshell, and the pitch-black kitten, Petal Pie, that Mary-Lou had found entangled in fishing line in a drain on her way back from school one afternoon. Most definitely not least of the animals on this list was the love of Mary-Lou's life: her horse, Copper Band, whose farm stabling needed to be paid for. Copper needed regular weekly exercise, and should she require veterinary treatment for any ailment, I was responsible for meeting those costs as well.

It all added up – and I haven't even gotten to the rent part yet, due beginning of February! In a nutshell, providing adequately financially for my family was of paramount importance and I'd better come up with a plan to ease the immediate situation.

So I needed a job and fast, with a quick return financially. There was only one such avenue of work that I could think of. But of course, everything has a price – mothers often have to do whatever it takes, come up with a plan to get through life; and sometimes do things they don't want to do.

I was proposing to sell my body, for money, on a temporary basis.

I'd never done anything like this before. I felt confused, afraid; could I cope, what would I have to do? So many questions.

I really had no idea what was entailed in an "interview" of this kind. I had visions of being asked to undress and parade naked, feeling humiliated, being told my body wasn't good enough. Maybe they'd let me keep my bra and panties on . . . my imagination was running riot, conjuring up all sorts of vivid images, and my gut wasn't coping with the onslaught of adrenaline. I'm nervous by nature, and my stomach felt like a snake eating its own tail.

This particular advert had been in the local paper for more than a week. I felt more comfortable – if that's the word – approaching a new agency than an established one. Maybe there would be other girls as nervous and as green as myself.

Must be kind of like jumping off a high diving board, I thought – close your eyes, rush of fear, adrenaline pumping, the voice inside saying, *Do it, just do it.*

Apart from having my gut in a knot from fear and anxiety, I felt saddened at heart as well that I should have to finally resort to earning an income in this manner; that it all came down to this. It was a momentous decision for me, but I realised it was the only way to get by right now.

Memory took me back in an instant to my childhood years on the equator in Kenya, East Africa – my country of birth. Now I sat in my little Nissan LDV all these years later, virtually on the southern tip of Africa, making a decision of this magnitude. Had the time in between counted for nothing?

My father was a dairy and maize farmer. All four children – my older brother and sister, my younger brother and myself – were sent to boarding school in South Africa, only seeing our parents during the three-week June and six-week December holidays. After Kenya gained its independence in 1962, my parents moved to a coastal town, where the warm waters of the Indian Ocean gently lapped the shores. They settled there for several years, operating a deep-sea fishing business catering for tourists. Then they moved to Angola and successfully farmed tobacco – fleeing in 1975 with the last escorted convoy of refugees when the warring factions plundered the Angolan countryside and towns, looting and shooting up the banks.

By the grace of God, my family arrived safely in South West Africa (now Namibia). Borrowing fifty rand from a friend, my father started life over yet again, finding work within ten days as a manager on a cattle ranch in this very beautiful country known for its vast, varied and oftentimes harsh landscape, with the most incredible dust sunsets the eye can behold.

I arrived in Namibia around the end of 1975, after a thirsty and hungry three-day train journey from Rhodesia (now Zimbabwe), where I'd gone to secretarial college and then worked for a year. I now found employment in Windhoek and lived in a rented bachelor flat

My marriages, divorces and re-marriages would take myself and my two children, Bert and Mary-Lou, to various destinations to set up home over the coming years: the desolate beauty of the Namibian coast; the cold Orange

Free State winters made bearable by the promise of memorable crops of blazing yellow sunflowers; back to central and then northern Namibia; and then back again to the friendly and very hospitable Afrikaners of the Free State. From there it was on to the gently rolling mountainous landscape of the Transkei, interspersed with the strangely spectacular multi-colours of soil erosion; then the Eastern Cape; and lastly, the splendid green surroundings of Cape Town with her sentry of granite, Table Mountain.

After nineteen long years of rebuilding his life, ranching with the majestic breed of Brahman cattle in Namibia, my father died of cancer in his own bed on the farm north of Windhoek in October 1994 – three months before his deserved retirement and the much-longed-for "golden years" of fishing.

Life is so full of pain and hardship, I thought, sitting in my little car this January day, the newspaper in front of me. Is this what it comes down to? Is it really worth it?

But to be fair, happy memories flashed to mind as well, and I allowed myself the pleasure of a few minutes of indulgence in snatches of blissful life gone by.

Snorkelling on the coral reef of the beautiful Kenya coastline as a school-child on holiday; eating enormous, juicy, hairy mangoes in the surf; being lost in the banter and excitement of bidding in the smelly fish market; waiting for my Dad's boat to come into the bay, the sea sand, flecks of gold, sticking to my feet and legs. The best ice cream in the world – sweet and creamy on the tongue, the cool whirly whiteness dripping from the cone in the heat of the day onto my salty fingers. Ice-cold Pepsi-Cola, intriguing dried palm-frond shop-fronts with matching roofs . . . oh, and the Arab dhows drifting gently homewards on the ocean beneath cloudless heavens – a sight soothing enough to entrance one to dreamy afternoon sleep. Magnificent, vibrantly coloured bougainvillea creepers in all their colours – the dark and lighter pinks, the purplish-violet ones, the pastel peachier ones – and coconut palms, all against a backdrop of endless blue skies. The sweetest oranges despite their green skins, hot fresh-roasted cashew nuts in rolled newspaper cones on our ferry trips to the coastal port of Mombasa . . . even an encounter with a green mamba on occasion seemed exhilarating, even if it was scary at the same time. We once found a sleeping cobra coiled in the airing cupboard!

So yes, there were treasured memories of life past, memories that made me smile dreamily and instilled some sense of purpose, some reason to carry on.

It was a warm summer afternoon, one of those idyllic days the Cape is known for, with just a breath of wind caressing the defined edges of the long, straight back of Table Mountain – on this particular day, without her "table-cloth" of cloud.

I was parked outside the Post Office at the small shopping centre, the noon edition of the paper propped against the steering wheel. Leaning forward in melancholy thought, somewhat downhearted once more, I folded my arms over the steering wheel and stared through the windscreen; a vacant stare. The continuous bustle of life before me was quite unaware of my existence, my plight.

"And anyway," I thought out loud, "why should anyone out there be concerned about me or my troubles? The world has enough troubles of its own."

Yes, my mind answered quietly, many others have stories of daily hardship, of their own struggle for survival – mine wasn't necessarily any harder than anyone else's. But it was mine, and mine to attempt to rectify.

I could hear my father's voice in my mind: "Life isn't always fair, my girl, and often not kind, but the Good Lord helps those who help themselves. Right now, you've got a big problem, so I suggest you get off your arse and do something about it."

Never minced words, my dad, honest and to the point. Not a religious man, he called a spade a spade, but he was the kindest, most honourable and fair man I've ever known. My father's dedication to starting over several times in life for his family, his ability to always make a plan and his spirit of getting up and getting on again were firmly imprinted in my being. I'd never known him to back down from a worthwhile challenge – he was always up and about before the early light of a day, and in bed by eleven at night for his much-needed sleep. His immediate family always came first and he never shirked his responsibilities. Dad had been my rock in life. I still missed him so; still wore his thermal vests as T-shirts.

"I'm glad you're not here to see me become a woman of the night," I thought, and then added, "Okay, to be blunt – a prostitute." I struggled with that word, but I didn't know any other.

I immediately realised it was a stupid thought – I felt my father's unseen presence so often, I was sure he'd know what I was going to do.

Leaning back against the car seat, I lit a cigarette, the smoke wafting out of the window. Giving up smoking would save a few bob, I thought, but not enough – and I didn't think I had the will to quit smoking now, not at a time like this.

Anyway, Dad was right. While there's life there's hope; your responsibility is to support your family, be they human or animal. And even though this way goes against your grain, girl, shit happens. It's time to put your pride in your pocket; it's only temporary, anyway.

My mind-chatter bounced back at me immediately in reply: if Dad had still been here though, in real life, this probably wouldn't be happening at all. But he wasn't, was he? And whilst he wouldn't necessarily like what I was going to do, I couldn't think of any other way to solve my problems.

Despite my anxiety I had to smile. Yes, my father may not have endorsed

10

what his youngest surviving child was about to do (my older brother was still living in Namibia, but my little brother, Alex, died at the age of eighteen after a motorbike accident, and my older sister, Meg, died of cancer at the age of thirty-five), but Dad had a fine sense of humour. To soften the blow to my pride, I could almost hear him say, "Bit old for a tart, don't you think?"

Perhaps, I thought whimsically, but I'll give it my best shot. You're never too old to learn something new. A perfect mother and person I most surely wasn't, but I'd always do the best I could to feed and care for my children.

At midnight it would be the 26th of January, the start of my thirty-eighth birthday, and the start of a period in my life as a female escort – a term I would soon learn and much prefer. Life certainly takes one on strange journeys, I thought. Hopefully, this side-road wouldn't last for too long!

Time was of the essence though, and I had a rather important and unnerving telephone call to make. "Better get going before you lose courage," I thought, and tore the ad from the newspaper, folded and put it in my purse. The rest of the unread noon edition I trashed in the pavement bin. Then I drove the five-minute trip back home in a state of increasing unease.

General met me at the front door of our home. It didn't matter whether I was gone for five minutes or five hours, his welcome was always the same: a joyous, jumping affair with barks and licks galore, after which he'd dash off to check if Petal Pie and Bart were okay. Both babies were orphaned – well, it seemed that way to General – and I found it most admirable how he took the responsibility upon himself, despite being a male dog, of caring for them: cleaning both kitten and pup, licking their coats all over, their eyes and even their nether regions, then patiently teaching them to walk through the kitchen and out onto the back lawn to do their business.

Chocolate the cat, on the other hand, took little notice of Petal Pie and even less of Bart the pup. She was by nature one of those exceptionally aloof cats: very loveable, but only when she wanted affection; more concerned with immaculately grooming her thick and beautiful fur whilst watching the family comings and goings from her perch in the sunshine on the window sill.

Opening the front door to our home and seeing my children and animals, our little family – sensing their trust and need for my support – reaffirmed my decision to try my best to provide for them, by whatever means. They were worth it. I'd make the call.

As luck would have it, Mary-Lou and Matthew said they were taking a walk to the shop, an excursion which usually took a while for these two youngsters. This gave me time to phone the agency. Teenage ears have an amazing ability to become stone deaf to requests to tidy a bedroom or help wash dishes, but a phone call of this nature would render them capable of perfect hearing, regardless of portable radio and television being on at the same time!

This was going to be worse than phoning a normal employment agency. But look on the bright side, I thought, perhaps this agency didn't practise affirmative action! Maybe they wouldn't mind about my age, maybe they would. There was only one way to find out.

Whilst boiling the kettle for a much-needed coffee, I gratefully swallowed a pink three-milligram Brozam tablet to calm the rising panic in my throat and the pounding of my heart. Then, mug of coffee in hand, and feeling much calmer for the tranquilliser, I walked to my desk – a fold-up camping table in the dining room – sat down on my old brown typing chair, lit a smoke and took the stashed advert out of my purse.

It wouldn't be just one phone call I'd need to make, but three – the first to the agency, another to my son Bert, and a further one to my boyfriend, James. And after that? Well, I'd then have to tell Mary-Lou and Matthew.

Bert had passed his final year of schooling in December 1995, with a university exemption – I'd been euphoric! He'd had to work exceptionally hard to obtain those outstanding results, for Bert was more a sportsman by nature than a bookworm. My little boy had over the years grown into a strapping young man of six foot three – handsome, responsible and eager to get out into the big world.

Now Bert had flown the nest, starting his journey through adult life. I missed him terribly, and was naturally concerned as he ventured out for the first time into the working world. Especially I missed the magic of Bert's deep, gut laugh, and his solid optimism.

From a young age, Bert had taken it upon himself to be the "man" in our family, always protective of Mary-Lou and myself. His father and I had divorced in 1979, and the child went through many years of pain caused by Jack not showing any interest in him whatsoever, forgetting his son's birthdays as well as Christmases.

Bert naturally turned to and found his father figure in his grandfather. They spent many hours together over the years, Bert happily sharing his grandfather's love of fishing and the outdoors. With pride I can say that Bert has grown to be the same fair and courageous man my father was, with the same essentially soft heart and fine sense of humour. I remain always grateful for this gift, my dearest little friend who grew into my dearest big friend; I could not make a decision to do escorting work without phoning the anchor in my life, my son, to let him know.

Despite having swallowed the tranquilliser, I still felt hesitant to dial the number. A decision such as this wasn't to be taken lightly – so to remind myself of why I was proposing to sell my body, my mind flitted through the folder of pertinent facts regarding my present dire financial predicament.

Taking Mary-Lou to her beloved horse, Copper Band, twice every weekend was a one-hundred-and-seventy-kilometre round trip. She'd ride, practise jumping and then groom Copper Band before we went home again. I'd sold my washing machine in 1993 and bought the horse for my daughter with the money.

Sometimes Mary-Lou entered horse shows, which entailed having Copper trucked to the show grounds on the day of the equestrian event. The horse still needed plenty of training as she often shied away from the jumps, but Mary-Lou wasn't one to give up, and the effort had proved worthwhile so far. Horse and rider had received various rosettes for their committed partnership on these occasions, and I stood waving and clapping from the ringside ropes as proud as punch as my beautiful young daughter with her neatly plaited ponytail graciously accepted her prize, and patted Copper lovingly and deservedly on her graceful neck. Owning a horse was a big responsibility – and trying to sell her at short notice was well nigh impossible and not an option for the moment anyway. I didn't want to break Mary-Lou's heart. If I could find some other way of keeping up with Copper's expenses on a temporary basis till things came right again, then that's what I'd do. I just had to keep abreast of the stabling costs for this rather enormous, but very beautiful, loved and dependent animal.

Matthew wasn't my own child, though I felt he was. A friend of Mary-Lou's, he'd been living with us permanently since about September 1995. Matthew visited often, and it wasn't long before his overnight stays in our home progressed to permanent residence.

It's really a very simple story. Having noticed Matthew was more in our home than in his own (which was in the same suburb), I sensed something was amiss. I then invited his mother for coffee – to one of the local cafes to discuss her son's welfare on neutral ground. In short, she said Matthew didn't get on with her new husband and that her marriage was very important to her; seeing as Matthew had now finished school he should make his own way in life, and she didn't want him back to live in their house – full stop.

Concerned about the financial burden I faced with another family member to support, I enquired whether she was able to contribute anything towards Matthew's keep. I received another simple explanation: she kept the maintenance money Matthew's father sent her each month, she said in a matter-of-fact tone of voice, "because he owes me a lot of money." I then pointed out that it was difficult for school-leaving children to find work. Her answers remained the same. Strange attitude she had, I thought, even more strange for a born-again Christian – not the slightest bit fazed, pained or conscience-pricked.

After a while, I simply quit – the youngster could stay with us, we'd just have to cope. I'd try to help him find a job. And that's what there is to tell about how Matthew became part of our family.

I myself had not received any financial assistance from Mary-Lou's father, Terry, since his death in 1992 from a car accident. Bert's father, Jack, had passed away in May 1995 of multiple organ failure, not helped by years of drinking – I'd had to make do without any maintenance from him.

That was it as far as maintenance from my two children's fathers went. There simply wasn't any, not a cent.

Last though definitely not least on my list of reasons for such dire financial circumstances was Sam – the agent who paid me my commissions on sales I made marketing investment products. Sam owned his own company on the foreshore in Cape Town. I'd started working for him in early January 1995, having experience in this particular line of business from my previous marriage.

My initial sales employment package with Sam had been very simple: one thousand rand per month basic salary, the rest of my income derived from commission on any sales I made, split with Sam. As employment was scarce at the time, I was initially delighted to have the sales position. However, about three months later, Sam suddenly announced that he'd declared himself bankrupt!

"So that my ex-wife can't get any more maintenance out of me," was his simple, toneless answer to my startled questions.

"The accountants have got it all sorted, and the lawyer," Sam assured me unconcernedly, scratching his ear with a pencil as I sat across the desk from him in his office. "Everything goes on exactly the same, only difference is that the ex can't get to the bucks now. You fret too much, Margaret, I'll let you know if and when things get worrying."

Things got worrying pretty much from the end of that month; I battled to get my basic one thousand rand out of Sam, let alone any commissions owing to me. This wore me down and left me severely depressed, to the point of feeling almost suicidal on occasion. Sam had two other women working for him at the time doing administrative and secretarial work, and their lives were also continuously, considerably stressed by their employer's inability to pay their monthly salaries by due date. Grace became a very close and dear friend. But there weren't other jobs to be had, so we just had to grin and bear it, and hope it would come right.

Out of the blue in October 1995, Sam called me into his office, told me he couldn't afford my basic pay any longer, handed me my last one thousand rand and told me to work from home. It would save on office expenses, he explained; I could carry on with the same work, transactions would continue to be done through his company and he'd still pay me my commissions.

There's not much one can do in a position like this, except work from home full-time and try to make as many sales as one can. And I was doing okay, although not marvellously by any means; I was still battling each

14

month to get my commissions out of Sam. It was a struggle, but I was hanging in there.

Until now, that is.

My end-of-month January commissions were due to be paid to me by Sam, but on checking with his secretary, she informed me that although the monies had indeed been paid to Sam's company from the various firms which we represented, Sam had unfortunately transferred the funds into his private account and gone on a much-needed holiday! He was not expected back at the office for three weeks at the least, and she had no authority or signing powers to rectify the situation until his return. It was a situation of like it or lump it for me – whilst Sam holidayed happily, probably sunning himself on far-away Palm Beach!

I felt pretty helpless and as mad as a snake in a pit. He'd done this once before, using my commissions to have his father's car fixed. I felt I could've punched dear Sam one on the chops if I'd seen him just then – but that wouldn't have helped matters either. The three thousand rand commission I was rightfully owed would've seen my little family through February – bills paid, children and animals fed; but it was not to be.

The flip-file of reasons why I was about to take up escorting ended there: no support for my children from their fathers, no income, and no additional savings of any kind – any I may have had having been slowly and surely surrendered over the years of financial struggle to support my little family.

Well, it's time to start on those telephone calls, I thought – can't put it off forever. I lifted the receiver and dialled the number. The lady on the other end of the line answered in a friendly manner, and I said a silent thank-you for her understanding.

"Good afternoon, my name's Margaret. I'm phoning in connection with your advert in the paper for staff," I said, in one long breath.

"Have you done this kind of work before?" she asked carefully.

"No, I haven't."

"Firstly, do you realise that you have to have sex with these men, if required, in return for the payment of the fee charged?" she responded, leaving no room for later argument or feigned misunderstanding on my part.

"Yes," I said after a pause, and cleared my throat self-consciously.

The reality of it now hit my guts like a stone plummeting down a well, and I pressed my free arm against my stomach as I felt the inner churnings of unease.

"Okay, come in this evening, Margaret," she advised. "The manager will be here any time after eight, and you can have a chat with him. Come prepared – you never know in this business. You'll need a change of clean underwear and – um, I suggest you bring some vaginal lubricant with you, KY's the best, you'll find it at any pharmacy." She paused a moment. "Okay with that?"

"Will you be there tonight?" I replied, trying not to sound too anxious.

"I'm working the day shift this week," she answered. "Tammy will be here this evening, she's on desk nights at the moment."

"What do I tell her when I get there?" I asked worriedly, rubbing my forehead, remembering how my mother would tell me not to frown so much because it gave me lines on my face.

"Tammy's been in the business a long time," she replied reassuringly. "Don't worry, she's very nice. I'll let her know to expect a first-timer, okay?"

"Okay, and thanks for your help and advice," I said. "How do I find the place?"

She gave me directions, which I scribbled on a piece of notepaper.

"By the way, Margaret," she added, "my name's Amy, and thanks for replying to the advert. Good luck, bye for now."

"Bye."

I replaced the receiver, my stomach in a knot despite the Brozam, and studied my scribbled notes. Well, she hadn't asked my age; I wasn't sure whether to be glad about that or not. And she hadn't mentioned anything about what to wear, or condoms. Or any kind of credentials for that matter!

Credentials – goodness gracious, the thought hit me, did one need any for paid sex with unknown men?

And what about HIV or HIV tests – would they want to know about that perhaps? It seemed hugely important to me if you were going to be doing work of this nature. Perhaps the manager would get to those details later.

I'd had an HIV test a couple of months previously, which was negative. This I've done as a matter of course every year or so since 1984, when I'd been hospitalised due to bleeding through the stomach, which all started from having my wisdom teeth removed – in hindsight, I think I should've kept the teeth and the only natural wisdom I ever had! Over a two-week period, the swelling to my face and neck from this procedure became quite grotesque. My stomach couldn't cope with the enormous amounts of anti-inflammatories and painkillers prescribed and I started bleeding internally, landing up receiving four pints of blood – for which I remain most grateful. Shortly thereafter the big Aids shock came to the world, and blood for transfusions had to be tested.

Me, being a worrier, became neurotic about it – you heard so many different stories – so I'd have the tests done for peace of mind. Just as well, I thought; in the "adult entertainment" business the boss might even want written proof that you weren't HIV-positive.

I'd better make a trip to the pharmacy, I thought, for that lubricant. On second thoughts, I'd better get some condoms as well – being more sorry than safe wasn't an option. I'd go to the local shopping centre after my next phone call, to James.

James was almost twenty years my senior, fifty-seven, and lived in Diep River, about forty minutes' drive from our home in Bothasig. We'd been going steady for eleven months.

I'd met him at a party one evening after I'd started working for Sam. Quite by coincidence, we were both in the same line of work, representing some of the same companies.

James had also had a bad time financially. At his age he'd had to start his business from scratch a little over a year before, also working from home, due to an unsuccessful trip to the States. He'd fervently hoped to get a work permit in the great land of opportunity and thereafter a permanent job, but plans had fallen through and his savings had dwindled, so he returned to the sunshine and greenness of the Cape to start over again.

James and I had discussed our finances in detail on numerous occasions. His business wasn't building as fast as he'd hoped, and his income wasn't sufficient to help me on a regular basis as well, much as he'd have liked to – so the topic of a "second income" for me had arisen. Neither of us liked the idea, but the possibility was certainly there that I might have to turn to escorting in the future. James is British, broad-minded, and naturally imbued with the fine and acute English sense of humour.

"If that time ever comes," he'd said, "at least you still have a good body, for your age!"

Still, would either of us be able to cope with the complex emotions that would undoubtedly enter our relationship as a result?

"Well," he'd pondered, "I guess we'll just have to cope. It's not as though you'd be doing it because it was something you liked – that I couldn't cope with. But out of necessity, yes, I'll cope."

James was also having a traumatic time in January 1996, dealing with the unnecessary and tragic death of his only child – whom we since always endearingly referred to as "Squire". On an outing together, Squire had died within minutes from severe internal injuries in front of James's eyes: a wall had collapsed on him, pulverising his heart and lungs as well as other internal organs. Legal proceedings were under way. Apart from the enormous and unimaginable shock to James of such a trauma, still so new in his heart and mind, he also possibly faced some hefty legal bills in the future.

Phoning James, I explained about Sam and told him the time had come for our contingency plan, and that I'd be commencing work that night. The gentle understanding James had shown in our previous discussions did not change, and I was grateful for his emotional support. However, he was understandably also anxious to hear I was to begin work "in the racket", and made me promise to phone him before I left home, when I arrived at the agency, before I left work and again when I'd returned home – no matter what time of the morning. I promised.

And last there was Bert. He was fine, working hard, learning plenty about ostriches on the farm where he was employed, and seemed happy and enthusiastic about his new adventure in life. First I gave him the run-down on the family and his pup, Bart; then I explained our precarious financial situation, and the work I was going to do to ease matters.

"Ouch, Mum," he said with concern. "You'll be careful, won't you?"

"Yeah, I'm sure I'll be fine," I said. "My biggest worry at the moment, though, is getting the condom part right – I'm a bit out of practice."

Making light of matters eased Bert's protective anxiety, and he laughed somewhat disbelievingly on the other end of the line – not about the condoms, but at the enormity of my proposal. Could I really be going to do such a thing for money? His mother! Bert knew I'd always done the best I could, but he'd never imagined my fertile imagination capable of resorting to a game plan like this!

"Okay, my boy," I said. "I love you lots, thanks for being there for me. I'll phone again soon and keep you updated on the news. Bye, Bert."

"Bye."

And so were the wheels set in motion on the 25th of January 1996 for the time in my life when I would come to be known amongst the girls as "Rachael."

It was my first step into another world, one I'd disapproved of before, and it was to be a good lesson for me. A lesson not to judge others too harshly – not until you've experienced their predicament yourself; for only when you've worn the shoe will you know where it pinches! My experiences would dramatically and forever change my views, instilled in me throughout my life by society in general. Instead, I would become enriched with a broader and better understanding and compassion, admiration and yes, respect for the women I worked with – and come to cherish the soothing caress of shared laughter.

But at the same time, the change to "Rachael" would also add a new and lasting dimension to what I, until then, understood as the sadness of the soul.

Chapter Two
Rachael Gets Going

There were preparations to make for the evening.

First of all, a change in attitude was required. If I continued dwelling on all my woes, down to the finest detail, on each and every aspect of my dire predicament, I might as well opt for digging a six-foot hole for myself in the back garden instead! Hearing Bert's laugh again on the other end of the phone had been a pick-me-up – even if it was a bit of a worried laugh, compared to his normal infectious gut laugh.

General lay at my feet as I sat at my desk. Music has always played an enormous role in my life, and music was what was needed right now. A good sing-a-long did wonders for curing my sometimes melancholy moods. Mary-Lou and Matthew weren't back from the shops yet, so I could do my personal rendition of Liza Minelli's "I Believe In Music", to the best of my ability. No interruptions and no need to feel self-conscious when I added my own trumpet parps to the recorded ones, with my most loyal fan and supporter, General, to encourage me – and tolerate my lively singing and antics. He'd perk up and behave as any good audience should at "mike time", his short, stumpy tail wagging like mad as I launched into my private show. The imaginary audience would swoon and scream at my strong, husky, voice – and General, my four-legged friend, would contribute significantly to the showbiz atmosphere in our sitting room with his intermittent enthusiastic barks. Sometimes I'd sweep him up in my arms – most accommodating General was, and patient in this regard, perched on my left hip, his one front paw in my right hand. We'd dance together – his keen sense of hearing no doubt impaired by my hearty off-tone vocals – after which I'd put him down once more on the carpet, and he'd retire in some relief, resuming a canine posture more befitting a Yorkshire terrier.

"Right, General," I said, "get ready, my boy. We've got to brighten up the mood around here a bit."

General's soft brown eyes followed me as I crossed the lounge to my old Blaupunkt hi-fi, which, with a separate CD player, sat on a shelf of the ornately hand-carved wooden wall unit I'd bought in Northern Namibia; the music centre I'd bought in 1989 with some money my godmother sent me from England. Perhaps outdated by now, but with two tall, two-way speakers of exceptional quality, this hi-fi has proved to be the single most pleasurable item of material value I've ever owned. Hours and hours of enjoyment I've had from this treasured gift – actually, I'd call it a blessing.

I put the CD in the player and turned up the volume on the amp – which sometimes did the crackle and pop routine for a few seconds – and braced myself, imaginary microphone in hand, as the opening bars played through the speakers. General's little stumpy tail wagged excitedly, and the look on his face said it all: "Here we go!"

"Music is the universal language, and love, love is the key
To brotherhood and peace and understanding
And living in harmony
So take your brother by the hand, and sing along with me
I believe in music, I believe in love . . ."

I was as usual pretty whacked after this number, and plonked down in one of the round cane lounge chairs to catch my breath again. Satchmo's "Mack The Knife" was another good song to unleash my vocal talents to, with plenty of wonderful trumpet parps. I'm pretty good at whistling to music as well – a talent I acquired in my first year of high school as punishment for whistling in the hostel corridor. The matron felt I'd refrain from this form of unladylike behaviour if I was made to stand in the corner at the end of the passage, where everyone could see me, and whistle loudly and continuously for several hours on end. She'd pop her head out of her office door at the slightest pause in my punishment and say in a firm and unnecessarily loud voice, "Whistle!" I refrained from this form of musical expression in the hostel corridors after that, but this now much improved talent I put to good use at every opportunity when I felt I wouldn't be caught – and my whistling has continued robustly ever since!

General hopped up onto the chair and lay down next to me now that the hearty sing a-long was over; the volume was turned down once more to provide soothing background music for my more relaxed thoughts in his gentle canine company.

The sex aspect of my new job loomed ahead of me, and I wondered if anything else I'd done in my life would be of help. I mean, if I wasn't too good at the sex stuff, perhaps I could talk about fishing – I knew a bit about tackle and bait, breaking strain of fishing line, rods and reels; not a lot, but it'd help with conversation. A bit about cars as well: head gaskets, dirt in carburettors, fan belts, distributor caps, radiator leaks – though I still couldn't change a wheel. And my secretarial experience in various fields of business could perhaps provide some gap-fillers – mining, a bit about legal matters, the food service industry, deep-sea trawling . . . I could possibly even throw in snatches about my job as an assistant buyer in the Free State, where I was responsible for ordering aviation fuel, and spares for Mercedes Benz Trucks, bulldozers and front-end loaders.

I could waffle a bit about sport in general as well – boxing I'd always taken an interest in, though I wasn't too clued up on the rules of soccer or rugby. Well, that didn't seem too daunting really – our Bokke had after all won the 1995 Rugby World Cup, and I'd still get the goose-bumps remembering the excitement of watching that first and the final game: our boys in their green and gold, Madiba's delight and beaming pride as he sported his number six jersey.

So, yes, I could make conversation if I had to, but success would logically depend largely on the sexual aspects of my life, wouldn't it?

Was reaching orgasm going to be of any importance? I'd accomplished this often in my life and had actually grown to consider it the right of a woman – having masturbated from my teens into my twenties whilst keeping an intense one-eyed vigil in the darkness for any impending plagues or devils, still waking up with all my fingers and both hands intact! I still partook of this most pleasurable indulgence on occasion – now utterly minus worries of doom. Plus, I'd eventually found the total sexual fulfilment I'd yearned for as a woman, and now enjoyed the best sex I'd ever had, all due to the last eleven months of James's caring, persistent and persuasive affections.

So was this sufficient experience to prepare me for sex with unknown men in exchange for money? Cripes – did this make me a condom fundi? No, in fact, I was totally out of practice with "French letters" – as condoms were known in earlier days.

"From a male point of view, it's like showering in your mackintosh," James had laughed, when we'd spoken about precautions early in our relationship, "or paddling with your Wellington boots on!"

James and I felt it was safe to have sex without a condom. I hadn't had any other lovers since my last marriage, I'd been faithful to my husband during my marriage, and I was also faithful to James. He had been in a long-term relationship prior to becoming involved with me and I had met the woman concerned. James, at fifty-seven years of age, clearly understood the dangers involved in sleeping around. Besides, he believed in the trusty old method of male masturbation "with Mrs Palmer and her five daughters" – which was totally safe, relieved an uncomfortable, aching scrotum without any reason for worry, and didn't cost an expensive dinner or a bunch of flowers either!

Being unused to condoms was bothering me a bit though – perhaps I'd make a mess of putting the thing on the client's penis, and feel terribly embarrassed. Or perhaps I wouldn't get it on properly, all the way down, and it'd sort of dangle too much at the end and quite possibly come off when we were doing the sex stuff.

Well, I'd just have to cope. Perhaps one of the ladies at the agency could show me how to put the condom on – Amy had been friendly on the telephone, and she'd said Tammy had been in the business a while; perhaps she could help me. It'd just have to do for the moment – if I got the job that is, I thought, and scratched General's head.

Bottom line, Rachael still had some preparations to make before the evening – so I'd better get going or I wouldn't be going anywhere.

Firstly, a trip was required post-haste to the local retailer, who would stock such paraphernalia as to equip Mother with the basic tools of the trade. I'd take General with me; he loved going in the car, and I'd give him a run in the park on the way. After that, I'd come home and take a little quiet time, peace time, reflection time – before the task of informing Mary-Lou and Matthew.

As it turned out, the two youngsters shuffled through the front door at that moment, somewhat de-energised and sweaty from the afternoon heat, and plonked themselves down in the lounge. Matthew sprawled out on the carpet, and Mary-Lou leaned back in my old typing chair, looking as though she needed life support. The plastic shopping packet dangled from her hand as she sucked absent-mindedly on some enormous round sweet, which went from one cheek to the other in turn, and rendered any form of normal conversation virtually impossible. I said I was taking General for a walk in the park, and asked them to stay home and look after the house while I was out – I wouldn't be gone for long. The two exhausted teenagers gave me a nod and an uninterested, simultaneous "Okay" in acknowledgement, and I left them to recover from their afternoon exertions. I called General, who, understanding perfectly the meaning of the words "car" and "walk", reckoned Mary-Lou and Matthew could take care of the kitten and the pup while he was out. Pa Dog – off-duty for the moment – bounced outside to the LDV with me and perched himself happily on the passenger seat, filled with great expectations of his walk to come.

First stop was the park, of course. General had a wonderful time – his energy was almost inexhaustible as he ran and ran, stopping for a quick pee on every bush, rushing off to meet other canine friends and then rushing back to check on me, just to make sure I was safe. On neutral ground, General was not a biter or fighter, and would rush up to each and every dog to say hello. Sometimes, he'd underestimate the friendliness of a large dog, and my heart would be in my throat as he beat a hasty retreat. Run time over, he'd flop on the passenger seat, tongue hanging out the corner of his mouth, panting from happiness, excitement and exhaustion. I adored this little chap. Tired as he was, he remained alert and would watch the car while I did my shopping. I parked in the shade of a tree at the shopping centre, told General to stay, left the car windows sufficiently open for him, and crossed the road to the pharmacy.

Embarrassed, I quietly declined the kindly help offered by the pharmacy assistant and found the aisle stocking the necessary items myself. The selection of condoms was amazing. I most certainly didn't want ribbed or fluorescent. Or strawberry flavour – I really had no intention of eating these things! One particular brand was called "Roosters". Goodness, what a name, I thought – hope the things that would fill them wouldn't crow! Well, I eventually decided on two packs of Roosters – with a brand name like that, I felt sure they were tried and tested – and another packet of cheaper condoms for practise purposes. That'd just have to do for now – then I remembered Amy's advice about a vaginal lubricant and added a tube of KY Jelly. Considerable thought went into the choice of a body lotion that wasn't too scented; maybe I'd have to give a massage. Everything right now was a "maybe", but Mother had to be prepared as much as possible for the inevitable. I hid the pharmacy package behind the car seat, and sat for a few minutes with General before driving back home.

Yes, I love animals and yes, they're considered part of my family. Some people don't like animals – each to his own. General was special. Although he couldn't speak, you could have a complete conversation with him. He paid attention and his gentle brown eyes would study your face intently as you spoke, his head turning from one side to the other, as though considering carefully what you were telling him. During the conversation he'd give either one or two barks – being a yes or a no – sometimes in the right places; and sometimes he wouldn't get it right at all and bark too much, and all at the wrong time. But it didn't matter; he was a good and attentive listener, and I could tell him anything. Yes, I talk to my animals. I also talk to my plants – they seem to like it as they grow like mad, and they love music. I even talk to myself. Call me cuckoos if you like, but that's me.

So, as I stroked his head, I felt I owed him an explanation as to why I wouldn't be at home during the nights anymore – if I got the job – because he always slept at my side. Little Bart, Bert's pup, would burrow under the duvet or chew my ears while I tried to sleep, but General always slept the night through with me, at my side, making sure I was safe. I knew his nervous nature wouldn't allow him a wink of sleep with me gone all night – especially after he'd had an exhausting day looking after Petal and Bart, and needed some well-earned shut-eye. I knew he'd lie, exhausted as he was, at the front door all night, waiting till I got home.

"So, General," I said, twiddling his ear, "with Bert gone now, and me away all night, and Mary-Lou and Matthew sleeping, I need you to take care of the family. Okay?" He silently watched my face. "I know you'll lie and wait for me all night at the front door, but try not to worry. I'll come home in the morning again and we can have our sleep together then. Okay?" He put his front paw on my hand reassuringly. "We'd better get home now – still some things to do," I said.

I got two enthusiastic barks as I started the engine, then drove home, General peering intently through the windscreen, his front feet on the dashboard. On the way a thought popped into my mind: Bert had mentioned my safety. What about some sort of protection? Some sort of, well, you know – weapon. And one that was easily accessible at that!

"Got it," I said to General with relief, and gave him a pat on the back. "For now, my steel nail file will do – it fits perfectly in my handbag."

Preparations were, indeed, coming together.

General rushed to the water bowl for a quick drink when we arrived back home, and then dashed off to check on his paternal responsibilities. I made a cup of coffee, poured myself a glass of "happy box" red wine, and sat down at my desk again, on my old brown typing chair. Quiet reflection time was what I needed now, before the task of telling Mary-Lou and Matthew of my evening excursion. I lit a cigarette and studied our little home.

The dining room and lounge were L-shaped with green fitted carpets. The lounge furniture was sparse, comprising two large and deep round cane chairs with big chunky cushions in pretty pastels – some of the buttons missing. They always looked cosy and welcoming to a tired body, and were marvellous to curl up in. The square glass and chrome coffee table came from my first marriage and was older than my son, Bert. Two cardboard boxes covered with a green sheet served as a table for the second-hand answering machine. Then there were my pot plants, which I loved – two ferns and two others I'd had for years, the correct names of which I still didn't know! I didn't like TV, especially not in the lounge, and had given my big colour set to my girlfriend, Marjorie – though my kids had their own small black and white sets in their rooms. The dining room was used as my office: my desk was a fold-up camping table. There were two pine bookcases for my files, as well as the dark-stained wooden tea trolley my father had made for my birthday many years before. His hands were never idle – even after a long day's physical farm work, rising at four or five in the morning; his leisure-time included hobbies such as carpentry and fixing up old cars, which he'd later re-spray to perfection. So my tea trolley, crafted by his hands, remains very special to me – a gift I would never part with.

Despite the sparse furnishings, I found the surroundings of our humble abode to be pleasant to the eye, welcoming, cosy and homely. After all, home is where the heart is! Off-white, full-length curtains borrowed from a friend completed the scenario – and of course, my treasured music collection.

Music complimented my moods – it could energise the body when I was in a happy mood, or in melancholy times it could gently soothe the sadness until the spirit lifted. There seems to be music for all occasions and I associate many times of my life with certain songs.

Sometimes over a weekend I'd pull out my long-playing records, many of which had belonged to my father and after his death had been passed on to me. I'd spend hours and hours playing old numbers. I was brought up on the music of Jim Reeves – who could forget his "Distant Drums"? Other musical memories from my childhood were Bing Crosby, Bert Kaempfert's "Swingin' Safari", "The Sound Of Music" with Julie Andrews, and my dad's absolute favourite singer, Engelbert Humperdinck.

These record-playing sessions would bring back floods of memories and alternating tears and giggles. For some reason I liked to lie on my back on the floor, upside down as it were – meaning I didn't face the speakers, they were behind my head. Sounded better that way! Sometimes I'd conduct the orchestral music with great gusto trying to get the soft parts right with gentle movements of the arms and hands, but no matter how many times I performed this ritual, the clash of the cymbals would still catch me off guard. At other times I'd dance around the lounge imagining I could have been a ballerina, remembering the old gramophone on the front farm lawn in Kenya when I was about six, me in my pretty pink flared party dress made by my mother. She used to say I had the sweetest voice, and in those days before shyness and self-consciousness set in I would happily dance my version of Swan Lake for her. I still have an old sepia photo of this free-dancing child – and wonder where she went.

General would lie on the carpet, salt and pepper head resting on his outstretched paws, his fringe shading the gentle attentive brown eyes, as he patiently endured another of my musical repertoires. After one of these record playing sessions I always felt happy, relaxed and at peace.

I could reflect forever I suppose, I thought, trying to put off the inevitable discussion that now had to take place with Mary-Lou and Matthew. I needed another tranquilliser to calm me first though – I really didn't know how they'd take my revelation – and swallowed the little tablet in one grateful gulp.

It would be going on five years now that I'd been taking tranquillisers – since about three weeks after my sister Meg's death in my arms in June 1991. She'd been diagnosed with cervical cancer three years prior to that; by that stage the cancer was already in her lymph glands, and it was too late. It spread rapidly and aggressively despite all medical efforts, and Meg died five days before her thirty-sixth birthday in a Cape Town hospital. About three weeks later I started experiencing terrifying and utterly debilitating panic attacks – anywhere, any time and for completely unknown reasons – and sought medical help. The little tablets worked fast to calm my pounding heart, racing mind, sweating, damp palms and severe anxiety, and I'd been taking them ever since.

Throughout our lives, and particularly as a single parent, I have always been honest with my children. They were always consulted and informed of our financial position. This would seem to some an unreasonable burden for any child to bear. More often though I found that they appreciated the openness, understood far better when things were tight, and with their consideration contributed significantly to our getting through life. We had many hard times, but the fun and funny times, not to mention our closeness and love, more than compensated. Some of the best times we ever had were when we were really battling financially. Not only were we open about finances, but about every other topic imaginable – including any aspect of sex that puzzled or interested them, and believe me, there were plenty!

I wasn't prepared to start lying to my children now. Lies just snowball. And I've always been of the opinion that you cope or understand better when you know what you're up against, as opposed to dealing with lies, deceptions and the dark abyss of worry – when your gut tells you something's going on, but you can't put your finger on it. Besides, how else would I explain why I'd be gone every night, maybe till morning light, until finances improved? Better to hear from their mother what she was going to be doing, than hear it from someone else.

The discussion between the three of us was held sitting on the bed in Mary-Lou's bedroom. General was, of course, present for this family tête-à-tête – brown eyes attentive, ears pricked up, head going from side to side as he followed the proceedings.

At first, the look on the two young faces before me said, "Oh, no! Not one of her lectures again – what've we done now?"

There aren't too many ways to break this kind of news – except to break it. Reaction was a couple of seconds of disbelieving silence, followed by Mary-Lou and Matthew rolling around on the bed with laughter, going "You?" with their fingers pointing in my direction, and then collapsing into hysterics again. The look on my face, however, confirmed the revelation to indeed be fact. Whereupon the two teenagers found the wisdom beyond their years to realise Mother needed some moral support right now and perhaps some tenderness, regained their composure and sat up.

"You're serious about this, aren't you, Mum?" Mary-Lou said, trying to keep a straight face, an inkling of suspicion in her eyes.

"Yes," I answered simply. Matthew remained silent.

"So I've got a bit of preparing to do for tonight – bath, etc. Perhaps you two could help me choose something suitable to wear," I said.

"No problem, Mum," Mary-Lou answered, after a short, deafening silence.

Matthew nodded in feigned solemn agreement – a slow smile creeping helplessly onto his face after a few seconds.

I'm sure it was a shock to both youngsters – that Mother, who would be turning thirty-eight at the stroke of midnight on the twenty-sixth of January, was proposing to do such work. I could understand that they found it funny too. Natural disbelief – until reality sets in.

"We'll give General and Bart their dinner, and feed the cats," Matthew said considerately, "and I'll make fried eggs on toast with baked beans for Mary-Lou and myself, while you get ready."

"Yuck," retorted Mary-Lou, "you don't make nice fried eggs."

"Oh yes, I do!" Matthew answered, somewhat indignantly. "They turn out just fine in your Mum's little frying pan."

The dreaded discussion over, I soaked in the bath, shaved legs and underarms, washed my hair, scrubbed toenails and then polished toenails – soft peach colour. I certainly didn't want to attract attention to my feet with dark nail polish: my big toe was exactly that, a big toe, rather like a paddle; my father always said that was the reason I was such a good swimmer! While I bathed, Matthew, of his own accord, made a box of sandwiches for me.

Matthew was a good kid and he'd had a tough time the last few months. He'd had an accident on his motorbike and fractured his ankle, and would be on crutches for some weeks, his leg now in plaster of Paris up to the knee. Matthew had understandably been somewhat depressed during this recovery period, not being able to get about on his motorbike and do the stuff he liked. Now Matthew was back to his old self again, and I encouraged him – and sometimes badgered, waking him by nine in the mornings – to start looking for a job. I pointed out that although we'd finally managed to get his dad to send the monthly maintenance money directly to Matthew instead of to his mother, a job would give him the freedom of independence, and he'd feel a lot better about himself as well. No more worries about trying to make sure his money for petrol and smokes lasted a month. He was trying hard, but still hadn't found employment; it was a positive start, anyway.

"You never know how long the night will be," Matthew said, grinning as he handed me my lunch box of fresh sandwiches when I emerged from the bathroom. "Besides, peanut-butter is full of instant protein!" He gave me a wink and let me get on with my preparations in peace and quiet.

It was a thoughtful gesture on his part, and I appreciated his concern. Peanut-butter was a regular on our home shopping list; apart from the fact that we all liked it, it also matched our budget.

Goodness, all this preparation was a most arduous affair indeed!

Next on the list came the clothes. I selected numerous outfits and had to parade each to the two youngsters perched on the bed. None met with the approval of the picky audience.

"Oh gross, Mum! I think you'll have to get some new stuff," said Mary-Lou, coming to the rescue – in her innocently tactless way – leaving me feeling slightly disheartened. I didn't have expensive clothing, but I always felt I'd been neat and sort of "with it" for my age. But perhaps she had a point, I thought; I had to try to look at myself through someone else's eyes.

Eventually, we settled on a knee-length cotton button-up black skirt, camel cotton blouse, black shoes with a medium heel, pantyhose-clad legs and a brown belt. So far, things were progressing relatively smoothly.

Equipped with my largest black handbag, which would later accommodate the pharmacy package containing my new "work tools" – still hidden behind the car seat – it was time to bid my family goodnight and *au revoir*.

"Matthew," I said, "you're to take care of Mary-Lou, okay? And Mary-Lou, you've got school in the morning, so don't go to bed too late – and I hope you've finished all your homework. You're both to look after the animals and the house, and I'll phone you from the agency later."

We were all standing at the front door. General was sitting on the carpet, his tail wagging in case he might just get to go somewhere, listening intently.

"It could be a long night – I don't know when I'll be home again. Try not to worry though. I'm sure I'll be okay."

With a goodbye pat and an ear-tickle for General, last minute hang-on hugs and kisses from Mary-Lou and Matthew, I drove into the new world in my little Nissan LDV. My sandwich box was on the seat beside me, the chorused, "Good luck, Mum," from Mary-Lou and Matthew still ringing in my ears, and my steel nail file in my handbag.

Puffing several cigarettes in rapid succession on the way, my mind was in turmoil. What I was about to do was illegal, which firstly bothered the honest nature instilled in me by my father, and secondly I was scared shitless, to put it bluntly, because logically my mind said it involved some kind of danger. The first and most obvious danger springing to mind was Aids. And what if I was caught and landed up in the tronk? I felt sure there were other dangers as well – no doubt I'd find out about those in time.

Well, standing on the street corner or at a set of traffic lights begging for kindness and help from society – and a largely unemployed society at that, with problems of its own – wasn't going to solve my immediate financial difficulties, was it? Especially if I said I needed donations to help feed and stable a horse!

And quite frankly, when it came to my pride, I'd rather die than face the personal shame of having a large, cardboard notice round my neck with black printed letters on it saying, "Please help, children and animals to feed – God Bless You." I'd earn my money myself, lying on my back if necessary.

Peckers and playgrounds have been around and together since humans evolved, arrived, or whatever, I thought, as I drove to the agency. I preferred to call a penis a "pecker" and a vagina a "playground", as my father had – it sounded softer.

Well, at this stage, I had three things to hope for. One – that I would get the job, and make the money we needed. Two – that the Rooster condoms would behave appropriately, despite my inexperience at fitting them. And three – that what would fill the "Roosters" wouldn't be any worse than the healthy carrots we gave to Copper Band on our riding visits!

Chapter Three
One Long Night

*I*t was about a twenty-minute drive. I was relieved that the agency was in the Durbanville area and not near my home. Hopefully, I wouldn't meet any of my normal business clients there – though finding me in such a place of employment, I thought, would prove more embarrassing for them than for me.

"Here goes," I thought, as I stopped my Nissan 1400 bakkie outside the front of the building, deliberately not parking directly under the flashing red "Open" sign. Amy's directions were good and I'd found the place without a problem. I switched off the headlights. My hands were shaking and my stomach, despite me having taken another Brozam tranquilliser, was a knot of anxiety. I took a last, long, desperate puff on my smoke, extinguished it in the dashboard ashtray, picked up my handbag and got out of the car. My peanut-butter sandwiches I left on the car seat to fetch later if the hunger pangs set in, and if such things were allowed.

It was a quiet evening, with the night lights gently twinkling below the brilliant white stars, suspended in the vastness of the cobalt sky. Tina Turner's "Private Dancer" played continuously in my mind – would the allure of the words hold true?

> "I'm your private dancer, a dancer for money
> Do what you want me to do . . .
> Deutschmarks or dollars,
> American Express will do nicely thank you
> Let me loosen up your collar . . ."

I walked up the steps with an exaggeratedly confident stride, through the open security gate and front door to the reception desk. Two male faces smiled at me expectantly.

"Hi, I'm Margaret," I said. "I spoke to Amy earlier today about your ad."

"Yes, Margaret, you can speak to me – I'm Marius, the manager, and this is Henry," he replied, indicating the young guy sitting on a stool to his left, who nodded slightly and said a quiet "Hello".

Marius leaned back in his chair as he spoke, his hands idly fiddling with a bottle top. He had a friendly, broad smile and his large blue-grey eyes studied me intently.

"Have you done this work before?" he asked, very directly and without the slightest hint of embarrassment.

"No, I haven't," I said, and after a slight pause added, "but I need to for financial reasons – and I feel very nervous."

"Yes, I can see that," he grinned. "Well, no need to worry. I'll introduce you to the girls, and Tammy can show you how things work around here, okay?"

"So," I faltered, "I mean, well, do I have the job?"

"Sure. Why, did you expect something else?"

"Well, I did, um, have visions of a more tricky kind of interview," I replied. "And this has been quick – if you know what I mean . . ." My voice trailed off uncertainly.

"Tricky, like what?" he grinned, giving me a wink, putting me on the spot a bit.

"Well, to be honest, I thought I'd have to undress to my underwear so that you could see if my body was in good enough shape."

That set him off laughing loudly for a few seconds; he had a very robust laugh. "No, no, that won't be necessary," he replied, smiling at me as he wiped his eye, having contained his amusement. "I'm a pretty good judge of what we require here – without inspecting underneath a lady's clothing. My, my, Margaret, you're really new to this, aren't you!"

I kept quiet and simply nodded my head, embarrassed. Marius threw the bottle top in the air, catching it deftly in his left hand. "By the way, what would you like to be called?" Seeing the blank look on my face he added, "In this business you need to operate by some name other than your real name."

"Oh," I paused. "I've always liked the name Rachael," I said, after a couple of moments of furiously hurried thought.

"If you like Rachael, then Rachael it shall be," he said most properly, and then immediately boomed, "Tammy!" in the direction of the curtain to his right. A petite brunette lady with a waist-length spiral perm and exquisite blue eyes appeared.

"Meet Rachael, our new lady," Marius said. "Show her around, give her the rundown. She's never done this work before and she's nervous." And then to me he added, "Tammy will look after you."

"Nice to have you join us, Rachael," Tammy said, giving me a pat on the shoulder. "Follow me and I'll show you around." I liked her immediately.

And so, having arrived at the agency as Margaret, within ten minutes I had become Rachael.

"Well, that interview was easy," I thought thankfully, as I followed Tammy through the bottle-green curtain, which she looped to one side with an ornate rope tie in a contrasting green.

"This is the kitchen on the right – as you can see," she smiled. Another girl walked in.

"Hi," she said in a disinterested way, went to the sink and filled a glass with water, turned around and leaned back as she took a sip.

"Christina, this is Rachael, another new lady who's just started," Tammy said.

Christina nodded in my direction said "Hello", swallowed the rest of the water and left. I heard more female voices coming from the reception area.

"This place gets really busy, and I mean *really* busy. Come with me, I'll show you round quickly. The other ladies are arriving now and I'm on the desk."

I followed Tammy on her quick guided tour of the shower and four "lounges", all identical. The rooms were very small – I'd always thought there'd be double beds in places like this. In each lounge there was a single bed pushed against the wall, and beside it a small square table with a lamp, a tiny electric fan and a glass ashtray. The walls and ceiling were painted a matte bottle green, with contrasting gloss-painted doors and skirting boards in deep apricot. The deep green wall-to-wall carpeting was definitely the hard-wearing kind (which I thought could really give a nice carpet burn) and almost looked black in the faint light from the lamp. The table cloth, falling to the floor in soft folds, and the fitted sheet were in peach, and the short wooden lamp-stand had a green shade with fringed edging. Each bed had four medium-sized scatter cushions, in deep green and peach tartan fabric. The idea, I later learnt, was to make the bed look more like a couch, which was why the rooms were referred to as lounges. A small white dust-bin was placed in the corner. There was a small window in each room, and on the windowsill a bottle of body lotion and a roll of toilet paper. Two wall-hooks and two coat-hangers; that was it. The temperature of the rooms was far from cool on this summer evening.

"Remember," Tammy advised, "after a booking it's each lady's duty to make sure the lounge is clean and tidy, with the sheet straight and pillows placed nicely. There are fines for not tidying up after yourself. Oh, and the white dustbin is for condoms." I nodded, paying attention.

As we left the lounges, Tammy added an afterthought: "And if the sheet is dirty, change it. The clean linen's in the kitchen cupboard, dirty towels and sheets go in the big laundry basket. The kitchen, toilets, reception, bar, ashtrays etc. are to be kept clean and neat at all times – including the magazines in the main lounge, which are to be in neat piles, always."

The phones were ringing. As I followed Tammy to the reception, I wondered how anyone was supposed to do any kind of sexual manoeuvring in a room with such limited space, and in that heat – the fan didn't seem big enough to provide sufficient relief. The rooms felt pretty claustrophobic and cramped and they didn't seem to be adequately soundproofed. I wondered if you'd be able to hear everything going on in the four lounges – that would be a bit embarrassing.

As Tammy leaned over the desk to answer the phones she said, "Go and chat to the girls and we'll talk later. This place starts going mad about now."

I walked over to the only face I knew so far, Christina, and asked if I could sit next to her. She nodded, and then rattled off the names of the girls in the main lounge.

"Everybody, this is Rachael – and that's Roxy," she said, pointing to the girl on the far left and then working round: "Shelly, Claudia, Vanessa, Kerryn, Janet, Kate, Diane and Lindy." They all said hello and then carried on chatting amongst themselves.

"If you want a drink," Christina continued, "which you get at staff prices, you have to tell Tammy so she can write it up in the book, and there's tea and coffee in the kitchen, free of charge."

"Thanks," I replied. "I could do with a cup of coffee. Would you like one?"

"Yes, three sugars, one and a half coffees and milk, please," she said, without further ado.

I walked towards the kitchen, stopping at the desk and asked Tammy if she'd also like some coffee.

"That'd be great," Tammy answered, dialling a number. "Black, two sugars and half tap water," she added, then started speaking into the receiver.

I filled the kettle, switched it on and leaned back against the kitchen sink, grateful for a few minutes to gather my thoughts. Janet breezed in as though the kitchen belonged to her, took no notice of me, opened the fridge and studied the contents carefully, then closed the door, somewhat disappointed. Next, she opened the microwave, closed it again, looked around – and spotted a take-away burger box on the corner of the kitchen counter, the contents of which she proceeded to ravenously devour. With the last mouthful of burger still being consumed and some chips in her hand, she finally acknowledged my presence in a casual, off-hand tone of voice: "If you're making coffee, I'll have some. White with three sugars." Then she pushed the burger box back to where she'd found it and walked out.

Being a waitress could be quite confusing, I thought to myself as I took the mugs off the shelf, repeating the various coffee instructions under my breath so I wouldn't forget them. I delivered the coffees as ordered and was just about to sit down on the couch when Tammy called me to the desk.

"Puff says you've got to sit at the desk tonight."

"Who?" I asked, confused.

"Puff – oh, Marius, the manager. We call him Puff. Bring your bag, here's a stool to sit on."

The phones were ringing and I fetched my bag and coffee, sat on the stool next to Tammy and waited until she had time to explain.

"You're not to do any bookings tonight, you've got to watch and learn. We'll chat when there's a break, but right now, I've got to get the girls to the out bookings."

Tammy had a cigarette burning in the ashtray on her desk – she smoked Camel Lights – so I asked if I was allowed to smoke and she nodded. I lit up with a long, deep, grateful drag, had a sip of coffee and surveyed my new surroundings in peace, quite thankful for the temporary shelter of the "watch and learn" process.

The colour scheme of the reception area was the same as the lounges. There were four stylish three-seater couches, in the same tartan fabric as the cushions in the lounges, each adorned with several plain peach and green scatter cushions. There was a small side table next to each couch, draped with deep green cloth, and a low square wooden coffee table in the centre. Numerous magazines were on the bottom shelf of the coffee table. Each side table had a tall wooden lamp stand, once again with a green shade and fringed edging. There were only four other lights in the main lounge – one above the bar, the spotlight on the reception desk counter, and two tall brass lamps in the corners of the room that shone gentle light up the walls toward the ceiling. Two enormous indoor palms, one just inside the front door and the other in the bar area, provided greenery. The reception desk was very large and U-shaped, with a split-level counter; the drawers had brass knobs and the finish to the entire desk was perfect peach melamine.

The receptionist's counter had two incoming phone lines, a coin-operated call box, a new, compact cash register, a credit card machine and a hi-fi – not to mention various hardcover exercise books, message pads, scrap paper and pens. In all, I found the atmosphere to be pleasant, relaxed and inviting, but felt sure the final touches would be a small vase of fresh flowers from the garden and a couple of small glass bowls for peppermints for the top counter of the reception desk. I made a mental note to bring some the following night – I didn't think they'd mind, and I'd ask permission later.

Tammy said I could use the call box to phone home if I wanted, and I called Mary-Lou and Matthew. How was it going? Had I made any money? What was the place like? And what were the girls like? I said I'd tell them everything when I got home – for now, I just wanted to check that they were okay. I then called James as well; he sounded relieved that I was watching and learning that night, and I said I'd phone him from home later. I didn't speak long, as that was another one of the rules. You weren't allowed to discuss agency matters over the phone at the desk either.

Some of the girls chatted amongst themselves, smoking, and others sat quietly reading magazines. They poured their own drinks and stopped at the desk to report what they had, to be noted in one of the exercise books by Tammy.

Various gentlemen came to the security gate and Tammy would press the buzzer to let them in. They would enquire in hushed tones at the desk about the rates and services performed by the ladies, sometimes being quite specific about their requirements, and then Tammy would invite them to have a drink at the bar. A different girl was chosen each time to pour the gentleman's drink for him, for which he paid cash there and then. He could then at his leisure mix and chat with the girls until he found one he wanted, his decision discussed with Tammy only. Sometimes the gentleman would have to make a second choice of escort – perhaps the first was already booked for "time" on the premises, or was leaving on an out booking in the next few minutes; or perhaps she wouldn't perform his specific request. Payment was made strictly to Tammy, and everything was noted; a cash transaction was slightly cheaper than payment by credit card or cheque. The escort concerned was called to the desk, advised of the time allotted with the client: half an hour, an hour or two hours. She then chose a lounge – again noted down, so that no one else would enter or choose the same room during a booking. There were two clocks, one on the receptionist's desk and another large one prominently positioned on the wall, so that the gentleman could verify the correct time – which was recorded.

Business transactions conducted, the lady chosen would open a small cupboard underneath the reception desk, remove some condoms and ask the gentleman to accompany her through the curtain to the lounge, to perform whatever request had been agreed to.

So far things had been quite busy. Several of the girls had gone through to the rooms. Another driver, Simon, had appeared, bringing three more ladies, and the first driver, Henry – the young guy I'd met earlier with Puff – had taken three escorts to out bookings, to addresses arranged over the telephone with Tammy.

I marvelled at Tammy's ability to handle all this commotion at once. The phones rang continuously and simultaneously; the drivers needed directions, drop-off and pick-up times; the girls had to phone in when they got to their appointments; drinks had to be paid for, rung up on the cash register and noted; credit cards correctly processed; problems solved.

Some girls were angry at times; some had home problems. Other girls were hungry and needed one of the drivers to collect food from a local take-away joint. I noticed that the driver earned five rand petrol money for going half a kilometre down the road and back to fetch one of the ladies a pie – which was more than the cost of the pie itself!

Then there were the men Tammy had to deal with – drunk and sober men, polite men, fussy clients, explicit clients, friendly gentlemen, aggressive and rude clients, old and young men, even obscene phone calls and prank bookings. I was amazed – not two customers were alike. Some were married, others single, some ugly or fat, others drop-dead gorgeous; there were clean and showered or sweaty after-work men, rich and poor. In the sale of sex, average didn't seem to apply. If you wanted variety, this was the place to be!

The clock had to be watched at all times, so we knew when to remind ladies of "time finished" on bookings being done on the premises. This was done by knocking on the appropriate lounge door and saying, "Five minutes left." Anyone over time could be fined. You also had to keep a keen ear on "happenings" in the four lounges, as any one of the ladies could need help with a difficult customer. Added to all this was the showering of ladies and clients, clean towels each time, replacing linen, toilet trips to check hair, lipstick, etc.

The smooth functioning of all this was the responsibility of the lady at the reception desk and I did not envy her the task – apart from the fact that she had to be bilingual as well. At times it was totally chaotic, with the girls literally running to appointments, grabbing condoms out of the cupboard before dashing out after the driver. Throughout all this pandemonium, Tammy had the patience of an angel. I was yet to learn that this endurance could be tried too far – the results of which I can assure you were not in keeping with her petite frame, for Tammy also had a black belt in karate.

All in all, it was a very involved business. Cripes, I thought, there is a mountain to learn about this work. And I'd thought it couldn't be too complicated. Wake up, girl!

The evening seemed to go in spates of wild activity, interspersed with quiet spells to catch your breath and sit in peace, or turn up the music and unwind a bit. I was able to have a chat to Tammy during one of the quieter spells. She kindly obliged my rather shy and embarrassed request for help with some condom practice – rolling one down over the rounded end of a pencil, and then giving me another one and asking me to do the same!

James had taught me to drink whisky "correctly", as he termed it – on the rocks – and it didn't affect me. I'd had two singles, duly noted with my name for payment later, and I'd refilled our coffee mugs twice. It was quiet now and I felt peckish. Remembering the peanut-butter sandwiches in my car, I fetched the sandwich box and Tammy and I shared the contents.

It was now twelve-fifteen and my thirty-eighth birthday had begun, but I kept this to myself. All the girls were booked except for the two of us, Tammy and myself. It was nice to chat to her after our short condom practice, but it was not to be for long, as another call came in and Tammy left within minutes with the driver, Simon.

Puff came out of his office to man the incoming telephone calls, and I sat with him at the reception desk, still perched on my stool as instructed several hours before. The ringing lines became relatively quiet, and he took the calls with ease.

"Can you say if you don't want to go with a certain man?" I asked, nervously.

"Yes, it's your body – as a woman you've got the right to say no," he answered, and then added with an enquiring smile, "Is there any particular reason for asking that, Rachael?"

"Well, I'm not quite sure how to say this – it being the new South Africa and all . . ." I fiddled with my skirt and Puff waited quietly. "Maybe it's, um, it's my upbringing – I don't know, but I'd, I'd feel better doing bookings with men like myself – if you know what I mean." I was struggling with this bit of conversation, feeling uncomfortable about my biased opinions, and added, "It's just a personal thing. I don't have a problem with any one else's preferences though."

"That's fine," Puff said, tilting his chair back on two legs and not looking directly at me. "I'll let Tammy know your preferences when she returns."

"Oh – and there's something else," I said hurriedly, "there'll be five days of the month that I can't work." Best to say all these things at once, while I had the opportunity, I thought.

He nodded and smiled. "Rachael, what's the definition of periods?"

"I don't know," I answered, after a couple of seconds of hurried thought.

"A bloody waste of fucking time!" was Puff's loud and hilarious reply.

"In this business I guess you're right," I mused in a quiet voice, "but I just can't do it."

"In this business, when in real financial need, one learns to do many things," he answered, more sombrely. "But it's your choice. Anyway, want some coffee?"

"Yes thanks, but I'll make it. How do you like yours?"

"Two heaped teaspoons of coffee, one sweetener tablet and a dash of milk, thanks."

I headed for the kitchen, heard the phone ring, and his answer: "We don't have any ladies at the moment, but there'll be some back in about twenty minutes."

Puff was, at a guess, about six foot four, slim bordering on thin, tough and wiry. He had a friendly open face, large blue-grey eyes and a broad smile with good straight teeth, albeit somewhat stained from numerous cigarettes – puffed on continuously to stay awake during the long hours of running a business such as this. His hands were like hams, big and strong, the nails clean although some fingers were tinged yellow from the nicotine, his shoes polished to a shine. He dressed neatly and in good taste, in a dark suit, the jacket and tie removed this warm evening and hanging in his office. His dark hair was cut in a short-back-and-sides style, with a matching moustache, trimmed precisely to the outer corners of his mouth. My impression was that cleanliness was a personal must with this man. He had a quick and warm sense of humour, coupled with a naturally protective – almost parental – caring attitude towards "his girls". His manners were exceptional on the phone and face-to-face with clients, but I felt sure it wouldn't pay to incur the wrath of this seemingly gentle giant.

"Oh, I've just remembered something I've got for you," I said, reaching for my handbag underneath the desk. I took out the paper that I'd concealed in one of the inner pockets and handed it to Puff. "It's a recent medical test stating that I'm HIV-negative. I just thought you might like to have some proof."

He glanced at the A4 page, said, "Thanks," and put it in his pocket.

The phone rang then, and he answered. It seemed there was some trouble with Roxy, one of the ladies. Puff took directions to her exact whereabouts and said he'd send one of the drivers immediately. Next he contacted Henry on his cell phone and told him where to fetch Roxy, adding, "Make it fast" before disconnecting.

Perhaps ten or so minutes later, the driver's metallic blue Opel screeched to a halt outside the front door and Roxy ran in, banging her handbag down hard on the top reception counter, then thumping her white stilettos down on the counter as well.

"Fucking bastard!" she stormed angrily. I noticed her hands were shaking. "But I broke his bed – should've broken his fucking head instead."

"Okay, calm down," said Puff, "and tell me what happened."

"First, I need a drink," she said, heading for the bar. The bar fridge door slammed hard, and she banged the bar counter with her fist. "There aren't any cold Castles in this thing, just my fucking luck!" Frustrated, she stormed through to the kitchen, reappearing in a flurry through the curtain, beer in hand, stood at the desk and took a long swig, her head tilted well back. Then she began speaking, fast and without pausing. I was gripped instantly and never even thought to utter a word throughout her tirade. Puff let her blow.

"He pulled the condom off twice – thought I wouldn't notice, stupid shit. I told him not to get funny. So I put another one on. Then he tries anal and I told him I don't do it, so he says he paid money to do it any way he likes and I told him we have rules. He said, 'Fuck your rules, I paid so I want what I paid for.' I told him he either sticks to the rules or I go. Then he shoves me against the wall, gets me round the neck and says, 'Listen, bitch, I paid for a fuck any way I want so you'd better do what I want.' I brought my knee up in his balls, hard, and he let go. I jumped onto the bed to get to my clothes on the other side, when I heard the thing bust under me – it must've been pine. So I jumped another one, real hard, and it broke in the middle."

Roxy took another swig of her beer, and Puff and I waited for her to catch her breath and finish her story, while Henry poured himself a drink at the bar.

"Anyway, he's lying on the floor moaning, holding his balls," Roxy continued, licking her lips then wiping her mouth with the back of her hand, "and I see him grab the side of the bed and start pulling himself up off the floor, so I grabbed my clothes and managed to get my broekies and top on and ran out of the caravan. I just ran till I saw a building and stopped to put my leggings on. Shit, then I just ran till I found a phone."

Roxy was about five foot four, well-rounded to plump, with a good-sized thirty-eight bust, maybe even a D cup, an attractive young face with a very mod short hairstyle, highlighted and bleached blonde. She wore shiny black stretch leggings to her calves with a loose, thigh-length white cheesecloth cotton top.

"All right," said Puff in a soothing tone. "If he phones in I'll sort it out. Don't worry about it though, just calm down now, have some coffee – maybe another booking will come in."

"He won't phone in, he knows he's in the shit," Roxy answered. "And I'm not in the mood for any more of this crap tonight. I'm going home. I'll just have another drink first, my nerves are stuffed." She went to the kitchen and came back with another Castle, gave Puff the nod and he entered her beer in the book.

"You'll be all right just now. It's just one of those bad ones, Roxy. Put it out of your mind," Puff reassured her.

"No ways," she replied defiantly, having another swig of beer. "I can't face any more of this shit tonight. Can I have my money now and go home?"

Despite Roxy's seemingly harsh exterior, I sensed that beneath it lay the gentle fragility of most women. Tonight she probably felt afraid, vulnerable and emotionally drained. I was sure some peace and quiet in her own home surroundings would restore a measure of inner calm and strength – to face this kind of work again tomorrow.

"Okay, I'll sort out your money and Henry can take you home just now." Puff realised she'd been frightened on this booking, and trying to get her to stay on wasn't going to be of benefit to either of them.

I felt relieved for Roxy. "Heck, it sounds dicey. This business seems quite dangerous. Is it always like this?" I asked her, as she stood leaning against the reception desk, finishing her beer.

"Some good, some bad ones. I've had worse," she replied, her anger seeming to have dissipated somewhat.

Her answer shook me. "Like how, worse – how do you get worse than that?" I said. I couldn't think of anything worse.

"Like the old guy that died on us," she answered, wanting to chat a bit now, as she leaned forward on the reception counter and looked at me.

"Died on you?" I said, incredulous. "Died – as in dead? Shit, I don't want that happening to me. What did you do?" She certainly had my interest with this story! I hoped she wouldn't be going home before she'd finished it.

"Another girl and I went to his place. Double booking, you know – wanted two of us. Turned out he was an old guy. Anyway, we were busy giving him the gears and he was on top of me, and next thing he's just lying on my chest, you know, heavy, not moving, like a dead weight. First, I didn't realise what was wrong. Shit, then it hit me. I rolled him off, and the two of us nearly died of fright ourselves. He just lay there on the floor."

"So what did you do?" I prompted. I think my eyes were out on stalks by this stage. This was hairy stuff. What had I gotten myself into?

She continued between swigs of beer. Roxy had a way of speaking fast – you had to pay attention. I wasn't going to interrupt anyway. "The other girl went to the bathroom and got the face cloth, soap and towel. We found a bucket in the kitchen cupboard and washed him all over, then we dressed him, combed his hair and sat him in his lounge chair with a magazine on his lap and a drink on the table next to him and left the television on. Then we tidied up the place real good, I mean, real careful. You know – like finger-prints and stuff. Then we left."

"You just left? Just closed the door and left? Didn't you phone anyone – like an ambulance or something?"

"Are you mad?" she said, looking at me as if I wasn't too bright for asking such a question. "It's illegal in this country, this stuff, and it was even worse at that time. We just left – pulled the door closed behind us. Then we went to the nearest bar for a quick stiff drink and called the boss from a phone booth. He said he'd take care of it if anything happened."

"Did you ever hear any more about it?" I asked. I liked Roxy. Apart from being intrigued by her stories, I liked the way she was so direct. I felt she was an honest girl and would defend a friendship vehemently – if you could get behind her tough facade.

"No, nothing, and we kept quiet. Anyway, he died of a heart attack, not from anything we'd done to him," she said in a matter-of-fact tone. "Most guys would probably like to die on the job anyway. But it can get real bad in this business and it stuffs up my nerves – like tonight. Why do you think I always wear these stilettos?"

I looked at the pair of white shoes still perched on the counter top, and then at her. They were well worn and scuffed, and the plastic heel cover was completely worn through, revealing the metal underneath.

"Take a look at this heel," she said, holding one of her shoes up for in-spection. "This is my protection. You've got to have some kind of protec-tion, always. Just one kick in the shins with these will do it, and in other places if necessary, and he'll fold in agony. If the knee in the balls doesn't work then he'll have to face these, and then he's going to feel sorry, and I mean, *real* sorry. Get my drift?"

"Well, do you always keep them near you, or do you always have them on?" I asked, hoping to glean as much information as I could before she went home.

"Fucking right I do," she said, with emphasis. "These two little wonders are always on. I might be totally starkers, but these things are always on. Men are funny creatures you know, they like a naked woman to keep her high heels on – kind of erotic or something, gets 'em going." After a quick last swig of beer she laughed and added, "Lucky they didn't break when I jumped on his bed. I suppose I should have the heels re-covered sometime, but I kind of like the metal. Anyway, must go, see you."

Roxy picked up her handbag without further ado, put on her stilettos and went through to Puff's office. I didn't feel as though I was being brushed off, it just seemed to be her way – everything short and fast. It had been an enormous help to be able to talk to her, and she'd been very friendly in answering all my questions so directly, without thinking I was prying too much – perhaps someone else would have thought I was way too nosy for a new girl.

"Okay, can I have my money now please Puff, I want to go home," I heard Roxy say from behind the curtain. "I'll see you tomorrow when I feel better. Right now, I need to get this shit out of my head."

Puff came through the curtain to the reception, opened the till and began counting her money. I felt this was sort of personal, so I went through to the kitchen and put the kettle on.

Besides, after Roxy's stories I needed some time alone to think and sort all this out in my head. It was really scary. Would I be able to cope with this kind of work? Well, I'd just have to, I'd just have to learn – I needed the money. I finished washing the glasses and mugs in the sink, tidied the kitchen and heard Roxy yell, "Good night!" as she left with Henry again. Then I checked that the four lounges, main lounge and bar were tidy, and collected any other mugs, glasses and ashtrays for washing as well. There was no draining rack for the washed glasses. I had a spare red one in the garage at home – I didn't need it; it could be put to better use here.

Another car pulled up and I heard a familiar voice, Christina's, saying, "Hi, we're back." She walked into the kitchen, smiled and said, "Oh, great, I'm just in time for coffee," and walked out again. I was beginning to feel like the coffee girl by this stage and was a little annoyed, but didn't dare show it.

I heard Puff and Christina at the reception desk discussing Roxy's ordeal. Christina said, "She's always in some kind of trouble. What's wrong with that girl?" From the tone of her voice, she didn't seem sympathetic.

I went through with coffee for Puff, Christina and myself. Before I could sit down on my allotted stool Puff said, "Hey, Rachael, get some glasses, we're having champagne. We don't have champagne or wine glasses, so any glasses will do."

"Yeah, and let's turn up the music as well to celebrate," Christina said, in a jolly voice.

"Any special occasion, Christina, or did you have a good booking?" I asked.

"Hell no, not the booking," she replied, grinning. "It's my birthday!"

"Well, happy birthday! That's quite amazing – it's my birthday too," I said, not meaning to detract from her special celebration – if I didn't tell her she might find out later, and feel odd that I'd kept quiet.

"Really?" Christina replied with astonishment. "The 26th of January?" I nodded.

"Okay, so get some glasses! Puff's getting the champagne from the fridge. Hey, Puff," she shouted, "it's Rachael's birthday as well, the same day as mine! That's some coincidence, isn't it?"

Puff came through the curtain, uncorking the chilled champagne bottle. "Oh, so it's a double celebration is it?" He smiled in amusement and popped the cork, which hit the ceiling. "Happy birthday, girls," he said with sincere joviality, holding up the champagne, and then added with a grin and a wink, "Here's my birthday wish for you two – may you both make lots of money!"

We all laughed. Puff poured and handed us each a glass, and we all said "Cheers" and sipped. Then the phone rang and he said, "I'll take it in my office," and disappeared with his champagne back through the curtain.

"Right, time for some music," said Christina, adjusting the volume on the hi-fi. "I just love the words of this song." With glass in hand she walked round to the front of the reception desk and danced and sang along to Tina Turner:

> "Some boys has got the look of the Greek Adonis
> And some boys just try to talk you off of your feet
> Some boys think they're God's gift to women
> And some boys just think they're sweet enough to eat . . ."

It had a good beat and the words sure were appropriate. I liked the song instantly – the mood lifted and things didn't seem quite so bad anymore, even after Roxy's stories.

"Hey, turn that down a bit!" Puff boomed from his office behind the curtain, and closed his door hard.

Simon, Tammy and Vanessa walked in then. Vanessa dumped her handbag under the desk and headed straight for the kitchen saying, "I'm starving," and Tammy took over the desk again. There was a loud bang on the kitchen counter and Vanessa stormed through the curtain.

"Who the fuck finished my burger and chips?" she demanded, hands on her hips.

I kept quiet, remembering Janet earlier in the kitchen.

"Is Dotty Dick coming back tonight?" she said to Tammy in a cutting voice, leaning over the reception counter to get her undivided attention.

"Janet's gone straight home from an out booking," Tammy said, looking up after studying the roster on the desk.

"Dotty Dick's our name for Janet," Christina whispered to me. "You'll find out why soon enough."

"The bitch!" fumed Vanessa. "No food's safe around here. She's like a bloody gannet. Can't you do something about her eating everyone's stuff?" Vanessa enquired with exasperation, pointedly leaning well over the top of the counter.

"In your defence, Vanessa, I must say that when another person takes what is not theirs, then that is not right," Tammy answered slowly, not looking up, her mind busy on checking paperwork. "However, you are aware of this particular problem with Janet, so perhaps you shouldn't leave your food around – but I'll speak to Puff again about it."

"Fuck!" exclaimed Vanessa, venting her anger at having lost her burger and chips to Janet's well-rounded girth. She was a bit hyped – quite understandably – and I must have had some kind of look on my face because she directed her next sentence at me. "What are you looking at? Never heard the word 'fuck' before? Well, you'll have to get used to it if you're going to work around here," she said, irritated, arms now folded on the reception counter.

"Fornication under consent of the king," Tammy said evenly, her eyes still focused on paperwork.

"What?" said Vanessa, perplexed but interested. I was as well.

Tammy looked up, momentarily studying the three of us – Christina, who'd kept quiet throughout the burger-and-chips episode and was also leaning on the reception counter, Vanessa, more contained now, and myself – and scratched her head with a ball-point pen.

"That's what fuck means," she said, "fornication under consent of the king." She smiled, relaxed, twiddling the pen. "Just thought I'd add that."

Not only was Tammy's comment enlightening, but I also sensed she'd subtly shifted Vanessa's irritation away from me.

"That's something I never knew," Christina said, chin on her hand. "I'll remember that for future reference."

"Me too – and in that case, if the king can use it, then it's good enough for us, isn't it?" Vanessa said with finality. She reached for her handbag under the desk and took out her purse. "Simon," she yelled in the direction of Puff's office, "I need you to go to the shop and buy me a pie, I'm fucking starving!"

"By the way, Tammy," Christina said, "there's some champagne for you and Vanessa. Rachael and I share the same birthday – today. Isn't that some co-incidence?"

"I'll get it," I said quickly, and went to the kitchen to fetch the bottle from the fridge.

Vanessa and Tammy had a bit of champagne and said happy birthday to Christina and me, and Christina called me over to sit with her on the couch and chat.

"So, how's it going so far?" she asked inhaling deeply on her smoke.

"I'm not sure," I replied. "Roxy's booking has made me a bit worried. I don't know if I can cope with stuff like that."

She took a drag on the Courtleigh, blew a smoke ring into the air and said, "Oh, I wouldn't let it worry me. She's always having problems. Anyway, most of the bookings are okay. You get some bad ones, but in a week you'll know enough to cope."

"How long have you been doing this, Christina?" I asked.

"For about two years," she said without emotion. "I was with another agency before, but I knew some of the girls who joined here. It's good to work in a new agency – means new clients." She puffed on her smoke and studied my outfit. "And I'd shorten my skirt if I was you. Guys don't like long skirts. And you're not allowed to wear pantyhose – only suspenders and stockings if you're going to wear stockings, but no pantyhose. Men hate pantyhose. And don't wear your hair up. You've got long hair, why don't you wear it loose?"

I listened to this advice, but changed the subject. "Why do you call Marius Puff?" I asked.

She put out her smoke in the ashtray on her lap. "Well, his real name is Marius Ulrich Frederick Francois Dietrich. You know the Afrikaners with their long names. Get it?" I shook my head and she repeated the names again slowly. Still, I couldn't fathom it out.

"Sorry, you'll have to tell me – I don't catch it," I said.

With exaggerated slowness she spelled it out for me. "Take the Christian names – M, U, F, F spells muff. Well, in this business it would be appropriate – except that we can't call him Muff, can we? So we changed it to Puff. Nobody calls him Marius. He's very protective about his girls and it's our sort of endearing nickname for him."

Although we shared the same birthday, it turned out Christina was nine years my junior. About the same height as me at five foot six, she was thinner and smaller breasted, with good slim legs and light brown, highlighted, beautifully groomed hair, and she was a neat dresser. Her most striking feature was her eyes – a beautiful blue, sometimes becoming darker or lighter, or even seeming to change to a shade of green, depending on what she was wearing. She had a full mouth with a natural mole at the corner. I imagined men would like a woman with a full mouth. But her fingernails were terrible, bitten down to the quick. I wasn't surprised; I felt sure this business could make you bite your nails.

Christina spoke without inflection in her voice, in a flat monotonous tone, without feeling. She appeared neither happy nor sad and showed no emotions, and especially no sympathy for Roxy. Only the music brought her any visible sign of pleasure. I later learned that money and what you could buy with it were her pleasures in life. She loved to shop and she loved to go on holiday.

I was sitting quietly next to Christina having a smoke when she remembered more advice.

"These guys will try anything to do it without a condom," she said. "Always put your hand down and hold his balls – that way you can feel if the condom is still on. If the condom breaks, well, that's another story, but always keep your hand where you can feel his balls. Oh, and watch out for fingers." I must have looked blank because she continued without any prompting.

"Fingers inside you, or finger fucking, as it's also known. When you let a guy put his fingers inside you, you're asking for trouble – you never know where his hands have been or what's under his nails. You can pick up all kinds of infections that way. And that's the last thing you need, believe me."

I nodded, remembering my own list for preventing dreaded fanny infections (not too many bubble or oil baths, cotton gusset broekies only, ease up on the pantyhose, rinse underwear properly, don't overdo the Stasoft) – I'd definitely take note of this extra advice.

"Are there rules as to what you have to do with a guy?" I asked.

Christina was a mine of information and quite easy about sharing it with me. I appreciated her openness – I needed all the help I could get.

"Everyone has their own rules, especially when it comes to anal. I mean, you either do anal or you don't – personal preference, that one. But we don't kiss. The majority of us have kids or husbands or boyfriends. Kissing is so personal. I don't want to go home and kiss my child if I've had to kiss some drunk I don't even know who's come for a fuck. A condom's a must – do it without a condom and you're asking for trouble. Apart from the health risks, doing it without a condom just fucks it up for all of us. I mean, the girl who's prepared to do that is going to make a lot of money and we others will hardly make a cent. And that's why we're here – so we can all survive. We've all got families to support." She lit up another Courtleigh, had a sip of her coffee and continued.

"Blow jobs without a condom are also dicey. And a blow job with a condom on tastes like hell – some condoms are really bitter and can make your mouth sore. So I guess that kind of narrows the field a bit. As well as no muffing. Doesn't leave much, hey? You might find this interesting – one of the drivers, Henry, reckons he can smell when a girl's been fucking without a condom."

This information was quite a lot to digest in one go. "It sounds so cold, so clinical," I said. "No romance about it at all. I suppose they're paying for sex, so that's exactly what they get. But surely they expect the rest of it when they book and pay? I find kissing very sensual – it turns me on, sort of gets things going, as it were," I said.

Christina smiled in a faintly amused way as she studied the length of her smoke, then deftly flicked the warm ash into the ashtray on her lap. "Listen girl, save the kissing for home, okay?" she advised carefully. "That's why you've got to have KY Jelly – it takes the place of being turned on. Instead of getting wet, just smack on a good dollop down there – but it dries quite fast. Sure they expect more when they pay, but you have to tell them what your rules are up front; then you shouldn't have any problems. If they don't like your rules they can always choose someone else who's prepared to do what they want."

"And how do you cope mentally?" I asked. Like Roxy, Christina didn't seem the least bit annoyed by my multitude of questions. "Do you see the guy's face or do you see only the money? I just don't know how to psyche myself about this part," I said hopelessly.

A little sparkle came to her eyes now. "Money. Dollar signs, that's all you see. Just concentrate on the money. It'll take a bit of time – in a week you'll know what you need to know and you'll just see money. Let's face it, the pay in this business is fantastic. If it's any help, take this bit of advice. Always come here for a reason – the reason is not just a fuck. You have to set yourself a goal each day. Like, for example, tomorrow you need to pay your phone bill and get some groceries, so let's say you need three hundred rand. Put this in your mind – *tonight I'm working to pay the phone bill and buy some groceries and I need three hundred rand.* Every time you walk into that room with a client, that's all you think about. You have to be totally focused on *why* you're doing it, not the doing of it. At the same time, you need to be totally alert – the dangers involved in this work are very real, very real indeed."

"I appreciate all your advice. Thanks," I said, standing up. "I'm going to get a drink, would you like a fresh coffee?"

Christina shook her head. "Just one other thing quickly, but it's important. Never be totally undressed before a client is – at least keep your panties on till he's starkers first. Could be a cop looking to bust you."

"A cop? God, do they come to these places?"

"Sure," she answered nonchalantly, "here, out bookings – you never know."

"I'll definitely keep that in mind then . . . though I don't know now if I'll cope with this work at all."

"You'll be fine, give it a couple of tries first." I nodded uncertainly, and she turned to chat to Vanessa, seated on the far couch.

I never forgot this conversation with Christina, and made a mental note: last undressed, no kissing, no fingers, no anal, everything with a condom, and hope no condoms break on me. Keep focused, focused; always have a goal.

I found the language of the sex-worker frequently punctuated by the word "fuck". Well, it made sense to me. In the fishing industry you'd use words like pelagic, sardines, shoals and trawlers; in the catering business, menus, head chefs, desserts and hors-d'oeuvres. Sex-workers say fuck – although their conversation is not often about fucking; sex is generally not even referred to. Simply put, the environment naturally prompts usage of the fuck word, which also offers relief from a multitude of complex emotions. The women face anger, frustration, fear, loathing, revulsion, excitement and happiness, physical and mental exhaustion and incredible stress levels, which produce constant adrenaline – which in turn can cause a breakdown in the average person's immune system. So although I only learned to say fuck when I was nineteen, quietly to myself and with some guilt and shame, I realised how fast I could pick up the frequent use of the word in such an environment.

It turned out that I was the oldest of all the girls at that time. Generally, I was pleased with my figure. After studying the other ladies, I noted that at thirty-eight I wasn't in bad shape after all.

During the evening I had constantly collected glasses, mugs, washed up, emptied ashtrays, straightened cushions and made mugs and mugs of coffee – trying to be useful and pass the time while I was learning, and also remembering the rule of keeping the place tidy at all times.

So for my efforts I now found myself christened "Granny" by Tammy. Granny I therefore became, along with Rachael – all in the same night! As the mood took them, the girls would refer to me by one name or the other. Having chosen Rachael as my working name, I was somewhat annoyed at how easily Granny seemed to stick in everyone's mind. Later my feelings would change – I realised that it was more a term of endearment than meanness. But that first night I misread it, and felt peeved.

By three-thirty in the morning I was exhausted, my chest heavy from the smoke. It had been one long night indeed, and I wasn't used to being awake during the early hours. I just wanted to go home and fall into my bed, with General sleeping at my side.

But four in the morning was closing time, and first we had to tidy up. All the lounges were checked again, condom bins emptied, glasses and ashtrays washed, counter tops wiped, bar and reception bins emptied, magazines tidied, tables and couches straightened, garbage bags put out, windows closed, toilets checked and tidied. Then it was time for the girls and drivers to be paid, and drivers organised to take the ladies home.

The girls were paid first and they all gathered in Puff's office. The split was fifty-seven percent for the lady per booking and forty-three percent for the agency. Then there were the deductions from the ladies' earnings – bar bills and petrol money for being fetched for work and taken home by the drivers, which depended on how far the lady lived from the agency. Sometimes fines were deducted as well. There was a board up in Puff's office with all the ladies' names on it, the top earner being Number One and so on. Each girl signed for her money. Then the drivers were paid and instructed who to drop off at home.

Just as everyone was ready to switch off the lights and leave, the phone rang – some guy wanted to book a lady!

"Here's the 'morning glory' call," said Tammy in a tired voice. "Well, he can fuck off and sort it out himself! And if he can't find a woman to ease his heavy load, he can bloody well use his hands." She picked up the receiver. "Sorry," she said, "but we're closed now. You can phone again at twelve to-day if you like."

"And what if the poor gentleman can't find a woman and doesn't have hands?" said Vanessa, in her sweetest sarcastic voice.

"Then he can crawl to the vacuum and stick his dick in the suction pipe. I don't know and I don't care, I'm too tired. I just want to go home to my kids now," was Tammy's fed-up reply.

Lights off and alarm system switched on, we all went down the front steps together. Goodbyes and see-you-tomorrows were said in weary voices.

I got into my little car and headed home, my tired mind in a whirl. Doesn't this business ever stop? I thought. Don't men ever sleep? I guess they do – it's just the penises that don't. They seem to have a life all of their own, I mused, exhausted.

Well, the girls were making money, and lots of it, so I guess they must be doing the sex stuff, I thought. There hadn't been any open display of sex. Men and women arrived and left clothed, they went into and came out of rooms clothed. There weren't people humping like hippos all over the place. The girls didn't walk around naked. The most naked people I saw were ladies and men with towels around them, going to or coming from the shower. The girls didn't compete with each other and compare underwear or bodies. None had their boobs falling out. A sexy outfit – a dress or top without a bra – was as far as they went. Nobody wore leathers or carried whips. All in all, it was a rather private affair.

I made a mental note to go to the mall later in the day when I woke up and see what I could get on my clothing account from the sale items, and pay it off. If I was going to make any money I'd definitely need to sexy up my dress code – especially as I had the added disadvantage of being the oldest.

The early morning was beautiful in the extreme and swathed me in a strange sense of peace and calm, like an invisible nurturing bandage, soothing my exhaustion, giving me renewed hope.

As I came over the hill on the N1 highway, the city of Cape Town lay before me, snuggled up and asleep in a blanket of a million colourful twinkling lights, the ships in the harbour floating still on their gentle waterbed. The early morning air felt fresh and clean from the hours of cooler night, as yet untainted by the morning rush-hour traffic still to come.

Table Mountain, in all her majestic beauty, was lit up – and stood like a gigantic armoured sentry over the resting city below: ever present, possessive and protective, guiding from far and near the peoples to her bosom. Guiding me home to my children Mary-Lou and Matthew, to General, waiting patiently at the front door for my return, and to Petal, Chocolate and little Bart.

Chapter Four
Rachael's First

I was up and about by ten-thirty that morning, after falling asleep with General at my side around six, as the early light filtered through my bedroom curtains. My birthday lasted until midnight. Maybe tonight I'd earn some money, I thought. Lord knows, that's the reason I got into this in the first place. And if I had to keep up this learning process any longer, I'd be bust by sunrise tomorrow!

I went to the mall, and it seemed luck was on my side – I found three new outfits and a pair of maroon suede shoes amongst the sale items, and put these on my account. Mary-Lou and Matthew nodded approvingly when they checked my purchases that afternoon. And Matthew, once again, made peanut-butter sandwiches for my supper.

Tonight I was better equipped. I had a neat hand-woven African grass basket at home that I used for magazines, flat-bottomed with overlapping handles, much like a large, wide briefcase. Packed neatly it could hold a multitude of items – almost the kitchen sink! Tonight it contained five clean G-strings, spare bra and my make-up bag. I added to this my short silk Chinese gown of rich blue with a red dragon embroidered on the back that my mother had given me as a gift some years before, and my "tool-bag" containing condoms and KY vaginal lubricant. To be properly prepared I packed in toothbrush, toothpaste, talcum powder, baby oil, body lotion and my flannel, wrapped in a small plastic packet. On top of all this, I folded a thin medium-sized towel.

My large black handbag I now swapped for my small black one, which could fit inside the woven grass basket, as well as everything else, without being seen. My small handbag contained only the immediate necessities – hairbrush, lipstick, perfume and identity document hidden in a separate compartment, together with my ATM card. The last and most important item in my little black bag was my metal nail file – never knew when I might need it. This method of packing would become second nature to me. The grass basket, however, could not accommodate the sandwich box, and this I would leave in the car to fetch when I felt hungry.

My preparations for the night ahead made me feel more positive and eased my nervousness. I'd chosen a thin-strapped, above-knee black cotton dress with the pretty floral design in shades of pink, and the high-heeled maroon shoes complemented the outfit perfectly. No pantyhose tonight though, per

Christina's instructions. I'd given my hair a fresh henna colour rinse, re-shaved my legs and applied body lotion with care to pamper any signs of age-ing or dry skin, and with the pink lace G-string nestled against my skin, I felt great. Yes, at thirty-eight, I felt pretty much like a million bucks. Fact was though, I hardly had *any* bucks.

James had introduced me to wearing G-strings, presenting me with "a little gift" one evening quite early in our relationship, and had then convinced me to have bikini waxes, torturous though they were! According to him, you couldn't wear a sexy G-string without having a "trim".

"No point, really," he'd said, "just ruins the effect with pubic hair stick-ing out the sides!"

It'd taken me a while to get used to wearing G-strings instead of full knick-ers – not to mention the further psyching I went through for the waxes – but he was right. I felt sexier, and James, being a healthy, visual male, was de-lighted with the progress I'd made from my previously dull underwear – this delight shown often, and further enhancing our sex life.

And I'd become even bolder this particular evening, perhaps in keeping with the mood of the new outfit. I've always loved hats, and my favourite remains one of soft greyish-brown velvet. I could make any style I wanted by turning the brim up or down, and I'd tuck my dark shoulder-length hair underneath. This hat was always with me from this night on – if it wasn't on my head, it was in my small black handbag.

I walked into the agency by seven twenty-five in the evening, with a more positive step, packed basket in hand.

"The hat lady's arrived!" laughed Tammy as she ran her fingers through her mass of long dark curls, then gave me a nod of approval and entered my name in the roster for the evening shift. The reversible velvet hat was to be-come Rachael's trademark, whether the girls thought the hat suited me or not – it was always Rachael, or Granny, with her hat!

Tonight the place was buzzing: phones ringing continuously, men al-ready at the bar, and a couple of new girls I hadn't met the previous night.

"Listen, Granny," Tammy said. "You're on an out booking – at eight to be precise – so prepare yourself. The driver will be here in about fifteen min-utes. And there's a bottle of champagne to take as well."

"Champagne? What's champagne for?" I asked, confused.

"New agency, good for business – so Puff says all new out bookings get a free bottle. Get one out of the kitchen fridge, I'll write it up. Oh, and the driver must give the champagne to the client, not you."

"But what about . . .?" I started.

"I'll speak to you just now, I've got to answer the phone," Tammy said.

I hurried through to the kitchen and switched on the kettle. Cripes, now it's a total attack of the jitters – panic rising up to my throat, guts in a knot like a mass of tangled fishing line, hands shaking and palms starting to get a bit sweaty. Must have a quick cup of coffee and a whisky, I thought, panicked – and definitely another half a Brozam. My mind was racing. Here it was – my first booking – happening faster than I'd imagined it would. Better check the lipstick and go for a wee, only fifteen minutes left before the driver gets here – oh, shit! Mad dash to the bar, pour a double J&B whisky, lucky there was still ice in the ice-bucket, don't need water, on the rocks was best, past the desk with a quick stop – "Tammy, one double J&B for me, thanks," and straight back to the kitchen.

"Hi, Rachael, how are you? What's with the hat?" Christina eyed me and started to giggle, a "this old girl's lost it" look on her face.

"Thought I'd try to look smarter this evening," I replied, somewhat self-consciously.

"Yeah, you do, I agree," she conceded, unable to hide her amused smile behind her hand. "And I'm glad to see you took my advice and shortened your skirt," she added more encouragingly, after studying my appearance for a few seconds. Noticing I had the kettle on the boil, she stopped at the kitchen door on her way out and said, "Oh good, you're making coffee! I'd love some – milk and two sugars. This place is going mad!" And out she went.

"Listen, Granny, it's a one-hour booking," said Tammy, walking into the kitchen and leaning against the fridge. I stopped Christina's coffee preparations temporarily, had a hurried sip of my whisky and paid close attention to her instructions. "The driver will check the place out and take the money. You don't have anything to do with the money. He'll note the time he leaves you there and he'll be back in exactly one hour to fetch you, so be ready, okay? Got your condoms, been practising?" she asked, giving me a pat on the arm. "By the way, I like the hat – and if you're making coffee, I'll have a cup as well please." And off she went back to the reception.

The phones were ringing wildly again when Tammy suddenly popped her head back through the kitchen doorway for a couple of moments. "Just need to check if you remember the agency phone number, in case you have any trouble?"

"Yes," I said, and repeated it for her.

"Okay – and good luck," she said encouragingly, and disappeared again.

I was pretty panicky by now. Half a tranquilliser went down with a swig of water followed by a swig of whisky followed by a couple of swigs of coffee, diluted with cold water. Quick dash to the loo, check the lipstick and back to the kitchen, swig of whisky, swig of coffee. Nerves pretty shot. When's the driver getting here? Oh shit, Christina and Tammy had wanted coffee, nearly forgot, the mugs were ready though – coffee, sugar – just need to pour in the water and milk.

I walked through to the reception with faked calm, there being clients milling around, gave Christina her coffee and put Tammy's on the desk next to her. Back to the kitchen I went – finished the whisky, slowed down on the coffee.

In walked Simon, the driver. "Ready to go?" he asked, without any emotion – we could have been going to the local shop to buy groceries, instead of him taking me to have my first paid sexual encounter as an escort!

"Yes," I answered, swigging the last of the coffee in my mug, then picking up my basket and the bottle of chilled bubbly.

"I'll give the champagne to the client," he said holding out his hand. "Right, let's move."

Simon was about thirty-three years old and drove a red VW Golf. We were at the client's premises within minutes. I thought I'd fall apart from fright, have a panic attack. He drove like hell, sometimes round corners on two wheels! Deep breath, I said to myself as the tyres screeched and I held on to the dashboard, applying imaginary brakes with my feet. We didn't speak much – Simon wasn't one for conversation. I had a few puffs of a smoke.

We pulled up outside a block of flats in Bellville and Simon told me to wait in the car. "Remember the fine if you're late," he said pointedly as he got out.

I nodded and watched him check the piece of paper, then go up the stairs to the top floor of the double-storey building, knock on the end door and then enter. After a couple of minutes he reappeared and waved to me to go up.

My knees felt a bit wobbly as I climbed the concrete steps and tried to walk calmly and sedately along the open passage to the flat. I stepped through the front door, held out my hand to the young guy before me and said, "Hi, I'm Rachael."

He had a firm handshake and introduced himself as Frans. While he spoke to Simon and they sorted out the fee for my one-hour services, which was to be paid in cash, I studied Frans quietly. About twenty-six years old, taller than myself, yes, nice looking, oh hell, short reddish-brown hair, and – oh cripes, nice build. Somehow, his being sexy made it worse! Now I really had the shakes and clutched the handles of my basket together in front of me with both hands.

Simon, having finished his talk with the client and counted the money – getting a cash tip for driving me there on top of my fee, I noticed! – left with the words, "See you in an hour, Rachael" and closed the door behind him.

Frans locked the front door, and not knowing what to do next I asked if I could put my basket and jacket down.

He turned, looked at me, smiled and said, "Sure – make yourself at home," then picked up the bottle of champagne that Simon had deposited on the kitchen table. "This is nice, I certainly didn't expect it – would you like champagne, or something else to drink?"

I said I was happy with the champagne and he immediately started opening the bottle. The room was a lounge-cum-dining room-cum-kitchen. An uncomfortable silence followed, and I had the feeling Frans felt a bit self-conscious with me silently leaning against the sink, watching him uncork the complementary bottle of bubbly.

I had a sudden horrified thought that, knowing my luck, the cork would rocket out of the top of the champagne bottle and hit me directly on the end of the nose or something – I'd just die of embarrassment if that happened – and I clutched the stainless steel of the kitchen sink behind me in a sort of petrified agony throughout the uncorking ceremony, with a very calm look on my face which belied my inner turmoil.

Thank heavens! Frans turned out to be pretty deft at uncorking the champagne without any rocketing, popping corks or overflowing, frothing bubbly. He took two glasses from the kitchen shelf, apologising that they weren't the correct ones, and poured some champagne into each glass – and I noticed with some relief that he too was a bit shaky in his hands.

"Shall we go through to the bedroom?" he said.

I nodded and followed him a few steps from the kitchen into the bedroom, champagne glass in one hand, basket in the other. The room was average size. Built-in cupboards along one wall, a double bed pushed against the other, nice chunky duvet in blue and white and a small bedside table. Leading off the bedroom was an en-suite bathroom with a sliding door that later revealed a toilet, basin and shower. The place was very clean and neat.

Frans put the champagne bottle on the bedside table and then sat on the floor facing the bed, leaning against the built-in cupboard, his glass of champagne on the carpet beside him. He leaned forward, patted the mattress and said with a smile, "Sit down and let's just chat a while, I feel a bit nervous. I need a smoke."

Temporary relief! "I do too," I replied without thinking as I sat down on the edge of the double bed facing him.

"Oh, I thought you'd be used to this kind of thing," he said, surprised, lighting up a Winston from the packet he'd taken from his shirt pocket.

"Actually not," I answered, taking my cigarettes out of my handbag. "I haven't been doing this for very long." He seemed to be waiting for me to enlighten him and after a few seconds I added nervously, "Actually, it's the first time."

He smiled easier then and picked up his glass of champagne; then I think he noticed my hands were shaking because he put his glass down again, leaned forward, took my packet of cigarettes and kindly lit a smoke for me. We chatted for a time, mostly about him, and he was easy to talk to. He tried to find out my real name, if I was married, why I'd started doing this and so on. He wasn't aggressive or pushy in any way, he had exceptionally good manners, and was so polite – even addressing me occasionally as "Ma'am". I had to smile at that!

I was out on his age by two years – he was twenty-four. He said it was the first time he was doing this kind of thing. Being in Cape Town on business, he felt lonely. And he wasn't married.

After a while, when we'd finished our smokes, he gave me a shy smile and said, "Okay, I think maybe it's time. Shall we try?"

"Can we shower first, please?" I asked.

"I've had a shower already, but it's no problem having another one," he said as he stood up and crossed to the bathroom. "I'll go first and leave the water running, then you can shower." He popped his head round the bathroom door. "This shower's a bit small, but it'll do," he said almost apologetically, and left the sliding door open.

I grabbed the bottle of champagne, poured a healthy dollop into my glass and gulped it down. Now I felt a bit better. I took out my tool-bag and left it open on the floor next to the bed, and put a few Roosters on the bedside table, together with the KY Jelly and body lotion. I then perched on the blue and white patterned duvet cover in my most calm, seductive pose – shoes off, feet up and legs crossed – when Frans suddenly appeared through the bathroom door without a towel around him, totally naked!

For a fleeting moment, I thought that the mixture of consumed tranquillisers, whisky and champagne were enlarging my natural vision. He gave me a broad smile and sprawled on the bed next to me, lying on his side. He was in fact an exceptionally well-endowed young man in the "privates" department – and beautifully so. Holy moly! I thought anxiously, I hope the Roosters cover that lot!

"Your turn," he said, putting his hand gently on my back.

I got off the bed quickly, picked up my basket and went through to the bathroom, pulling the sliding door closed behind me. I had a very quick shower, dried with my own towel and put on a clean G-string – white lace – and my blue Chinese silk gown, tied loosely at the waist. Frans silently watched me walk to the bed and moved over. I sat next to him on the duvet.

"I'll give you a massage," he said gently, breaking the silence and leaning round me to pick up my bottle of body crème from the bedside table. He then slid the silk gown off my shoulders, his gaze resting momentarily on my breasts, untied the belt and said, "Now lie on your tummy." I did. I certainly wasn't in charge here! Frans was being assertive now, but in a very sensitive manner; I was actually pleased that he'd taken the initiative, as I hadn't a clue what I'd have done next to get things happening.

This sexy twenty-four-year-old guy then sat astride my buttocks and squeezed the cool body lotion onto my back. I could feel his penis strong and hard against my bum. His hands were gentle; starting at the nape of my neck and carefully moving my long hair aside, he massaged the crème over my shoulders, down my back and teasingly around my G-string. "Turn over," he said softly. I did.

I plucked up a bit of courage here and rattled off my memorised rules. "No kissing, no oral sex, no anal sex and all sex with a condom," was my re-hearsed and hurried statement.

"Yes, I notice you've got a good supply," he said, smiling shyly. "Okay, close your eyes." I did. He removed my G-string, kissing my legs in turn, from my bikini line to my ankles. I felt his fingers on my lips, the soft sweetness of the champagne. His hand lifted my head and I felt the glass on my lips. "Keep your eyes closed," he instructed softly. I sipped and he gently put my head back on the pillow, and again the sweet soft champagne fingers on my lips, now in my mouth, on my tongue.

Champagne drops on my nipples, first the one then the other, his lips and tongue, gentle, nibbling, lingering, a champagne line drawn down the cen-tre of my stomach to my navel, the tip of his tongue following the little beads of sweetness. Then his hands – all over, caressing gently and evenly, my breasts, my chest, my stomach, my inner thighs – closer and closer to my now severely aroused and moist softness.

"This isn't supposed to be happening!" I thought. At this rate, I'm defi-nitely not going to be using the KY Jelly! I must be sick because I don't need a dollop of the stuff. Maybe it's the champagne. Oh, stop making excuses, girl, my mind jumped back at me – can't deny it forever: this guy turns you on, even if he's not supposed to, and you turn him on too! This is a case of simple, electric, beautiful body chemistry.

"I think we must put on the condom," Frans said, his lips brushing and lingeringly kissing my neck, so sensually taunting that I felt my skin get goose-bumps.

I longed to bring his face to mine and kiss him properly, on the mouth, but I'd better try to keep to at least one of Christina's rules, I thought; I sure don't seem to be any good at this type of work if this is what's going to hap-pen, I concluded ruefully. I leaned over and picked up a Rooster, tore the paper with my teeth, hands shaky, checked which way, reached forward, held the little titty, positioned it and tried to roll it down. Frans helped me immediately and pulled it down properly himself. I noticed with some dis-may that the condom didn't seem quite long enough. Too bad and too late – not much I could do to remedy that now.

I lay down again on my back on the bed and he next to me, on his side, first studying my body, then caressing, kissing my neck, moving against me, our damp skin electric. Suddenly with one fluid movement he picked me up and put me on top of him. I was amazed he had the strength to just lift me onto him like that. His hardness in me, he pushed me back slightly, fondling my breasts and our gaze held – gentle but intent. I moved on him, smooth and slow, watching his face.

Then he whispered, "I want to lie on you." I got off him slowly, checking the condom was still in place, and lay on my back.

His body covered me. Our aroused nipples caressed, wet with champagne and sweat in the heat of the summer night, on top of the duvet. One moment his face was in my hair, the next his mouth was on my neck. Our movements together were seductive and slow at first – in time, together, then faster, his hands in my hair, our mutual wanting, thrusting, now desperate – my womb aching for his hardness, aching for the infinite, exquisitely sweet split of atom to orgasm. It was me who came first; then Frans raised and supported himself on his hands – and our eyes held as I watched him come, watched his release, his expression as he filled me.

Even though I'd been paid to have sex with him, the strangeness was that this first experience hadn't felt shameful at all! If I said it hadn't been a beautiful encounter, that he wasn't a good lover, that I hadn't felt aroused by him, I'd be a downright liar. Frans was an exquisitely sensual man and an utterly delectable, sensitive lover!

He rested on my chest a while, our sweat dampening the duvet, his fingers lightly tracing my side, lost in the afterwards of warm wetness. Then he rolled over and lay next to me, gave me a wink, and closed his eyes.

I sat up and looked at his penis. Then I looked between my legs. Then I looked at his penis again, and touched it.

"Where is it?" I asked.

"Where's what?" Frans replied, eyes still closed.

"The condom," I said – now annoyed, the pleasure temporarily forgotten.

He opened his eyes, sat up and studied his penis. "I don't know," he said, rather perplexed.

"What do you mean you don't know?"

"I mean I really don't know where it is," he said, trying to convince me.

"Oh! No!'" I gasped in horror, suddenly registering. "Maybe it's inside me!"

We both jumped up then and searched the duvet. No condom. I made a mad dash to the toilet, pulling the sliding door closed behind me. I put my fingers inside my vagina – total panic – felt around, and felt, and oh yes, thank heavens, I could feel it! I tried to get it out, but couldn't. Well, there was no way I could walk around with this thing stuck inside me, I thought, so out it must come!

I opened the bathroom door and leaped onto the bed, spread my legs wide before Frans and said, "I've found it, but you'll have to take it out."

Disbelief, shock on his face. "I can't do that."

"Oh, yes you can," I replied forcefully, now more worried than embarrassed. "I can't get it out, so you'll have to."

"I don't know how to. How do I get it out?" he said helplessly.

"You put your fingers inside me and you fiddle around until you find it, and then you pull it out. That's it, okay?" It wasn't a request, it was a demand.

Somewhat gingerly, and with some nodding encouragement from his booked lady, Frans slowly put his fingers inside me and gently felt around. I sat spread-eagled, waiting anxiously. Seemed like hours – though it was really seconds – that he spent digging around in my vagina.

"Got it!" A little excitement in his voice. "Hold on – got to get a good grip . . ." And out it came – the soggy, used Rooster!

Relief flooded us both and we fell back on the bed together, laughing in disbelief, Frans shaking his head. Despite the obvious fear of possible ugly little monsters hanging out somewhere – which I think flashed through both our minds – it was actually very funny.

He sat up then, had a swig of champagne and fell back on the bed laughing again, quite relaxed and unashamed of his nakedness.

"I hope I didn't hurt you getting the condom out," he said after a moment, looking at me, in a more serious and concerned tone of voice.

"No, you did great – really, thanks a lot, and I'm sorry about that mishap," I answered, not able to keep the smile from my face.

"Okay, so all's well that ends well then – but I'll never forget it. I don't suppose you will either, me being your first client."

"Nope," I agreed, "and I'd better have a shower now, before the driver gets back."

Frans had a smoke while I washed and dressed, ready just in time within the allotted hour. With his boxer shorts pulled on he held out his lit smoke and gave me a few puffs before he opened the door to Simon's knock, first leaning forward and kissing me with slow, sincere tenderness on my cheek.

"By the way, I like your hat," he said approvingly, and gave me a wink as I left.

I returned to the agency with a certain amount of guilt for having actively enjoyed my first booking. I was thankful my first client had been a decent and gentle man – understanding and sexy to boot! I headed straight for Tammy at the reception desk.

"Tammy," I said, standing next to her and speaking quietly, "these Rooster condoms I bought don't seem long enough. What are the ones like that you keep in the drawer? The ones we practised with last night – do they fit big men?"

"Sure they fit big men," she replied looking directly at me. "They fit every size. We've found they're the best. Why? How did your first booking go?"

"It was fine," I answered. "But we had a bit of a problem at the end which I don't want to happen again. The condom got stuck inside me and he had to get it out."

"You asked the client to get the condom out? How – with his fingers?"

"Yes, well I tried, but I couldn't get it out, so I asked him to," I said as casually as possible.

Christina walked up to the desk as Tammy leaned back in her chair and laughed and laughed, her arms folded behind her head.

"What's so funny?" Christina asked inquisitively, peering at the two of us, not to be kept in the dark for a moment about whatever was going on.

"Granny's just been on her first booking and the condom got stuck inside her, so she gets the client to pull it out!" Tammy said, wiping her eyes.

"I told you you'd learn fast," Christina said, grinning and leaning on the reception counter.

Tammy opened the reception desk drawer and took out a supply of about five condoms. "Keep these in your handbag, Granny, and bin the ones you bought, okay?" she advised, smiling at me. "And when you need more, get some from the drawer. I'm going out on a booking now, so Christina's taking over the desk," she said, standing up.

"I'm going to make some coffee now. Want some?" I asked Christina.

"Yes please," she replied, "milk and two sugars, remember?"

I nodded and Christina shook her head as I walked off to the kitchen with my hat on. I don't know if she was shaking her head about my hat or about the stuck condom – and I wasn't going to ask either.

Christina called me to reception about an hour later. I was in the kitchen at the time washing some glasses. A gentleman I'd seen about fifteen minutes earlier when he'd arrived at the agency was standing at the reception desk in front of Christina with a drink in his hand. She informed me that I had a one-hour booking with him, which was to be on the premises and which started immediately, as the gentleman had paid for me already.

In my mind, I went into panic. Puff had said he'd advise Tammy of my "preferences" as discussed with him the night before. But Tammy wasn't on the desk at the moment – she was out on a booking, so obviously someone had not told Christina. It was too late to remedy the problem – the client had chosen and paid for me, and I wasn't able to now discuss the matter with Christina. I'd just have to do the booking.

My one hour started at eleven and I escorted my client to the cubicle, my mind racing. I'd chosen lounge number one, and once we were inside and I'd closed the sliding door, I gave him the rundown on my rules: no kissing, no oral or anal sex, no fingers inside me and a condom at all times.

"Sure," he said quietly and agreeably.

I remember he had a pleasant, friendly face and had spoken politely to me at reception. Further I can't describe this client, as I don't remember. Neither do I remember his body.

"Please would you take a shower," I said politely, and handed him a clean towel. I'd shown him the shower on the way to the cubicle. "I'll wait here for you," I said as he turned towards the door.

"No problem," he answered, taking the towel from me and pushing the cubicle door closed behind him.

I undressed to my bra and G-string (remembering never to be totally naked before a client was), hung my clothes on the hanger, put two condoms, the KY Jelly and body lotion on the bedside table, and sat on the bed. I could hear the shower water start – and then stop again, it seemed almost immediately. I didn't like that. He couldn't have washed his body properly in that space of time.

The cubicle door opened and he entered, towel wrapped around his waist. He bent down and put his clothes in a pile on the floor. Then he leaned forward and began stroking my breasts gently with one hand, and with the other hand he pulled off his towel and dropped it on the end of the bed. His penis was fully erect. He put his hands around my waist and lifted me from the bed, so that I was standing in front of him.

"I want to do it doggy style – from the back," he said, wasting no time. "Turn around facing the wall and kneel on the bed." The words weren't harsh – he spoke softly.

"Condom first," I answered carefully.

He smiled obligingly, reached to the table, took a condom, tore it open with his teeth and masterfully rolled it down over his erect penis as I watched. I squeezed some KY Jelly onto my fingers, reached down and put it between my legs. Then I turned and knelt on the mattress, facing the wall as he'd instructed.

"Move a bit closer this way," he said, "nearer to the table."

I did and knelt again. He immediately put his penis inside me and began thrusting, slow and hard. Suddenly one of his hands held me by the back of my neck, pushing my face forcefully forwards and then holding it sideways against the wall, while he continued thrusting his penis into my vagina.

I remembered Christina's words and managed to put my one hand between his legs and feel his balls, and feel the end of the condom to be sure it was still on. It was.

"You're hurting my face," I said, trying to move my head. His grip on my neck tightened.

Suddenly I heard a cigarette lighter flick. I froze. Then I felt the heat of the cigarette against the skin of my back. His right hand kept my face squashed against the wall while the thrusting of his penis continued, increasing in rhythm.

I didn't dare move. Terror filled me. The hot cigarette was being moved slowly across my shoulders, down my back and onto my buttocks, so hot, almost touching my skin, stopping now and then, being held still deliberately so he could be sure I felt the heat of the red-hot coal. I was too terrified to move, to make any noise or protest. I knew he'd burn me. I realised that was why he'd been so insistent on me kneeling on the mattress so close to the bedside table – that way I wouldn't notice when he picked up the cigarette lighter or the cigarette, because he had my face so firmly forced the other way, against the wall.

It seemed to last forever. Finally he climaxed – forcefully and aggressively, but without uttering a sound – and then withdrew his satiated penis, letting go of me abruptly.

I turned slowly on the single-bed mattress, avoiding any fast movement which might cause him to do something else, and also because my face and neck hurt so much. With his left hand he stubbed out the cigarette butt in the ashtray, and with his right he pulled off the soggy, limp condom and dumped it into my hand. Then he leant down, picked up his clothes and started dressing.

I immediately deposited the used condom in the white bin at the end of the bed, reached for my towel and wrapped it around me, then remained seated on the edge of the mattress, not offering him any assistance with his clothes. He could dress himself. Neither of us spoke. Perhaps my hatred and disgust showed in my face.

Stopping at the cubicle door, he turned and stared at me deliberately for a few moments, and I felt I could read his thoughts from the look of loathing in his dark, almost flat, glassy eyes.

"Think your white skin makes you better than us, don't you? Well, I've just fucked you the way you deserve – shit-scared and submissive. Stupid fucking whore. You'll remember this, won't you?" With a last look of dismissal, as though my life and feelings were valueless, he turned and left.

I stood up, pulled the door closed and latched it. Mechanically I tidied the room, gathered my things together and went to the shower. I stood under the warm water, letting it rain gently down my back. Then I washed and washed myself, my face, all over, everywhere – trying to wash him off me, trying to wash his sick mind down the drain, trying to wash his face from my mind so that I'd never, never have to remember that meanness inside me; but it just wouldn't go, the memory of him stayed, like a blanket of menacing fog falling from the night. Eventually, I had to turn off the running water – someone else might need the shower.

I dried, put on clean underwear and dressed. I'd redo my make-up later. Right now I needed a quiet smoke. I needed a quiet place. I found Puff at the bar checking the stocks of beer in the fridge.

"May I sit in your office for a few minutes please," I asked him. The question was flat.

"Sure," he answered. I nodded my thanks and walked to Puff's office.

Inside the peace and safety of the manager's office, I pulled up the spare chair and sat. The time was twenty minutes past midnight by the clock on the desk. My thirty-eighth birthday was over. I lit a smoke. My emotions and movements felt mechanical. I was filled with a vacant, dead nothingness. I thought I'd feel something – anything – even thinking about nothing would be better than this dead place inside me I'd gone to. No revolt now, no anger either, but no tears as well. No tears? I thought there should be tears. But none came. Just the dead place. Some birthday, I thought: from one extreme to the other. First a good booking, then this second terrifying one, all in the same night.

"Want some coffee?" It was Puff. I think he had an intuition seldom seen in men. I nodded. He put his hand on my shoulder and gave it a gentle squeeze. "How do you take your coffee?" he asked quietly, in an even voice.

"Milk no sugar, please."

When he came back with the coffee, I said, "I need to ask you something."

As always, Puff was there to listen whenever one of his girls had a problem. I told him about the second booking in detail.

"No, Rachael, it shouldn't be like that," he assured me. "Next time anyone treats you badly, scream, just scream, and we'll be there. Smack the sick bastard. Kick him. We can hear from the front and we'll help you." I nodded and lit another smoke.

"Thing is," I answered slowly, "I was too afraid to scream, plus my face was against the wall. The doggie-style position with the lit cigarette didn't give me room to move. I just froze – and my mind and voice froze as well."

"Sit a while quietly – and then go and do your make-up again," Puff said comfortingly, smiling gently. "I'll leave you alone now, I must check on a few things in the front. And I'll tell Tammy and Christina to advise any lady who's on desk duty about your preferences. Remember Roxy's bad booking last night? This one was a bad one for you, Rachael, but the majority aren't bad ones."

He stood up and put his hand on my shoulder again for a moment before he left the office. "By the way, I like your hat," he said, and gave me a wink.

"Sit a while quietly," Puff had said – and he was right. I'd sit a while quietly and get some perspective. And what was it he'd said to Roxy the night before, after her traumatic out booking? "It's just one of those bad ones, Roxy. Put it out of your mind."

Roxy was white, and the guy she'd been with had been white, and he'd treated her abusively. So what was my deadness about? Was it just about skin colour? Was it because my first bad sexual experience as an escort was, co-incidentally, with someone contrary to my personal preferences?

No, that didn't seem right in my mind. Born and brought up in Kenya, having lived in Zimbabwe, Angola, Namibia, the Transkei – without doubt, many of my most enriching experiences from childhood onwards had been with people of other races and skin colours. So perhaps that's partly where my confusion lay now – in the fact that I was so angered by having to face this other side, the opposite of what I'd known.

That wasn't it though. I felt so emptily pained because it was sexual – where the soul lies in its most vulnerable nakedness, the body giving of its most fragile physical offering. New, quaking terror swamped my natural senses. What is normal sex anyway? I thought. I didn't know. What pleasures one person, may well not pleasure another, so somewhere within the realms of sex, unfortunately, lies abuse. Further than that, I couldn't find words – the deadness remained.

So, lessons were coming thick and fast for Rachael. What you'd call a learning curve, I guess. Trying to figure it out didn't seem to help much either; quite simply, I needed the money. As Puff had said: put it out of your mind, it was just one of those bad bookings.

Nevertheless, I'd now add a new rule to my already lengthy list of rules for clients. I'd shower with every man in future and wash him myself, so I'd know the washing was thorough and not a five-second effort.

As for washing the clients from my mind, I'd learn that too – and not just because they'd been "bad ones". Granny had another booking after midnight that night. To this day, I don't remember it and I don't remember that client. I don't know if it was good or bad. I'd hit a blank. Even though you're alert at the time, later the mind just eradicates portions of memory – leaving this blank space of deadness within your being.

I learnt that night that you can't judge a book by its cover; that survival's the name of the game; and that aggression and sickening fear – your guts always in a knot – were part and parcel of the sex racket.

But the pay was good – real good. I earned almost three weeks' grocery money on my first night, though it wouldn't go far enough – not when one is trying to feed a horse as well. Mary-Lou's love, Copper Band, had a somewhat larger stomach than the rest of my little family put together!

On my way home in the early hours of the morning, I cried to my Mountain in a new confusion and loneliness, and she soothed my soul on the breeze:

"Margaret, remember the words of wisdom the minister spoke at Squire's cremation. Just as the grain of sand nestles in the soft flesh of the closed oyster for years until it matures to perfection and beauty, so too must you mature and sometimes cry. For the tears that fall are those that form the pearl in your heart, to sustain you on life's long journey. Never forget your pearl, Margaret."

General's own special kind of loving met me at the front door when I got home. After we'd said our hellos, I made a cup of coffee and went to sit at my desk to give James his promised phone call – just as I'd done the previous morning. And so began a new and added trauma. I was tired, but so was James.

"I haven't slept. I can't concentrate at all – on anything. I've tried doing some paperwork, but that didn't last long. I can't even watch TV, not even the sport," he said in a desperate voice.

And he wanted to know everything – everything – down to the tiniest detail. Psychologically or emotionally I didn't feel that it would be good for him to deal with all the details, and said as much, which just resulted in a fight. It was obvious he wasn't coping after all – and I wasn't either, really.

"I'll deal with the situation a whole lot better if I know what's going on, what you've been doing all night," he yelled down the phone. And so began my nightmare morning telephone calls to James – to relay, exactly, under pressure, what had happened, how much money I'd made, etc, etc. He refused to say goodbye until he knew the lot.

Now utterly exhausted after the heated and painful debate with James, I headed straight for the kitchen – to find the only method of survival I could think of that was better than the steel nail file in my handbag, which hadn't been one bit of use against the second client that night. I hadn't even been able to get to my handbag – and even if I had, my mind could never have imagined that I'd need to use the nail file against a man holding the red-hot coal of a lit cigarette against my naked body.

Bert had suggested I carry a small firearm for protection, but that would be utterly useless, even if I got one manufactured especially for a woman. Firstly, I was in this temporary form of work to feed and support my family, and I didn't have extra money to go buying a firearm now. Secondly, even if I had the money, I'm terrified of guns – I wouldn't know how to use the thing properly. Bert wasn't here to show me and even if he was, I'd probably shoot my own foot off, or worse, shoot the client dead by mistake instead of injuring him.

Yup, it would have to be the frying pan, I thought – my little cast-iron one that you could just manage to fry two eggs in at the same time. I took it out from the top shelf of the cupboard below the kettle, and studied it carefully. If I needed help in the future with a difficult client and my voice froze again, or I couldn't manage to kick him in the groin or something, then I could try to use this instead.

Well, it certainly seemed perfect – the round base of the pan was about the size of a saucer. I fetched my tape measure from my sewing box. The pan was seventeen centimetres across, while the circumference was fifty-two. The handle was only eight centimetres in length, just a tiny bit longer than the middle finger of my right hand. And the entire weapon was solid black cast iron. I sincerely hoped I wouldn't have to use it, but if things really got

bad, I reckoned the frying pan could inflict enough damage to stop a man –
dead, if it came to that.

All in all, the idea of a firearm was definitely out – and the little frying pan
was in!

General studied me intently as he sat on the kitchen floor, his head moving from one side to the other. I wrapped my new survival weapon in a thin
white plastic packet and put it down the side of my basket, the handle pointing upwards so that I could grab it easily if necessary.

The frying pan stayed there forever, from that morning on, within reach –
for the next sick bastard that I might encounter in the scary business of paid
sex.

"You pay for my body," I thought, "but your money doesn't buy my soul –
so welcome, dear sir, to my little cast-iron frying pan. May you always be
kind to one another!"

I went to sleep that morning with General faithfully beside me, so grateful
for the gentle peace and comfort of his love – the same feeling I had about
God. And my last thought before I drifted off was that if I turned the word
"dog" back to front, it came to the same thing: man's best friend.

Chapter Five
The Girls

I suppose it would make better reading if I said they weren't nice. The girls, that is. After all, that's what people probably expect to hear, considering the stigma attached to "women of the night".

The "night" part is not quite correct though, as the girls work during the day as well, depending on the income needed to provide for their families and whether they've made target or not.

These women have rent to pay each month, electricity and water bills – just like anyone else. They stand in queues at the bank, have school-going children who just hate porridge for breakfast and want strawberry pops instead, and even get evangelists knocking on their doors, trying to convert them! A host of normal problems fill their lives, just as for any other woman: pimples, period pains, thrush, backache, headaches and exhaustion. They have to juggle their hours in order to get kids to school and still have time to sleep, clean house, wash and iron, and remember to put out the garbage in time on collection days. Sometimes the washing machine's on the blink, and sometimes their kids get sick – flu, chicken pox, gastro-enteritis, tonsillitis – and let's not forget homework or visiting teachers or attending school sports days. And on top of all this, most of them have partners, and when they get home in the early hours the husbands or boyfriends want their sex as well!

Some have little oddities. Who doesn't? But at a quarter to three in the morning, no one appreciates more the true value of a shared peanut-butter sandwich and a good laugh.

I'd struggled to say the word "prostitute" even before I'd become one. And I'd always disliked the words "whore" and "slut." These three words I now found to be utterly distasteful, quite simply because they imply that women who sell their bodies for financial gain also have naturally low morals or poor characters – a gross misjudgement of the girls' characters.

Of course, there are male prostitutes as well – men that render this service to other men only, to women only, or to both men and women. It's not just women who sell their bodies.

Despite the work the girls did – or rather, had to do – these were nice women that I worked with, good people with decent characters. I find it strange how elements of society require the whore's existence, seeking and paying for various sexual services – yet she is denied the legal right to earn a living in this manner.

Now, let's get on to the girls. First, Cindy. Cindy is a self-confessed nympho-maniac. I never met another sex-worker like her – who really enjoys what she does. She needs sex – and lots of it! But she hasn't always been this way sexually; in fact, quite the opposite. Her story is very sad, but ultimately, I find Cindy most courageous. The memories of her childhood rape still come back to her, but even with the replays, she can't remember it all – and not because she was only in primary school at the time of the incident; I think because her mind wiped much of her inner pain from memory.

As she walked home from school across the field one day, a dark, scruffy man had stopped her near a big clump of bushes and asked her where the shop was. He said he was hungry and wanted to buy a bunny chow. The only other memories Cindy had were the hand over her mouth, replaced by a stinking cloth tied tight around her head, the soil beneath her and the bushes above. The rest was gone from her mind. She shut her eyes tight, tight to block it out forever. Her panties were completely torn down one side, but she put the shredded garment back on and tied a knot at her hip to keep it up.

When she arrived home, no one noticed anything amiss – there were more than six children in her family. She bathed, changed into her afternoon clothes and lay on her bed. And just lay on her bed. By evening, her mother felt her forehead to see if she was "ailing". By morning, Cindy was still the same and her father came and sat next to her on the bed before he left for work. The fourth oldest and favourite of his children just stared – a blank stare. Something in her vacant look said, *let me be*, and her father kissed her fore-head and informed her mother that Cindy was to stay home from school for the rest of the week.

Cindy left home at the end of Standard Eight, when her mother died, to work and help support their large family. Cindy was in nursing for a num-ber of years, followed by a spell in credit control and then as senior super-visor at a laundry. To this day, Cindy still helps support her father.

After being married for a week to her first husband, they'd still not had sex, and Cindy was referred to an elderly psychologist who helped her come to terms with her fears and traumatic childhood experience.

The result of this marriage was a drunken husband and three children for Cindy. He fell in love and left her for a beautiful, refined and sexy woman of mixed race. Considering Cindy's childhood rape trauma at the hands of a dark-skinned man, this caused her almost unbearable emotional pain at the time – like rubbing salt in an open wound. And due to this intolerable drunk-en marriage, she never again drank alcohol of any kind, at all, ever.

Cindy's second husband, in time, revealed his sexual preference for men. Personally, I do not find gay relationships to be distasteful in any way – love is love between any two people – but I would imagine this revelation would be quite a shock to any wife. Accepting and dealing with such a situation must take time and leave the wife perhaps feeling humiliated, cheated on and lied to.

Eventually, when affirmative action was enforced in 1994 in our new South Africa, Cindy was made redundant. Without maintenance or a job, Cindy and her three children were forced to live on a pocket of potatoes. That's all they ate: just potatoes. She'd cook them in every different way she could imagine. However, this diet began to affect their health, and the kids were continuously ill with some ailment or another. There was only one way to improve the situation and ensure survival for herself and her children. And, Cindy decided, if this was the only way out, she'd make sure she was the best, the absolute best sex-worker! She read everything she could to equip herself for this new task – and still today, she's up to date and equipped with all the latest gadgets. She knows it all and does it all.

Cindy started out on the streets. One night a seven-series BMW pulled up; the guy at the wheel was well spoken and expensively dressed, and Cindy agreed to go to his home. Conversation in the car was pleasant and relatively easy. The electric gates opened and closed behind them, as did the garage door; he parked, came around and opened her door for her, and then in to the kitchen they went.

And that's where Mister Nice Guy ended. He pulled out a set of five razor-sharp kitchen knives and put them down one at a time on the expensive kitchen counter.

Looking directly at the inexperienced Cindy, he said, "If you don't make me come within fifteen minutes, I'm going to use these on you, one at a time, until I get what I want."

Cindy couldn't speak from terror and remained, as if fixed in concrete, where she was standing. Her mind raced – there was no way out of this guy's house.

He picked up one of the knives, stepped forward and pointed it at her throat. "Understand? Fifteen minutes, starting now."

Cindy says she has no recollection of what she did to him then – but he came within the fifteen minutes. He then let her out of his property via the electronic gates, and she walked until she could find a taxi to get her back home.

After this terrifying experience she never worked the streets again, and immediately went in search of an agency, which offered a far higher degree of personal protection.

Cindy has five vibrators: two electric plug-in and two battery-operated ones, and one that no longer works. As she says with a grin, "They wear out before I do!"

I admire Cindy's courage and determination in conquering her fear of sex, which stemmed from her traumatic childhood experience, in order to support her family. She turned the ordeal around, faced it head-on (excuse the pun) and made her fear a mastered obsession. Never again would she be at the mercy of any man. He would be at *her* mercy. And, I believe, she is really good at what she does. Cindy is now a medically diagnosed and self-confessed nymphomaniac; but what a nice woman – and interesting!

I know a few men who need some "Cindy treatment." In the beginning she is every man's dream – but she'll become his nightmare. Because when she's finished satisfying him and his penis is soft, floppy and content, that's when she wants her turn – and out will come her penis pump. She'll mount and ride, softly across a rolling mountain and then hard like an outlaw on the run, until she's content. Oh but believe me, within an hour she'll want more!

Any man that walks through the agency door is a challenge for Cindy. Don't say you're impotent. Don't brazenly utter such things as, "You'll never get me to come." Don't whisper that you "just want company and a chat". Cindy is sexy, sensual and insatiable – and if you don't treat her right you could die from a broken knob!

Next, we move on to Amy. I remember well one night the look in her eyes, tears caught in the corners as she said to me, "I wish I could find another job" – and bit her lip to keep from breaking down and crying like a child.

Amy has a Standard Ten and secretarial qualifications, including some years' experience as a legal secretary. She too was retrenched.

Amy has exceptional telephone skills, is a natural "people person" and is capable of doing about five things at once, with utmost efficiency, when on duty at the reception desk. Even though she's slight of build, don't mess with this woman. She has a very firm but polite way of saying "no" – which cannot be mistaken for anything else. But her heart is gentle and kind, and as well as her two children she loves animals. Amy is very attractive with long, thick, red hair, good legs, tiny neat ears, and a lovely deep, husky voice, which the men find irresistible. They also find nibbling her ears irresistible, which drives her mad. She loathes the work she has to do. She can't stand men touching her anymore. Given her natural flair for handling people, I'm sure that Amy would be a top earner in any other sales position. The only way her mind can cope with the stress of the agency and the work she has to do is to have a joint now and then.

One day her new puppy became ill. "Beatnik" was the name she gave him. She'd chosen him because he was the runt of the litter, but the vet later found he had a liver disease and despite initial home treatment, little Beatnik had to be hospitalised. Amy was distraught and desperate to make "target" to cover the vet's bills – anything to save Beatnik. One night, Amy had worked a double shift to make extra money. When she arrived home in the early morning she stayed awake in order to phone the vet for a progress report when the surgery opened. Only there hadn't been any progress, because Beatnik had died during the night. His liver had been eaten away by the illness. Amy had her little four-legged companion cremated, and scattered his ashes under the big tree in their garden – the tree from which hang her many and varied wind chimes – so Beatnik would always hear the soothing tinkles of the chimes in the breeze in their shared "peace place". Then she smoked a joint to numb her brain and dull the pain of losing her puppy.

Next in line, we have Christina. She has two children, has never married and says she never will, but lives with her children's father. Christina's mother ran off with another man when she was just a little tot, still in a crib. Her grandfather was a wealthy farmer, but her father was poor. Granny was deceased, so her granddad brought Christina up until she was fourteen; then she went back to her father. Her grandfather ensured a safe and happy childhood for his granddaughter, and his sudden death when Christina was eighteen left a gap in her life that couldn't be filled by anyone else. But his strength of character was a constant inspiration to her, and she completed her Standard Ten and became a hairdresser. Her hair always looks super and the style changes often – one day curly, one day straight. I asked her if it took hours each day to keep her hair looking that good.

"Not when you know how!" she said confidently. Being a hairdresser, she knows all the tricks for quick beautiful locks which hold all through the night. But her nails are a total mess, bitten so short that I sometimes imagined her fingers must hurt. Even when you can see there's hardly any fingernail left to bite, she's still got her fingers to her mouth, nibbling away constantly.

Christina never met her mother and wouldn't want to now. Once I asked her about the long-term effect on her of her mother running away and leaving her when she was a baby.

"Firstly, I have a constant fear of being left homeless, even at my age – it's difficult to explain. I love my children dearly, and no matter what happens in life, I could never just run off and leave them," she replied. "And I still miss my grandfather – he was both mother and father to me, and I adored him."

Christina is materialistic and almost a "shopaholic", but in this endless shopping lies much generosity. She's been known to give away many of her home furnishings to others in need, including an entire lounge and dining room suite, and then go out and buy more! And if you have nowhere to stay the night, you are always welcome to bed down in her home – Christina hating the thought of anyone having no place to go.

I found Christina to be very helpful and generous with advice about working in "the racket", and I reckon she's got a good, sensible head on her shoulders. It's a pity that I'm not as sensible as she is, considering that we share the same birthday; I'm far too emotional.

Now we get on to Claudia. Claudia has a large silver stud in her tongue and another in her belly button. She's petite and very sexy, with shoulder-length pitch-black dyed hair and hazel eyes, shaded by incredibly long and thick lashes – totally natural. She wears little make-up, dresses casually and loves bell-bottom pants and chunky high-heeled shoes. The men go mad for her.

Claudia has three children and receives no maintenance from her alcoholic ex-husband. "I've hunted and hunted for jobs, and walked until my ankles and feet had blisters – to no avail. So here I am!" she says in her naturally optimistic way. She would dearly love to be an actress and admits to rehearsing on the quiet, at home, in front of her full-length mirror – which, she says with a giggle, gives her a lot of fun and laughs. Her other wish is to form a women's group where members could meet once a week to stitch a quilt together, a really big quilt, and just talk or sit in silence and creative peace.

Claudia's father died at sea and she finds the ocean very soothing to the soul, like he's out there in the great calmness. She's not churchgoing, would like to be, and prays often – with a self-inflicted sense of unworthiness due to the work she does. Claudia's simple joy at the dawning of each new day is as exuberant as spring following winter. Of all the girls I have met, Claudia has the most incredibly electric, happy, positive character. She literally shines, like a gemstone.

Sandy is in her early twenties and comes from a poor, unhappy and broken family. Slowly but surely, her thirty-something layabout husband is eroding every shred of self-confidence she has. He cannot find a job, and her work at the agency supports them and their two-year-old daughter. So why doesn't she just leave him, you may ask? She's tried. Trouble is, he won't let her. Somewhere in his hatred of the work she has to do, is the knowledge that he cannot function without her – and he takes his self-loathing out on her every day.

"Whore!" he screams at Sandy. "You're nothing but a no-good whore!"

Sandy's suffered extreme depression, combined with terrifying panic attacks, during which she was convinced that the world would end. She woke up one day literally unable to see. Thankfully, the blindness was temporary, and with help she has learned to cope better with her depressions and fears. Still, she is always agitated and nervous, and once in the beginning she even ran away from an out booking.

She sometimes throws things when her anger gets the better of her. Since the birth of her baby, she has absolutely loathed sex and is tired of selling her soul to support her family.

Sandy has what I can only imagine must be a turn-on to any man, a magnificent pair of breasts – natural ones. I've never seen them unleashed, but

I'm sure many a man would love to bury his face in their fullness. She has a cute face with large round brown eyes and a big friendly smile – which masks her tortured mind – but I think it's her breasts that make her so popular with the men. Sadly, her self-confidence is so eroded she only feels good enough to go with old, wrinkled men. Somehow, old men don't frighten her as much as younger men do. And had she the choice, she'd go with none of them at all.

Mandy is a sexy big-breasted brunette with a need for fun and laughter, and a very quick and sharp sense of humour. She walks as confidently as a model in her high-heeled stilettos (of various colours and styles), and could make a man cringe if he belittled her or any of the other women in the agency.

I remember Mandy coming back from a good booking with a young, handsome guy, and walking through the agency door as if she was on cloud nine. Her hair was somewhat tousled, a loose strand hanging down across her cheek, make-up looking a bit worse for wear – but her face and eyes aglow! Yes, a good booking with a nice guy is a bonus, and there are times when you get turned on by a client. Most of the girls won't admit it though, except Mandy. As she says, "Even in this work, there must be some perks!"

At the bar stood a forty-something man who'd been there well over an hour, his seven-series BMW parked outside, blocking the driveway. We'd started to ignore him by this time, as he'd remarked that he couldn't find a single woman there that he liked! Mandy pranced across the floor to the bar and poured herself a drink. She was in a really good mood.

The fellow studied her dishevelled appearance as she clinked the ice blocks into her long glass, then leaned forward on the bar counter and said loudly and with obvious disgust, "Jy lyk net soos Liewe Heksie."

This bloke was asking for the end of Mandy's sharp tongue – and he got it. We all kept quiet; the whole place just hushed, dead still for a couple of seconds as we waited for her reply. And a good one it was!

Picking up her glass with practised sophistication and charm, little painted fingernail pointing outwards, Mandy slowly raised her eyes to meet his and in her sweetest possible voice replied, "And you, my darling, bear a striking resemblance to Dracula!" Whereupon she gave him a little nod, eyes never leaving his face, said, "Cheers," with a big smile, and had a good swig from her glass.

That was it! Manners and "discreet behaviour in front of clients" flew right out the window – sorry, forget it, Puff – as we girls just about collapsed laughing; to the extent that the client plonked his glass down in a huff on the bar counter, marched out and screeched off in his BMW. We really didn't need his shit – funny how men think money and a snazzy car are all it takes to get a woman! After his comment to Mandy none of us were interested in doing a booking with him anyway. Luckily for him, Cindy wasn't around at the time or he might never have been able to drive his BMW – she'd have ridden him till his back was finished!

Lindy started escorting when her business went broke due to her constant gambling – or more correctly, her gambling addiction. One-armed bandits cost her everything: her house, her car, the lot. All the years of hard work were fed right back into those slot machines at the casino; whether she won or whether she lost, she kept going back.

Eventually, with nothing left, she came to the agency at the same age as me, thirty-eight. She didn't have the greatest figure, and not the greatest looks either, but she still made money. I asked her if she'd use any of the money from her sex work to go back to the slot machines. She said she wasn't sure; sometimes the temptation seemed overpowering. I found her honesty admirable: it's very difficult admitting to an addiction, let alone having to admit to falling off the wagon once in a while, and I wished her well in her quest to quit gambling.

I could understand addiction – me popping tranquillisers for almost five years and not knowing how or if I could ever stop. How would I ever get through a day, an entire twenty-four hours without one? Especially right now with the sex work – I was taking more tranquillisers than usual. I was aware of it and didn't like it; but how else would I stop my hands shaking, or get some calmness inside me? Perhaps, if circumstances became easier, I'd try to cut back.

Cathy sits quiet as a mouse, reading magazines non-stop. She's a very smart dresser with beautifully manicured nails, her shoes and handbag always matching. Despite a lack of outward liveliness, she's popular with the men.

Melanie is in her twenties, noisy and mischievous with auburn curls and blue, blue eyes. She never wears dresses – always jeans. She has quite a few regular clients.

Some girls came and went – like "Dotty Dick", work name Janet, who used to eat everyone's food. I kept a close watch on my sandwiches while she was in the agency. She was quite overweight, and insisted on wearing a very short, white, stretchy frock covered in black polka dots, which gathered up into a white bow at the back, just below her bum. The outfit was completed with black pantyhose, regardless of the fact that we weren't allowed to wear them. She too was popular with the men. "Dotty Dick" alternated between daytime and night shifts, so I didn't see her every night.

Nancy was a lively, attractive and very popular coloured lady with three young children to feed. She had a university degree, but couldn't find other employment – she was either "under-qualified" or "over-qualified"! When Nancy started at the agency, her husband had left home about six weeks before, saying that he was going to look for work in Johannesburg; this he apparently found – along with another woman. He hadn't come home, and didn't send any money either.

Naomi was an exquisite-looking young woman of smooth ebony skin, small-breasted and quiet. She was a hit amongst the men, her mass of dark, perfectly braided hair swept up fashionably atop her head. She literally vanished after some weeks and we never heard from her again.

Vanessa – another lively character! Vanessa was really sexy, with her dark kohl-rimmed eyes and long black hair. To work up courage, she'd down two beers before doing a strip show. Vanessa could move her lithe young body like a cobra dancing to a flute. Sometimes a group of men would book her for a strip show: the front door would be locked and the lights turned down, and we other girls were allowed to watch. The guys were enthralled – first shy and a bit embarrassed, then courageous, aroused, noisy and never disappointed with one of her shows. She'd undress to the music – her knee-length black boots being the last item of clothing remaining on her body – then put her small breasts in the men's faces, sit on their laps or bend over in front of them, with only her skimpy black G-string on!

Between working hours Vanessa usually got high on something or other. This was her method of coping. I am pleased to say that someone had the sense to see her other qualities, and after about five weeks she was offered a regular job.

Shelley was a very sexy twenty-two-year-old with a doll-like look; together with Cindy, she was the top earner. The blackboard in Puff's office showed a neck-and-neck weekly competition between these two. My name was usually at the bottom, and perhaps once or twice was I second last. It didn't bother me that I didn't earn as much as the other ladies, as long as I paid my bills. Tammy would often smile and shake her head at me when I told her I needed to sit quietly for a while with my smoke and coffee before I agreed to another booking – after I'd had the necessary shower and make-up check, or been to the loo for the umpteenth time, or eaten a sandwich!

Shelley really messed things up in the agency for a while, until word got out about what she was doing. Apparently, she wasn't insisting on condoms. When she started getting sores all over her body the guys began passing remarks. I never asked her what the sores were; everybody sort of steered clear of the matter. It was a touchy subject due to the fact that she earned more than everyone except Cindy – any comments could have been construed as jealousy. We passed our remarks on to Tammy, and she in turn passed them onto Puff; the issue was receiving attention, we were informed.

The sores were round, large, inflamed and pink, with no head – like a boil before it's ready to pop – and were on her chest, shoulders and back; I never saw the rest of her body. I felt uncomfortable when she walked around behind the curtain in a towel after doing a booking on the premises. We all had to use those towels. Even though the linen was taken home and washed daily by Puff's missus (his common-law wife, called "Mrs D" by the girls), I still felt squeamish about what might have gotten onto the towels from Shelley's body sores – so I only ever used my own towel for showering. Unfortunately, I couldn't supply one for the client; he had to use the agency towels.

Then the complaints of money missing from clients' wallets or pockets began. Shelley would often blatantly show us the "tips" her clients had given her – sometimes up to four hundred rand. Considering how much the clients paid to book Shelley, I could never figure out how they still had that kind of money to tip, however fantastic she was. Eventually, she was caught. There were no first or second warnings or written warnings about stealing from agency customers – the first time proof was to hand, Puff fired Shelley immediately and quietly behind the closed door of his office. Shelley left without any fuss or bother, as though she was going home normally. We were all told to take note of what happened if we stole from clients.

I felt sorry for Shelley in a way – though earnings were more balanced after that for the ladies. She was a truly beautiful young woman with an exquisite body; she was also intelligent and very friendly, always smiling. Her dress sense was fantastic, and she always looked like a million bucks – she didn't clothe herself with off-the-peg or sale items like I did. But I never heard her make an adverse remark about another lady's clothing; quite the opposite in fact – she always made a point of saying you looked nice. Shelley was also a generous woman and had a couple of good friends at the agency, and would often buy them drinks.

Sheena was from England. While some of the girls – myself included – balked at the idea, she would quite happily announce to prospective customers, very clearly and directly, in quite a loud voice, that she "did it all – including anal". Never batted an eyelid or twitched a facial muscle either as she said it. The girl had guts, I thought. After a couple of weeks Sheena also just vanished, and we never heard from or saw her again. I know she had a young child that her parents had taken away from her, and I'm sure this emotional pain was part of the reason for her disappearance.

I've yet to see a truly perfect girl in the agency. Some have looks. Others have beautiful hair. There are those with good legs or fat legs, big breasts or small; some have beautiful eyes or a full mouth (men love a full mouth) and some are slim and some are fat. Every lady has male admirers. Even a mole at the corner of the mouth can be a turn-on to a man. And there are guys who love feet – polished toes they want to suck – or nice ears they want to nibble and put their tongues into!

Escorting has taught me that there is indeed a lid for every pot – a most important lesson; a woman's inner sensuality shouldn't be submerged or suffocated by relentless images of thin, good-looking models. Plentiful bosoms, large hips and well-rounded curves are just as sexy! When a woman loves herself, loves her body, is proud and accepting of her own natural beauty and sets her sensuality free, she exudes a charm as alluring as jasmine to a bee – regardless of her size, shape or looks!

When I was working there, the ages of the girls ranged from eighteen to forty or so. The majority of my bookings were with younger men; the older men seemed to like the young girls.

Some girls stay in the same agency for years and some get fed up with certain rules and join another. Yes, we have arguments and there's the normal bitching; but it's no different to any office situation; I've actually experienced more petty squabbles in other positions of employment than during my time as a sex-worker!

One evening, Granny Rachael got fed up with being "chief coffee maker". I'd brought it on myself, as everyone knew I drank coffee continuously. Anyway, I wasn't in the best of moods and felt like some peace and quiet so I went to the kitchen, made myself a cup of coffee and then sat down on one of the couches and began reading a magazine.

Cindy walked up to me and said, "Hey! That's nice – only making coffee for yourself, and not offering anyone else a cup."

I didn't feel like her shit. I looked up from my magazine and replied, "Well, I'm actually sick and tired of always making everyone's coffee around here. Perhaps people should make their own more often."

"Keep your pants on, Rachael, there's no need to be like that," she said and as she walked past the reception desk I heard her remark to Tammy, "Boy, is Granny not half in a bad mood tonight!"

Well, it seemed to resolve the problem. News travels fast. After that incident, the other girls often offered me coffee.

There are plenty of rules in this business and it is far more complicated than outsiders can imagine. Stress levels are naturally high and worse if you don't reach your personal target. Of the many different forms of work I've done in my adult life – telephonist, secretary, sales agent, assistant buyer, vehicle spares dealer, even working in a corner café – I can say in total honesty that I've never experienced such a difficult form of employment; it's really tough, earning your money as an escort. I used to feel that my packages in those previous jobs didn't match what I was rightfully due, for whatever reason – until I became a sex-worker. Did it not half make me realise, in hindsight, how blessed I had actually been at the time!

The escorting "employment package" goes like this: no letter of appointment, no pension, no paid sick leave, no paid public holidays, no unemployment benefits and no paid pregnancy leave, no company car or car allowance, no bonus, no medical aid, no housing subsidy, no free drinks except tea and coffee – and zero danger pay.

One fair perk – no restraint of trade! Condoms are supplied, and toilet paper, fresh towels and soap. Sometimes the soap runs out and someone brings a bar along. In the beginning, I even took shampoo and a nailbrush for the shower – Tammy just shook her head and laughed at me. "You'll learn soon enough," she remarked.

It didn't end there. There were fines too – for sitting on the desk, or being overtime, or for not tidying the room after you, or forgetting to empty the condom bins – which are deducted from your pay at the end of a shift. There were restrictions on what you could wear. And each time you were collected from or taken home by one of the drivers, petrol money was deducted from your earnings immediately.

Street prostitutes operate differently and charge different fees to agency escorts or home sex-workers. From one escort agency to another, the fees and the split of income between worker and employer can also be different. Quite simply, you only earn when you work; and this particular escort agency was closed on Sundays. Sometimes you could get an advance loan against future bookings. Pay-time was four or five o'clock in the morning, sometimes later – depending on when the last booking finished. If you wanted to go home earlier you could, given permission.

One night, Granny had a set-to with one of the drivers when we got back to the agency from an out booking. I'd heard the drivers made good money. I'd also heard that when the client was paying cash for an out booking, the driver would pretend to have too little or no change. The client, being embarrassed and in a hurry to have his time with the lady as the clock was ticking, would usually say, "Oh, it's okay, you keep the change."

So Granny got to thinking. First, there were set rates for the bookings, of which the lady earned a percentage and the balance went to the agency. If the booking was not on the premises, petrol money was added, the amount depending on how far away the client lived – and some bookings were right up the west and east Cape coast, or inland. And let's not forget about the extra five rand a girl had to pay the driver for going half a kilometre down the road to get her a pie when she was hungry. On top of this, the driver then deceitfully misled the client!

Fuck this for a joke, I thought! It's my body being sold here, not the driver's. Me lying on my back or with my legs open is what's paying his salary – all he's doing is driving the car! So if he's going to deliberately lie about the change and get the tip, then by rights I deserve half of that tip!

So we had it out in the kitchen: Granny Rachael leaning against the old white fridge, hat on, bee in her bonnet. Here she goes! I wasn't about to give in without a lengthy debate. I won my argument; the driver threw in the towel after about ten minutes and I got half the money – dumped begrudgingly in my hand – and was understandably not very popular with the drivers for a while. The other girls all agreed: it was a far more fair distribution of the driver's tips, and our incomes improved slightly after that.

Some husbands and boyfriends have no idea what kind of work their partners are doing. This causes numerous lies and problems, not to mention increased stress levels. I preferred to be honest with James and my children. In fact, my children were most supportive and understanding, especially when I needed sleep, and they knew that I wasn't doing "the work" just for fun. James, on the other hand, was a different kettle of fish.

Apart from the psychological problems of being a sex-worker, living two lives wears the entire system down: the long nights, stress and eating takeaway foods at odd hours take their toll on the body.

On cold nights we'd all huddle round the oil heater, which wasn't good for business – despite desperately needing the money, we were loath to move away from the warmth when prospective clients walked in. So the heater was removed by Puff. I needed extra showers on chilly nights just to keep warm and to stay awake, let alone undress and sexually perform in the freezing hours at a moment's notice – having to smack on a dollop of lubricating KY Jelly down there between my legs, which by then felt as though it was bordering on a temperature slightly above zero! Nipples instantly erect – and it certainly wasn't a case of "are you pleased to see me?" No, just plain cold!

Apparently, some prostitutes inject a solution made from a Schedule 7 tablet directly into the vein in the groin or the vein behind the knee, in order to feel absolutely no pain and be able to "do" up to ten men a day. Sadly, this method of dulling the pain can result in gangrene for the sex-worker concerned – though I must hasten to add that I never saw or heard of this being done in the escort agency I worked in. Drugs were not allowed on the premises.

However, because of the work they do, sex-workers are also good drug targets – illegal work, stress, exhaustion, desperate need for emotional and physical relief . . . it can add up (though definitely not always) to being the perfect drug buyer. Which in turn makes for a pretty perfect police bust. Apart from the other stresses, the prostitute must still work with the constant threat of being arrested, perhaps jailed, fined or having her children removed due to her being considered an unfit mother. To my mind, policemen who approach a prostitute with the view to deceive – asking sexual favours or enticing her to commit a sexual act for money and then arresting her – are accomplices to the act. Surely they have better things to do, better ways to spend the state's money?

I've seen girls continue working while they're pregnant – up until a month before the baby's due – because it's their only means of financial support. This particular aspect of escorting made me feel very sad. One girl strapped her stomach in so that her pregnancy wouldn't show, and fainted on several occasions.

There were requests to urinate on the client – a "golden shower". Some guys preferred one step further – politely known as "emptying the bowels on demand" on the client's stomach or chest! I am relieved to say that I was never asked to perform either of these two acts. The former I believe is quite good for curing athlete's foot or relieving chilblains. The latter, however, should only be done in toilet bowls and the results safely flushed down the s-bend afterwards. Once again, however, each to his own!

Some girls continue doing sex work during their monthly periods; they stick sponges up their vaginas, and the client is none the wiser. I never took much note of specifics of this procedure – inserting the sponge correctly – as it gave me the heebie-jeebies just thinking about it. Amy once got a sponge stuck inside her and she had to insert tweezers up her vagina to pull it out – you've got to be pretty tough to do that. But who was I to judge when a girl could or could not work? Many people have sex while the woman has her periods – some women find they get turned on more during menstruation. Myself, I'm not particularly taken with the idea; and with Aids being so easily transferable through blood products, I reckoned a menstruating vagina was really dicey and steered clear of the agency during my monthly time.

The health risks are high in sex work, even if you're careful. You learn to study penises and bodies without the men noticing. And you can never judge a book by its cover: murderers, stranglers and prostitute-killers don't walk around with warning signs on their foreheads. You need a level head every time you walk into a room with a man – there have been occasions when their pals have hidden in the cupboard, or under the bed, until the driver has left. You'd thought it was just the two of you, and suddenly it turns out it's not. Some girls have faced guns and knives and jumped out of more than a few windows to get away.

One of the girls was once booked by a guy – for his guy! The man that had booked the lady intended to watch her and his boyfriend together and get turned on in the process – and then he and his guy could do whatever, and then perhaps the three of them could do whatever. Except that the bloke that arranged the booking hadn't figured on jealousy creeping in, and became enraged instead when he saw his guy getting it on and enjoying himself with the agency girl.

This particular booking then turned out to be dangerous – as in guns and a fast getaway kind of dangerous! With the girl stark naked and into the swing of things with the boyfriend, the one that had booked her suddenly pulled out a firearm and pointed it at both of them. His partner then tried to ease the situation, apologising profusely for becoming so sexually excited by the young lady, and offered to phone the agency and have her removed immediately. He was handed the telephone and the girl gave him the memorised number. With the gun to her head, still naked, she waited while the situation was explained over the phone and the driver was sent to fetch her. She then asked if she could use the toilet, and was followed at gunpoint to the bathroom – where, behind the closed door, she jumped out of the window into the flowerbed below, twisting her ankle, and hid while the arguing continued in the house. When the driver screeched to a halt outside, she dashed to the car and arrived at the agency still straightening her clothes.

The young girl was still terrified out of her wits – she'd been told she'd get her head blown off if she so much as looked at the other guy again! Poor thing, she was in a right state. If it had been me, I think the opening to my vagina would have temporarily closed from fright reflex – rendering my immediate potential as a sex-worker null and void! Sort of like the "temporarily out of order" sign on the ATM screen.

But that's unfortunately part of what a sex-worker's job entails – you never know what's going to happen and you've just got to cope as best you can, or you could land up dead.

One of the girls was regularly booked by a guy for his wife – husband would watch the two women in the double bed, thereby getting turned on himself, and then have sex with his wife. The wife wouldn't allow him to have sex with the escort however – she was required to watch. The girl hated these particular out bookings, but the guy always insisted on the same lady.

I remember a foreign bloke one night who fancied me. While I was sitting in front of him on the pouffe, a lady came and sat next to him, and eventually they went off and did a booking. Then Christina very pointedly had a chat to me, not angry with me but a little irritated: why had I just given my booking away like that, when I could see full well that the bloke wanted to go with me? Well, there was nothing wrong with the guy and I'd have gladly done the booking with him, but the other girl hadn't made bucks yet that night and I had – it seemed no skin off my nose, so the longer he sat, the less interest I paid him; I'm not a remotely competitive person.

The girls never fought over clients – it was understood that we each tried to get the booking in a nice, discreet way, but you backed off when you saw another girl making progress.

There were some other very refreshing qualities to the girls. Personal "woman things" – were openly shared: "Oh fuck, Rachael, I tried to wax my fanny last night, fuck does it hurt! – so I've only done one side. Have a look at this –" Giggle, giggle, giggle.

"Hey, Cindy, I've just bought a new lipstick that would look great on you – here, try this – if you like it, I could get you one tomorrow."

"Anyone want this top? I bought it last week and I don't like it any more . . ."

The lack of female rivalry was incredible. One would think there'd be jealousy, considering that we all earned our money from sex, but actually it was the opposite – nothing like in the normal world.

If you had a problem about sex – something that hadn't worked quite right perhaps, or that you weren't sure of or shy about – you could quite happily ask any girl, and she'd easily chat about it and give her thoughts, without you feeling remotely silly, embarrassed or stupid. She'd laugh if she thought it was funny, but the laughing was never *at* you – and we laughed plenty.

Sex discussions amongst us girls were like a breath of fresh air – you could say anything you wanted, and no-one batted an eyelid. There was none of this western, conditioned closedness on the subject – you could go from discussing blow jobs to some recipe for curry without taking a breath. It was lovely to feel so free in the speech of sex.

But we really didn't gossip among ourselves about actual sex with clients; I cannot ever recall any lady discussing a client's genitals – big or small, or the manner in which he "did it" – not even difficult bookings.

I remember arriving back at the agency from a one-hour out booking during my first week, leaning on the reception counter and saying to Amy, "I feel a bit buggered. That guy wanted it again, but I still had to shower before Henry picked me up."

"How many times did you do it?" she asked me, peering over the reception counter.

"Twice," I answered.

"In that case, I'd say you're feeling fucked, not buggered," chipped in Christina, leaning on the counter and laughing.

She didn't miss a thing, Christina. "What's she find so bloody funny?" I thought to myself. "It's none of her business anyway." I kept quiet.

"Granny – listen carefully. And watch my lips," said Amy, loud and clear so I wouldn't misunderstand: "One hour, one fuck. Got it?"

I looked at her, disgruntled. "Thanks for telling me now."

"Can't expect us to remember to tell you everything – you learn as you go along, Rachael!" laughed Christina and walked off to the kitchen.

"If he wants it again," Amy continued, "then you must negotiate with him right then and he must pay what you ask before you do it again. Okay? And that extra money is yours only – none of it goes to the agency."

I kept quiet, at a loss for words. Amy pondered a moment, then said, "If you keep up with two fucks for one hour, firstly you'll be doing yourself out of money and secondly, your other lips, the ones between your legs, are going to get worn out." She smiled and shook her head at me.

"So I take it then that two hours is two fucks, right?" I asked her. I couldn't afford to mess up again on such a matter; better to ask direct questions and get direct answers.

"Right," Amy said as the phone rang.

Life for me became measured by fucks. Need to pay the electricity bill? Then you need one fuck, and you'll get six rand change! The groceries were twenty-two rand more than one fuck. A tank of petrol gives you one hundred rand change from a fuck – depending on the car, of course. Feel like a pizza tonight? Well, that's one fifth of a fuck. Want to go to the movies to sit with the rest of society to enjoy yourself, have some time off? Have to get a fuck first!

To pay the rent each month is on average about twelve and a half fucks. That's twelve and a half times a tortured mind. Not to mention school fees, doctor's bills for bladder infections, medicines and regular checkups, clothing, water and telephone accounts, car insurance . . . and don't forget the psychologist or psychiatrist's bills either, if you should land up needing one because your head's fucked up from all the fucking.

Of course, one could beg. I believe that some people make as much as eighty rand a day from begging, and don't even bother looking for work. I have my own ideas on the subject; maybe they aren't fair. If a jobless person tries to earn a living in whatever way – car washing, housework, playing a violin on the street, gardening jobs, making and selling marmalade, picking up trash off the streets, whatever – then that's fine with me. The universe needs give and take, though, to keep harmonious balance. While generosity and kindness are necessary, continuously taking without any form of returning isn't enough to keep the equilibrium. So able people who simply stand around with cardboard signs begging for money and help (and I've seen some doing this wearing leather jackets and smoking), don't have my respect like the girls do.

So call us whores or prostitutes, or be kinder and call us escorts or sex-workers – as far as I'm concerned, these women are as deserving of rights as any other employee. At least they're earning their own money to support themselves and their families. They're not living off other people's hard-earned cash or expecting Welfare to support them or their families. And I wonder if Welfare *would* support a sex-worker and her children – or would they take her kids away and put them in foster care until she could find a more "acceptable" job?

Being in the racket gave me what I consider a wider, more expansive view on the sale of sex. It's a service offered or a commodity.

Sometimes the girls would discuss the images portrayed in adult magazines and blue movies. The majority of us felt that what is being put across to the public in these features and tapes does not correctly represent the sex-worker's life at all. The viewer of such material often expects from the sex-worker what he or she has seen in this material. But the manufacturers, photographers and actors of these "visual features" have entirely different concept of the sale of sex to that of the actual sex-worker. However, they too offer a commodity.

More than any other attribute, more than a good body or big breasts or a lust for sex, what a woman needs in this business is a sense of humour. But everything in life has a price, and sometimes even with a sense of humour, some girls get swept up into black pain, prisoners of their own minds. It can be a one-way ticket to paying the bills – or to a broken mind or body, or both.

Once in the racket though, it's difficult to get out. Firstly, you need the money, and secondly, the adrenaline highs of escorting become addictive. The pump of adrenaline is silent and not noticeable to anyone else, but it starts pouring into the bloodstream each time you prepare to go to work and increases as each client arrives to choose a lady. Eventually, it's something you need – something you must have to function, like needing a fix. When you stop the racket you go into subconscious adrenaline withdrawal – it took me a while to realise what was missing.

This work has had a damaging effect on my personal sex life – to the extent that I can quite happily go without sex for some time now. Yes, I can still be lustful and passionate on occasion, but for now I prefer the old-fashioned, romantic way – lots of gentle and passionate kisses, touching, easing into matters, wining, dining and dancing: sex and the soul stuff. I think it'll take some time for me to get back to wanting regular sex. For the moment I'm quite content touching myself, if necessary. That way it's always perfect, always safe, without stress, without pain, without fear, relaxed – and without guilt! I'm hurting no one, and no one else is hurting me.

Apart from the pleasure of a shared peanut-butter sandwich, a piece of pizza or a pie and sometimes crying together, the girls also taught me to appreciate the joy of simple, honest, unaffected laughter – totally non-judgemental, and priceless to the soul. And some people think the only other things we do as adult female sex-workers is paint our nails and drink ginger squares while we wait! When there were no clients around, we girls would turn the music up and dance together in a group, kick off our shoes, sing, play silly buggers and laugh – just laugh.

And no man can put enough money on the counter to buy even one of these shared laughs I had with the girls – laughter from caring, kind and compassionate women of good heart, despite the work they do or the labels society has given them.

Chapter Six
The Nymphae Soak, Brozam and God

I was exhausted out of my mind doing two different jobs in every twenty-four hours.

About ten days now in the escorting racket, I was in overdrive – the night stuff was killing me. Your whole system's upside-down. When you're supposed to sleep, you're awake. My chest burned. Nicotine, being a stimulant, helped keep me awake, as well as the copious mugs of coffee, but I'd have to switch to lighter smokes – sometimes I felt I could hardly breathe.

And what about my stomach – I mean bowels? Whatever happened to my morning "regular"? Bum didn't know its arse from its elbow. Come sunrise, it usually wanted to go to the loo. However, sunrise would come and its owner would be asleep, so now it has to wait. Eventually, when its owner wakes up, with all the waiting it's now got stuck – tight as a cork in a bottle. We'll have to add more fibre to the diet, I thought, otherwise I'll land up with haemorrhoids! Sitting on the loo was kind of like trying to play the trumpet I used to own, but could never get a sound from – except without the trumpet! Cheeks once again like a hamster, but pushing and straining, as opposed to blowing. Nothing. Time was a consideration as well: extended stays on the loo for a nil result were time wasted, as I could have watered the garden or checked sales paperwork or done half a dozen other household chores.

And what about the other things – the penises? Exhausted, I'd close my eyes for sleep, and here they'd come, out of the dark. "You've had my body, now leave my mind alone," I'd say out loud. Cocks – just cocks. No faces, no bodies, not even money; just cocks. Didn't they have anything else to do? Light ones, dark ones, thin ones, fat ones, long ones, short ones, skew ones, big-headed ones, pointy ones, veiny ones, warty ones, un-foreskinned ones, foreskinned ones – all dancing around, victorious.

"For fuck's sake, can't you leave me alone?!" I said angrily, burying my face in my pillow, trying to blot out the images and get some sleep. Little Bart, Bert's pup, had wriggled under my sheet nose-first like a mole, and General raised his head from the mattress beside me, studying me with concern – he was pretty tired as well, and I gave him a tickle on the ear.

"Perhaps we need a restful holiday," I said in a quieter voice. Yeah, how about a slow boat to China – with Mary-Lou, Matthew, General, the two cats and Bart on board. We could stop at some unknown island on the way and

83

stay there. China wouldn't miss us and we probably wouldn't have found it anyway! Quite an enticing idea, really, for a much-needed rest – except I then remembered to add Copper Band to the entourage, which finished this alluring concept once and for all. I'd need Noah's Ark, and that's long gone!

Bert's laugh popped into my mind, and that always cheered me up. He'd phoned the previous evening to find out how things were going. I gave him a further general rundown on my new employment, but when I told him about the guy who held the cigarette against my body, Bert became extremely concerned.

"Hell, Mum, this sounds dangerous," he said anxiously. "You can't do this work without some form of protection, especially after a client like that."

"I know you're worried about my safety," I answered, "but I'll be okay, really – I've got the little frying pan now and carry it with me in my basket all the time."

"You've got the *what*?"

"The little cast-iron frying pan – you know, the small black one we fry two eggs in at a time."

"Yes," he answered slowly, "and what exactly are you going to do with it?"

"Well, it's small, solid and very hard and it fits in my basket perfectly. I'll hit the next guy on the head who tries shit like that with me," I said convincingly – sounding a lot braver and more confident than I actually felt.

Bert couldn't help himself at this revelation and erupted into peals of laughter on the other end of the phone.

"Yes, I know it sounds ridiculous," I countered, "but I feel more comfortable having a frying pan instead of a gun, and I think it's a pretty good weapon."

"It's not ridiculous, Mum," he answered, gathering himself at last. "But it does seem funny – an escort, my mother, walking around with a frying pan for self-protection! What do Mary-Lou and Matthew say about it?"

"They think it's amusing, but a good idea as well."

"Okay," Bert said agreeably, not able to keep the twinge of mirth from his voice. "Try the frying pan, but if it doesn't work well enough, I think we'll have to look into a lady's handgun for you, okay? I've got to go now." I could hear his laugh again before the call disconnected.

Anyway, thank God for the Nymphae Soak – the term I'd now given my bath routine. I'd become a water baby out of necessity: having always had a strict standard of personal hygiene, I was now neurotic about cleanliness. The soak in the tub was a vital cleansing of the body, and very necessary to soothe the mind to some sense of normality.

The female genital anatomy is more complex than that of the male human; the labia majora and labia minora now needed to be soaked in salt and bicarbonate of soda on alternate days. Too much of this wasn't good either;

while the sodium chloride was a natural disinfectant, overdoing it could result in an imbalance of the necessary bacterial levels in the vagina, thereby causing infection – apart from the possibility of drying up and turning into salted snoek! And in the escorting business, the last thing you need is a shrivelled purse.

Then I needed to douche with Betadine as well to definitely kill any lurking little monsters which the salt may have missed. The bicarbonate of soda on alternate days was marvellous for soothing a worn-out, sensitive fanny that had been subjected to thrusting penises that couldn't afford to stop momentum to re-lubricate with KY Jelly.

I'd done some reading on bacteria and viruses – which gave further cause for my initially logical, now obsessive, need for the Nymphae Soak. Showering before and after each booking with a client was also an absolute must. Consider a few things here: our bodies, both inside and out, are covered in hundreds of different kinds of naturally beneficial and friendly bacteria necessary to normal, healthy living. It is important not to upset this truly amazing balance of nature and the human anatomy. While kissing wasn't done in our work, about two hundred and fifty types of bacteria are exchanged in a French kiss! Most of our resident bacteria, for example, are in our guts, and the human colon contains up to five hundred species, weighing around one and a half kilograms altogether. The examination of a single human pooh, to identify all the different bacteria contained therein, can take up to a year! What a novel way to solve unemployment, I thought – thousands of people could have a permanent job, just studying human pooh!

I remembered Cindy and I having a chat about anal sex one night at the agency.

"Rachael," she enthused, "for the most fantastic orgasm you'll ever experience, you must try anal. Believe me, it's the best there is."

"No ways," I answered. "And please don't take this personally. I don't mind anyone else having anal sex, but I'm not interested, not one bit. In fact, I take it as a personal insult to my femininity that a man would prefer to poke his knob in my bum when I've got a fanny. Why do they want to, as a matter of interest, anyway?" I asked her.

"It's tighter," she answered simply. I so admired Cindy's direct honesty with regard to sex. "You know – a tighter fit around his penis, more sensation for the guy, especially if his partner's had a child."

"Yeah, I bet it's tight all right," I answered, ready for a bit of humour, "kind of strangulation method – unless he's got a thin knob." I couldn't help laughing.

"Don't be stupid," Cindy replied seriously. "You start slowly and carefully with plenty of lubrication, you don't just shove it in."

"I couldn't give a hoot about the method of penetration, I'm not going to try anal sex, no matter how much you try to convince me," I said. "I've had kids. In my old age I can already look forward to the possibility of wetting my pants when I cough or sneeze – I don't want to add dirtying my pants to that as well!"

"Really, Rachael, you can be so dogmatic at times – just like a granny!" she replied, exasperated. "Anyway, I think you should start doing exercises to tighten your fanny – I do, every day."

"Oh yeah, and what do these exercises entail?" I asked, having a puff on my smoke and vaguely hoping I could be more co-operative about this new aspect of sex that had suddenly popped into our conversation.

"I use a pencil," Cindy replied in a matter-of-fact tone of voice as she picked up her cup of coffee and took a sip.

"A pencil, you mean a writing pencil?" I asked, dumbfounded but certainly interested in another of her enthralling revelations.

"Yup," she replied evenly, without the slightest hesitation. "You put the pencil in your fanny – not the sharp end, of course –" I was relieved about that and couldn't help the smile that crept into my face! "and then you tighten and relax your vaginal muscles. Once you can hold the pencil steady in your fanny for about two minutes at a time, your muscles will have firmed sufficiently."

"Goodness me, that's amazing," I replied more seriously, pondering the matter a moment. "Well, some of the first sailors to go to the North Pole died from lead poisoning, from the tins containing the baked beans they had on board. So I think I'll skip the pencil, Cindy, but thanks!"

She eyed me seriously from her seat next to me on the couch. "Nothing's happened to me yet and I promise you, it works." Obviously, Cindy wasn't about to give up on what she felt was sound advice.

"Yes, but at my age, I might need quite a big lead pencil," I said, laughing and wiping my eyes.

"Sometimes you're utterly impossible, Rachael," she replied, fed up with my silly wit, reaching for her handbag on the floor. "I'm only trying to help you." She took out her purse. "Anyway, I need a burger or something, I'm starving and I still don't see what's so funny about the pencil – but it's alright, you don't have to take my advice."

My anus, I thought, was and will always continue to remain purely for the elimination of my own waste material. What other people did was their right and their business, but I most certainly was not going to allow any erect penis to stretch or tear this muscle of mine – no matter if the object in question would have its dreams fulfilled. No matter how much its owner, or Cindy, assured me that I would experience an orgasm of cosmic proportions. And I definitely did not want my five hundred species of bacteria buggered up by some thrusting knob.

I took the long Nymphae Soak after I came home from work and also before I left home in the evening – without it I would not have been able to face the night in a controlled state of mind, as this was not only a ritual of cleansing for myself, but necessary "psyching" time for the hours of paid sex ahead. I often found my psyching in the bath would be quite aggressive, and on these particular evenings I would cope better – a sense of anger imbued me with a false sense of self-confidence.

I then showered with each client before a booking to assure myself that the gentleman was clean. It also killed some of the allotted booking time, and half the battle was won on the sexual front – the client sufficiently aroused by the time we returned to the lounge, making what followed usually less physically tiring and stressful for myself; the act itself accomplished quicker, giving us time to chat a bit. Then I'd dress him and he'd leave. But for me, it was back into the shower again!

Puff had said that I'd soon be able to service seven men a day. What a dreadful expression, I pondered. Service? Service! May as well be a motor mechanic. Need a brain service instead at this rate! However, no matter how much money was at stake, I could never do more than three men in any twenty-four hours – my mind simply could not cope.

When I arrived home as the sun came up, I'd sit in the bath and soak for ages, and time seemed to stand still. My brain went into shut-down – total blackout – and for no apparent reason the tears would fall, mixing with the salt or bicarbonate of soda in the bath water. I didn't sit and sob – just a silent crying, in the solitude of my water world.

Then there was James's stress – understandable, but still a cause of considerable stress to myself. Constantly on the phone, he'd demand that we talk, regardless of whatever else I was doing at the time or had to get done during the daylight hours. And now I had to phone him from the agency before I did any bookings as well, stating how long and where they'd be; and don't forget his questioning of every detail when I got back home. What did the guy look like? How old was he? How big was his penis? How did he like doing it, did he enjoy it, did I, did I get turned on, what was I wearing, how many clean G-strings had I worn, had I worn the white one he'd given me?

I didn't want to discuss these matters in length, but he decided otherwise, and arguments ensued if I wouldn't comply. Regardless of how tired I was in the early mornings, James flatly refused to put the phone down until I'd answered all his questions. He then started telephoning the agency and plaguing the girls about my bookings. I in turn was called into Puff's office and told to sort out my boyfriend – or else. I relayed this message to James, which only made him more incensed. Then I'd start to cry from the fighting and shouting and trauma on the phone, and he'd insist on jumping into his car and driving to my house immediately to comfort me. I'd tell him I didn't want sex right then (I knew James's idea of comforting would include sex) – that I needed to be left alone for a time before he touched me.

"Yes," he'd say insistently. "I understand, I won't try anything, I don't want sex right now – I'll just lie next to you and comfort you."

Oh God, and then it'd start – the penis up like a warrior to battle, and I'd sit up in the bed and scream every obscenity at him I could think of to put him off. Nothing worked – he wanted his sex. If I could have it with other men then I could have it with him, now, when he felt like it too. I just could not seem to get through to him that after a night at work I just wanted to lie next to him, that I needed some space to get my head together, to separate my mind and rid myself of "them" first, before I could cross to "him".

Since I'd met James, he'd consistently demonstrated a stable character and even temperament; he was an avid bridge player and also a member of the Lions Club, doing charity work in his spare time. Quite the opposite of me in terms of life and personality, I'd often thought. Until now, James had always been a quiet type, and Mary-Lou often said he looked like an owl with his spectacles perched on the end of his nose. I was the more boisterous, verbal one, singing and chatting – though his English sense of humour was wonderful. He didn't hum or sing in the shower for example, whereas I'd warble along gaily to music wherever I happened to be in the house, or talk to the dogs, or the plants for that matter, and James would shake his head at my antics when we were together.

I was the more spontaneous decision-maker, James needing to mull things over first for a while, sometimes days. He was exceptionally intelligent and especially mathematically inclined, able to do mental arithmetic in seconds, quite unlike myself, who needed a calculator.

James didn't smoke either, and rarely had an alcoholic drink – I'd only seen him drunk once. His favourite English soccer team won the cup in 1995 and James had invited some friends over to watch the match and have supper. With his faithful supporter's scarf and cap on, James had become increasingly sloshed as the match progressed on the television, and unable to conceal his absolute joy at his team's achievements, had taken to sipping everyone's drinks.

After a while, staggering from the concoction of quickly consumed al-coholic beverages, James started making a right banana of himself – hug-ging the women, making pathetic jokes with the men. I didn't envy one bit the hangover I reckoned he was going to have the following day!

James was also totally against taking medication of any kind, unlike me – not even for a headache. "Fresh air cures that," he'd say without further fuss.

This new obsessive, incensed and somewhat volatile behaviour of his – though understandable to a point – left me even more emotionally wrecked and physically exhausted than I already was. James, on the other hand, seemed to be charged with physical energy, and quite frankly, I didn't know how much more of his over-the-top possessiveness I could handle. His behaviour with regard to sex seemed inconsiderate and extreme to me, rather like that of a tom cat – it was as if he needed to mark his territory, to put his mark on me, in me, to show that although I'd been with others sexually, I still belonged to him.

Anyway, there were some blessed early mornings without James's palaver – when he'd accept my answers to his questions on the telephone, and not drive over to my house.

These were my private peace ceremonies, when I could be alone with my own thoughts and talk to General, or to myself, think about my Dad or my sister, Meg; feel God in the stillness of the new day and cherish the quiet; fall in love with my bed; or try to straighten out my muddled head at five past six as the approaching light filtered through the bedroom curtains. Lots of jumbled thoughts, one after the other in no specific order, about the things I loved, the things I hated; various worries and emotions.

General would lie next to me listening to my ramblings as I gently stroked his head, or fiddled with his ears and rubbed his tummy – he had long nights, waiting patiently at the front door for my return from a night at the escort agency, guarding Mary-Lou and Matthew and our house.

I'd indulge in some self-pity as well on these occasions, and present myself with a medal for courage and bravery. What a martyr! What a wonderful mother! Such a kind person! Yes, I honestly felt utterly dejected and sorry for myself at times, and the self-awarded medal presentation lifted my flagging spirits.

"I'm not surprised I was born six weeks overdue," I said to General. "Female intuition, I suppose – I probably knew what the world had in store for me and decided I'd rather stay where I was!"

My grandfather (my dad's father), son of a sawyer, was born in north-west Aberdeen, Scotland, in 1854. His highest education was equivalent to a modern South African Standard Two. His family travelled from Britain by ship to South Africa when he was still a boy, his father (my great-grandfather) initially finding work in the Forestry Department. During this sea journey, the family met members of my mother's side of the family on board ship – which would be how my own mother and father came to know each other and marry, so many years later.

Being an astute youngster, while tending sheep on a farm in the Cape, my grandfather taught himself to read and write, keeping detailed journals, and in time came to correspond with Winston Churchill, never forgetting Churchill's birthday.

Grandfather was one of the first people to be granted land in Kenya, and in his will left farming land in that country to my father. The majority of

Grandfather's income was made as a transport rider, taking supplies to and from the diamond mines and the coast – Algoa Bay (Port Elizabeth), Kimberley, Johannesburg and Delagoa Bay (Maputo, Mozambique).

Grandfather also married three times, fathering a total of seventeen children, and adopting another two. His first two wives died natural deaths; then at sixty-seven he married my grandmother – she being of pure German descent, living and working in the Transkei as a hospital matron, and twenty-six years of age. My grandmother had four children: the first two died of peritonitis and diphtheria; the third, a son, passed away in 2001, and the fourth was my father, born in 1930 – making my grandfather seventy-six years old at the time of Dad's birth!

When Grandfather became ill, my Dad was taken out of school in South Africa at seventeen and sent to Kenya to manage the family's farm there. Grandfather later died at the age of ninety-four in East London.

My little brother Alex would sit entranced at my grandmother's feet, eyes never leaving her face, while she related over and over stories of those early wagon trips, which fuelled Alex's young imagination considerably. He in turn enthralled young school chums with exaggerated stories of ferocious lions roaming free right outside our house in Kenya, even getting as far as crocodiles in the bath!

Grandmother died in 1984 in her sleep in East London, also in her nineties; the last years of her life were extremely isolated and lonely, alleviated only by the kindness and visits of her Church congregation. She was incredibly gifted at piano playing – I was the only grandchild who inherited her musical abilities, although I couldn't play nearly as well as she did; I was also the one that inherited her large nose. Sometimes I've thought about my similarity to her, not least our "loner" qualities, and I wish I'd never been so afraid of her, and been able to spend more time with her in her old age. Unfortunately, Grandfather's detailed and very informative journals were accidentally left in Angola when my family fled with the escorted convoy out of that country in 1975.

On my mother's side of the family, her mother also owned and ran a farm – yes, a woman – in the same area of Kenya at that time, and had divorced her second husband, my mother's father, who was born in Natal; my mother never saw her father again from about the age of seven.

After the Second World War, this grandmother was often sent soldiers from the British army who'd either lost their own families in the blitz, or who were considered convalescents, and she'd give them a home on her farm in Kenya until they felt they could cope again in the outside world. My mother recalls family stories of how very poor they were in those days – making all their own clothes and shoes, sometimes using old newspapers as blankets. This grandmother, originally born in Alice, South Africa, later died in Kenya of pneumonia at the age of seventy.

My own parents married in Kenya in 1952, my father at the age of twenty-two, standing at six foot three – and my mother eighteen years old, five foot one, virtually able to stand beneath my Dad's arm. The year of their marriage coincided with the start of the Mau-Mau uprising in Kenya, which would continue until 1962, when the country gained its independence under Jomo Kenyatta.

The farm in western Kenya is where my first memories come from.

I learnt to ride a bicycle, my Dad pushing me down a gentle slope of the garden and me tottering and falling, many times, with a crash into the flower-beds.

We had a wonderful old nanny, of the Tiriki tribe, who came to my mother when she was already in her fifties; parts of her clothing were still goat skins. She just loved us four kids – my mother would sometimes find her giving Alex a quick suck on her "dry" breasts.

I also remember well our kindly old Kikuyu ex-Mau-Mau gardener, who saved my older brother's life when he tied a hemp rope around his neck and then jumped from the roof of the summer house. Walking past, the old man was met by the sight of this child hanging by the neck, blue in the face, and quickly chopped the twined rope with his panga.

Meg was pumped full of fuel once, diesoline I think – out playing around the fuel supply with two young boys, she put the pipe in her mouth as she was told to, then swelled alarmingly and fell over! I apparently swallowed an entire bottle of malaria tablets at the age of three and had to have my stomach pumped – though I've been given no details of why or how I came to swallow these tablets.

These early years included our wondrous safari holidays – the only memories I have of a united family, when we were together continuously. Other memories include the pet pink pig we had, and the ferocious bull named Ben.

After independence, the British Government bought my father's farm and my family moved to the Kenya coast, where my parents started their deep-sea fishing business – and where I landed my record one-hundred-and-thirty-one pound black marlin, single-handedly at the age of nine, in the Children's Annual December Fishing Competition, and received a trophy cup with one hundred Kenya shillings under the lid for my prize! The equivalent of ten rand, it was a lot of money for a kid in those days and I had the most wonderful shopping spree – it was well worth the hour it took me to land the marlin and all the blisters I had on my hands afterwards!

General rested his head on my tummy and I scratched behind his ears, which he just loved – still listening to my jumbled ramblings, because this was our private time and I wasn't ready to sleep yet; understanding my need for reminiscing, for trying to find sequence to all the muddled thoughts, past and present.

I had to keep General's hair clipped short all over, quite contrary to a Yorkshire terrier's natural hairstyle of flowing, soft, groomed locks. His hyperactive adventurous spirit had him ferreting under every bush, running and rolling in every patch of grass when we went for walks; he'd land up a tangle of knots and burrs in no time at all.

"Still, you're a most handsome chap, even with your short-back-and-sides," I assured him quietly.

Sometimes I'd talk to my dad as well. Although he was gone, I found it soothing to just chat to him anyway in the peaceful early morning light. Even with our strict and distant upbringing, I'd always been able to talk to my dad – over the years, we'd had many conversations my mother, brothers and sister never knew about; he took more interest in my emotional welfare than my mother did, and never beat around the bush or told me to "just pull myself together" the way she did.

I've never known any human being with the ability to make my six-foot-three, strong, sensible and stable father cry – except my mother.

As a child and a teenager, I always thought it was my dad who was the boss of our home and family; in my twenties, I realised it was my mother. When she'd go off on her world-trip holidays, I'd take my children and go and look after Dad on the cattle ranch in Namibia – his health wasn't good; the first signs of cancer appeared some ten years before his death. I've sat nights with my father in his heartache, as he filled his whisky glass many times; listening until he'd poured his inner pain out, and poured a good deal of the whisky bottle out as well, before going to bed. There'd apparently been some infidelity in their marriage, and my father remained in a state of anxiety for years.

I've never seen my dad drunk except on these occasions, and his distraught and depressed state, while my mother holidayed, bust me up inside – writing these words now is difficult; I've hidden it so long.

Yes, Dad would be pleased the way Bert and Mary-Lou were turning out, despite all the hardships; he understood the difficulties of trying to support a family single-handedly.

My father had been a keen horseman and excellent polo player, representing the Kenya Polo Team in his younger days. Mary-Lou had been crazy about horses since she was tiny, and her riding and horse-jumping skills had improved dramatically since I'd bought Copper Band for her.

It wasn't too easy at the moment, though, with the addition of my new work, to get to horse riding twice a weekend. Travelling to the farm and back where Copper was stabled was most time-consuming. Mary-Lou would usually sulk when I complained that she hadn't polished her riding boots, saddle or tack. This was an ongoing nag on my part, to little avail. These were expensive leather items and needed polishing regularly. Sometimes I'd notice that Copper's numnah – the shaped and padded material that goes beneath the saddle against the horse's skin – was hard and stiff from sweat, and tell Mary-Lou to put it in the car to wash at home; she'd then leave it lying in the bucket, until I washed it. Apart from that she needed jodhpurs, ones for normal riding and others for horse shows. I really could not afford any further riding gear.

If her grandfather was still around, I thought, she wouldn't be allowed to go riding until her gear received the required attention. But he wasn't around anymore, was he.

I'd always been guilty of giving in to Mary-Lou since she was tiny, and it didn't necessarily pay off all the time; but it kept the peace because I utterly detest friction and discord in the home. Bert did the same, though he was the only one she listened to regularly or who could get her to tidy her bedroom and cupboard.

Thinking about my father and horse riding brought back the sad memory of his death in October 1994.

I'd left Mary-Lou in the care of my husband when I took the bus home to Namibia to say a last goodbye to my father – there being perhaps only months left, due to his aggressive lung cancer.

As always, Dad was sitting in his favourite maroon swivel chair at the round kitchen table. This time, though, his breathing was painfully laboured and shallow, and his eyes lacked their usual sparkle. Dad had put all his affairs in order so that my mother could continue her lifestyle: she didn't have to work; she had house help; she never had to worry about a roof over her head or fret about how to feed herself or her companion animals; she could still have her holidays with friends and family.

"Have you given up smoking yet, my girl?" he asked, looking me in the eye across the table.

"No, but I'll try to some time," I answered, averting my gaze – it was hard to look at him, it being time for me to leave again for Cape Town. Dad understood only too well that the end of his life was drawing nigh – would he ever see his remaining two children, my older brother and myself, again?

"Well, I think you'd better get going, otherwise you'll be late for your bus," he said, trying to ease the emotional situation.

There were no words to answer this, and I pushed the stool back and crossed to his sad, tired frame, slumped in his chair, put my arms around his big shoulders and kissed him on the forehead, loving and stroking his thick, white hair. Always short back and sides for my dad.

"Bye, my girl," he said.

"Bye, Dad." My throat closed. I walked to the kitchen door. I didn't dare look back – but I couldn't do it, I couldn't just go; I stopped and turned around. So many confidences we'd shared . . . Dad's arms were folded before him on the table, his head slightly bowed, this great man's quiet acceptance showing in his eyes; he was broken and in pain, but without complaint, silent tears on his cheeks – in our hearts, the shared knowing of his ending life.

"Oh, Dad," I choked, and ran back to his chair, put his head on my chest and held him. And we cried together a while. But buses don't wait and somehow, sometime you have to end this embrace, and face life and a coming death.

"Go now, my girl," he motioned gently, wiping his eyes with his handkerchief.

I didn't dare look back a second time as I walked to the kitchen door, to the waiting Ford Cortina at the back garden gate, ready for the long trip over dirt roads to the waiting bus.

On the 19th of October 1994, my mother telephoned me around eight-thirty in the morning to say that Dad was on his deathbed and that I should get the plane home immediately – they would pay the fare. With such short notice, and there being only sufficient funds for a ticket for myself, I once again had to leave Mary-Lou in the care of my husband.

On arrival at Cape Town airport, we found that my plane had been delayed some hours, and after a further slow and anxious night drive of two hours over dirt roads, I arrived at the isolated cattle ranch too late. My dad had passed away three hours earlier, a couple of minutes before seven in the evening, my mother having administered his last pain injection, their three dogs with her at his bedside – while I had been in flight over Namibian airspace.

A gauze bandage was tied around my father's head, under his chin, to keep his mouth closed, and another bandage was tied around his ankles, to keep his feet straight and together.

"For when rigor mortis sets in," my mother explained gently, to ease my initial alarm at his appearance.

I sat with my dad in his bedroom, in this new and unfamiliar quietness of his, and talked to him awhile, his dear face upon the pillow, at peace. I was relieved he was free of pain – but the finality of his passing reminded me of how many things I wished I'd shared with this dear friend and father of mine, now so vividly before me in body but no longer with me in living spirit.

Twelve hours after his passing, with a clean pair of pyjamas for his cremation attire and strict instructions to the mortuary attendant from my mother, Dad disappeared into the Namibian morning inside the undertaker's white van, strapped onto the stretcher and covered with a purple cloth, his still-warm heart housed within his cold body.

Standing at the garden gate with my mother, my gaze never shifted from the white van growing smaller and smaller in the distance, my heart clinging to the trail of dust rising into the still air. I longed to reach out and cup the cloud of powdery fine brown earth in my hands, to hold it close forever, this last memory of my father. Then it was gone – the van, the dust – and though the day was clear, in that moment I didn't think I could see "forever"; instead it was replaced by an inconceivable emptiness.

Within minutes, the mystery of the bush telegraph had the farm staff and labourers gathered at the garden gate to pay their last respects. The men solemnly dipped their caps to my mother, and the women sobbed as they embraced us. We spent the rest of the morning under the outstretched arms of the big thorn tree in the front garden, comforting each other and drinking tea together, whilst the plentiful variety of birds and hornbills, with their arched beaks, perched on the branches and fed from the tray of bird food above us.

And in the next couple of days, somewhere amidst all this sorrow, packing and loading of boxes for this leg of my mother's life without my father, no one noticed Dumbo, my dad's aged, black cross-sausage dog, her muzzle grey and her hearing bad, as she stood waiting patiently for her regular ride in the powerful 4x4 farm truck. She couldn't hear the Ford as it reversed, neither could she understand why her master wasn't there looking out for her as he always did.

I could only stand next to the hole they dug for her, dear Dumbo, later that day – between the fruit trees, next to the duck pond that evaporated in the sweltering Namibian summer heat and froze solid in winter – and stare at her lifeless form, as lifeless as my father's; a further heartache filling my being – as if a hand came down and numbed my shocked mind. They went together, but apart – Dad and his dog, Dumbo, as faithful as they'd been to each other in life.

After my father's death, Bert, Mary-Lou and I shared a house with my mother for a few months when she came to Cape Town in early 1995. She helped me all she could financially, but by mid-year she left for her second marriage, settling in a Cape country town.

Love, affection and companionship are quite natural needs and desires, and although not six months had passed between my father's death and the new man in her life, I did not find this remotely perturbing – quite the opposite in fact. My mother had not only lost her husband, but outlived two of her children as well, and had lived an isolated farm life for many years; but her depression was greatly lightened by her new romance, and she seemed once again full of life, optimism and energy, making new friends and having some fun in her new city surroundings. Whilst her new husband was a tall man, like my father, and also English-speaking, I never thought to compare them further – there was, after all, no one who could ever take the place of my father, either in my life or his grandchildren's. Of slight concern was the fact that this man had little wealth of his own, whilst my mother had been adequately provided for by my father; perhaps an added worry was that he had been married several times before – but then again, so had I. What counted most was that Grandma was happy again – Bert, Mary-Lou and I would often giggle at her radiating joy.

I'd talk to God too on these peace mornings of mine, when I needed His gentle solace. I talked to God a lot when I felt down, particularly about death. Being dead I wasn't afraid of, it was the part in between alive and dead that bothered me, the part you went through to get to being dead. There'd been so much death around me in recent years, particularly the last five years – my younger brother Alex in 1979, Meg in 1991, Mary-Lou's father, Terry, in 1992, Dad in 1994, Bert's father in 1995 and James's son in 1996 – and most of it felt like wasted life to me, gone too soon.

Meg had told me she had some severe period problems – continuous, heavy bleeding – and I harped and nagged at her for about two years to go to a doctor for a check-up and a pap smear. She wasn't a smoker and didn't take the contraceptive pill; she had the injections instead. Being a single mother, holding down a job to support herself, her son and her horse, Meg's life was pretty hectic. Between the work and everything else, she said she didn't have time to see a doctor and kept putting off making an appointment.

By the time she eventually went to a doctor, it was too late – even though she had an immediate hysterectomy, the cancer was already in her lymph glands. Meg's "ticket" was five years to live with treatment, and three without. With heavy cancer therapy, done at a Cape Town hospital, Meg lived a further three years.

By this time, she had met and married her third husband, Ian, a marvellous man – the opposite of Meg's noisy, lively, "on the hop" character.

We read up on anything and everything we thought would help during Meg's illness, did all we could think of to ease her going. One felt so utterly helpless watching as her beautiful long hair fell out, leaving her bald. She vomited continually and her breathing became more and more shallow, almost seeming exhausting at times, rasping or rattling within her chest. But she never gave up hope, never gave up on her son or her horse, and I never once heard her complain. Weak as she was, Meg was out there caring for and riding her horse. Her husband, Ian, was truly wonderful – supportive, caring, considerate, compassionate and very brave throughout; her medical costs were never an issue. Meg was Ian's love and life.

There were times I couldn't look directly at Meg because she was so brave; her courage in the face of adversity was so great compared to my own fear and weakness at seeing her so helplessly ill and in such pain. No matter how much you think you're prepared for a death – when it happens, you're not. And death has a smell all of its own, not unpleasant, but distinctive; when you've smelt lingering death, you'll never forget it.

I found Ian at Meg's Cape Town hospital bedside around eleven on a Sunday night, utterly exhausted and reluctant to leave his wife for a minute. She'd collapsed in the late afternoon – my mother had informed me by phone from Namibia, and asked me to do for Meg what she would do for her. I'd been sitting on my bed studying for my legal secretarial exams that started the following day when I received my mother's call, and went straight to the hospital, returning home the following morning.

Meg had confided that her greatest wish was to get back home to Namibia. I'd privately discussed the matter and her condition with her doctor and Ian – and was informed that Meg's time had come, that if it was her wish to get back home then that was what should be done. The long flight, however, would be very taxing in her frail condition, and the doctor was concerned that her heart might not cope with the take-off and landing. I spent most of the Monday arranging her flight and medical assistance on board – while a long trip by car lay ahead for Ian, alone.

My mother had left the cattle ranch and gone to Meg's house in Windhoek, arranging home assistance from a Namibian hospice. So far, so good, I thought – things were happening the way Meg had hoped.

I was in constant contact with Ian, and received a specific message from my sister: to please visit that afternoon to relieve him a bit, and also to be sure to bring some chocolate – two kinds particularly, Bar One and coconut – as well as coffee. Meg hadn't consumed either chocolate or coffee for about two years, being utterly rigorous about correct diet to alleviate her illness – and so her specific request gave me an uneasy, niggling sensation in my stomach; but I made a thermos and stopped at the shop on the way. It was essential she have whatever she wished.

Ian left his wife's side with reluctance, Meg giving him lots of smiles, kisses and reassurances that he should go off and have a bath, freshen up and get a bit of sleep – she'd be fine.

When we were alone she said, "Could you give me a bath later? I hate being bathed by the staff, I feel so helpless and exposed like this, it's my body and it doesn't feel private, if you know what I mean. Oh – and please wash my hair as well, it feels awful."

I assured her I'd do both for her, and then she asked to eat her chocolate. "And my coffee too," Meg said, "I haven't had coffee for so long, I'd love a cup."

I unwrapped one of the chocolate bars, put it in her hand, poured the coffee from the thermos and told her she'd have to wait for it to cool down a bit. She nibbled her chocolate and I gave her sips of coffee through a straw, holding her head for her to drink, keeping her flannel constantly cool and clean wiping her mouth and forehead, gently playing with the dark little curls of her hair.

She couldn't manage to finish the chocolate, and handed it back to me with a cheeky look, pointing her finger to her mouth. "You haven't wiped my mouth properly." I did it again, until she was sure her mouth and face were presentable.

Then she perked up and chatted, so much, about lots of things: first and foremost, when she got home and felt well enough, she'd be back on her beloved horse, riding again – and she'd make sure she'd win the cup that year. I was starting to get anxious about the amount of talking she was doing. I felt sure it would tire her tremendously; but she seemed so happy chatting away twenty to the dozen.

Then her voice changed and she suddenly asked me seriously, "I'm not really such a bad person, am I, Maggs?"

The question took me off guard – I hadn't expected it, after her happy chatter. Of course she wasn't a bad person; but I felt an uneasy sensation in my stomach.

"You? No," I answered, trying to make light of her question and averting my gaze slightly. "Just a bit stubborn and full of shit sometimes – like me, like the rest of the family." Then I added more seriously, "No, you're not a bad person, Meg. I think, though, that you should get a bit of rest now, you've been chatting for ages and we need you to be rested for your flight home tomorrow, it's important not to tire yourself too much."

"Okay," she answered simply and surprisingly. Normally she would have argued, but now she agreed to rest, closing her eyes.

I sat in the big chair next to her bed, holding her hand, and started to page through a magazine, checking on her restful face every few seconds. Her breathing was steady now, still shallow, but steady. I felt a bit easier. I'd only got to the third page of the magazine when it happened.

Meg suddenly sat bolt upright in the bed and grabbed at one of the tubes. I caught her in my arms as she fell back, her heart unable to take any more. Oh God! Find the bell – it was stuck under her. Oh God! Her oxygen mask had come off and I tried to get it back on properly with my shaking left hand, her head in the bend of my right arm. Oh God, ring the bell. Oh God, she's pulled out one of the tubes, maybe *I've* pulled out one of the tubes by mistake.

"It's alright, Meg, I'm here, Sister's coming now," I said as reassuringly as possible.

Then I looked at her face again. "No, Meg, *no!*" I screamed in utter panic.

The lady in the opposite bed rang her bell for me and the staff came running. One sister immediately helped on the other side of the bed, while another ran to phone Ian – and returned saying there was no answer. What number did you ring, I asked – wrong number. I couldn't believe this was happening; I scratched in my handbag for Ian's correct phone number and gave it to the nurse, keeping Meg's head in the crook of my arm throughout, then lowering it gently onto the pillow, as Sister instructed.

"I want my morphine," Meg said quite clearly.

"It's coming now," Sister answered.

"And turn the oxygen up please, I need more oxygen."

"The oxygen is turned up to its maximum already," Sister replied. The morphine arrived and was injected intravenously. "I've given you your morphine now," Sister said to Meg, touching her shoulder comfortingly. Meg nodded.

"I think one of the tubes came out and I couldn't get her oxygen on properly again," I whispered to Sister across Meg's bed, panic-stricken.

She looked me straight in the eyes and said quite firmly but compassionately, "It's not your fault, don't blame yourself. There's nothing more you or anyone can do – we've been expecting it. Just hold her."

I did. I talked to her, my sister, told her I loved her, that we all loved her, that Ian was on his way; I played with her hair with my other hand and helplessly watched her die in my arms. I noticed she'd gone before Sister did. She confirmed Meg's death and noted the time – in all, it took about eight minutes. It seemed forever.

I asked that all the tubes be removed before Ian arrived, and helped Sister with this, as I felt the still-connected medical equipment would be further distressing to him when he got to his wife's bedside. I also then requested that Meg be allowed to lie on the pillow, as she was when she died, her face uncovered and at peace, and that they not disturb or move any of her bedding, more than straightening the sheet over her body, before Ian saw her; I owed him this much. And then I left them alone, husband and wife, as soon as I saw his heartbroken face around the curtain.

Using the call box in the hospital passageway, I phoned my mother in Namibia. Meg's twelve-year-old son answered the call and I kept my voice normal; it wouldn't be fair to break this kind of news to him over the telephone – he would need his grandmother's support and comfort when he was told. I asked to speak to Grandma.

My mother sensed immediately what had happened, the moment I said hello to her. "Has she gone, Margaret?"

I told her about Meg's last minutes, assuring her I'd done everything within my power to do for Meg what she would have done for her at the end, had she been there herself.

Sister came and talked to me comfortingly in the staff lounge after I'd phoned my mother – saying if I wanted to scream, cry, whatever, I should do it then. I could only sit and cry quietly though.

Ian came into the room after a time, gave me an affectionate hug and a kiss and said, "Thank you, Margaret. I'm going home now. I've taken Meg's wedding ring off and packed her other things."

I felt so guilty. He hadn't wanted to leave her that afternoon; she'd said she'd be fine. I was with her instead.

Meg died on the Tuesday, shortly before the seven o'clock evening visiting time, and I was advised that her body would not be fetched until about nine-thirty that night. I refused to budge from her bedside until I'd seen for myself that she was taken away with dignity and care.

Sister bathed and prepared Meg gently, talking to her continuously. "They can still hear for a time after death, you know," she said to me.

The curtains were closed around the bed and Meg was wrapped in a white sheet, but I wouldn't allow them to cover her face. She looked truly beautiful with her short curls, and totally at peace. I talked to her now and then and stroked her hair. Before the mortuary attendants arrived with the stretcher and put the domed lid over her body, I kissed her cold forehead, and put my right hand on her heart; it was still warm. My only consolation at the time was that I'd done as my mother had asked. Even if my mother hadn't asked, I'd have done it anyway.

Ian's sister gave me a lift home later that night, back to cancel Meg's flight booking, the specific oxygen requirements, the ambulance to the airport, etc. We drove in silence most of the way – she'd given me a hug at the hospital.

"Did Meg say anything about God before she died?" she asked carefully, breaking the quiet of the night drive.

"No."

"Are you quite sure? It's important, you know. Can't you remember her saying anything about accepting the Lord, or God – something, anything like that?"

"No," I said evenly. "She didn't say anything like that. But not saying it doesn't mean she hadn't."

Later that night, I stood in the quiet on the little balcony of my flat in Wynberg. I knew it, in my heart, within my being, around me, next to me, above me, in me: Meg was safe and free of pain, in a world of new and unconditional love, nestled in arms as great and wondrous as clouds of cotton wool.

Still, I couldn't sleep with the lights off that night. I returned to work the following Monday and don't remember doing my job at all, or much of the three weeks following Meg's death. The phone seemed to have died as well, a few days after Meg, with little emotional support coming from my mother. She had pain, I understood that, but so did I.

Then I started having sudden terrifying panic attacks – hands shaking, heart pounding in my throat, pulse racing, breaking out in sweats; being afraid of traffic, afraid of speaking on the phone, afraid of writing anything in front of another person; hyperventilating on occasion. I just felt afraid of everything and everyone, and I went to see a doctor. A tranquilliser, Brozam, was one of the medications prescribed.

I was surprised to pass both my legal secretarial examinations, a month or so after Meg's death, with Honours.

But it didn't help with trying to fall asleep after a night of escorting if I dwelled on these sad events, and I went through to the kitchen to make a cup of delectable rooibos tea, put Bart and the kitten out for a quick wee in the back garden and then piled into bed once more, General at my side.

Sometimes my mind was so wide awake, so hyped, that even after a long night at the escort agency and one and a half tranquillisers it still raced, and I'd lie dozing until I finally fell into a shutdown of desperate sleep.

Yes, what a life I've had, I thought – from watching hundreds of flamingos in Kenya, to catching a calf as it slid from its mother's womb in Namibia at four in the morning, or rescuing tortoises on the R27 Cape west-coast road; from saving an injured though magnificent white cockerel on the N7 high-way near Moorreesburg – he'd fallen off the back of a moving lorry – to dodging pigs and goats and pot-holes as I drove home through the Transkei, many times late at night, after settling Bert and Mary-Lou into boarding school in the Cape

Since my first bachelor flat at seventeen in Rhodesia, at a rent of fifty Rhodesian dollars a month from my pay of one hundred and fifty – sparsely furnished, but I'd had money left over to buy a new LP every month to add to my music collection – I'd moved house, um . . . my mind churned over the calculations. Cripes, a total of twenty-nine times!

Well, one must go where the husband goes, I suppose – and go where one has to as a single mother to find work to feed your kids and yourself when there's no longer any husband.

Yes, we'd certainly been around the block more than a bit. I never actually thought of our life as unstable; more as interesting. We'd met many different people and seen new places – that was experience and knowledge in itself, I reckoned.

Through the years, Bert and Mary-Lou had been my two little pillars of strength, offering me the continuous encouragement, love and support that gave me reason to get up each morning. Bert was the "man of the family", and Mary-Lou called us "the three musketeers"!

It wasn't always possible to have my children at home with me during their school years, much as I wanted to, for I understood the pain of family separation; but they'd done damn well all things considered, especially with all the moves.

I giggled remembering some of Bert's antics as a boy. You needed eyes in the back of your head! He was right into spanners and "man stuff", and would try to take the washing machine, and various other things around the house, apart – and putting it back together again was impossible. And accident-prone! His little feet seemed to go faster than the rest of his body, so we had quite a few stitches – he fell down the back stairs onto his big blue-and-red plastic lorry, which meant stitches on the chin; then he fell onto his grandmother's dog basket, which meant more stitches on the chin. Then he made a roaring fire with my discarded old paperwork, which I was busy sorting through in the dining room, with flames to the ceiling. That one was touch and go – I was pregnant with Mary-Lou at the time, and got such a fright I thought I'd lose the baby; anyway, Bert was fine, thank heavens, and I managed to put out the blaze.

He'd been quite a hyper handful alright – sometimes when he was upset with me he'd pedal away frantically on his bicycle, BMX helmet on, legs whizzing like mad on the pedals, little brown school case packed and strapped tight to the back.

"You're an ugly mummy," he'd shout. "I'm leaving."

An hour later, Bert would be at the kitchen door, case in hand. "I'm sorry, Mummy, can I come home again?"

He really had a very kind and gentle heart, did my Bert, despite his tough shell.

Bert was the sporty one of the two children – soccer and cricket, as well as being offered a rugby bursary for high school and playing first-team hockey in his final years. Bert never failed a standard academically either, although he'd had a tough time in 1995, his final year, what with his father dying. After all the years of disinterest, it was quite weird how Jack decided to live in the same country town Bert went to boarding school in – sheer coincidence, but at least they'd got together a bit. Then Jack landed up in hospital a few months later with a burst spleen, the years of alcohol taking their toll, and died after a long and painful illness in intensive care, leaving his son a suitcase of clothes and thirty rand – which the hospital never found, despite noting it as having been handed in!

Strange how life turns out. After all the years of no financial support from Bert's father, the mortuary authorities decided that I should have the responsibility of disposing of his body, even though we'd long since divorced. Bert, his father's next of kin but not yet eighteen, was not allowed to sign any papers regarding this. It was a painful discussion and decision for Bert, but as we did not have the finances ourselves, Bert agreed that I should sign his father's body over to medical science. That way, he'd be given a cremation, though we'd never know when.

Nevertheless, Bert's father deserved an acknowledgement of having lived and passed on, as everyone does, and I bade him this simple respect by first spending some quiet minutes with Jack's lifeless body before signing the necessary papers at the mortuary. It was the least I could do, not only for him, but for Bert as well. Compared to the dignified state of my Dad's and Meg's bodies at death, Jack's was horrendous; it took me some days to overcome this experience, and I will always remain grateful that Bert never saw his father this way.

Mary-Lou wasn't into the sport stuff, apart from being "horse crackers", due to suffering so much from chilblains on her hands and feet in the winter. She was the brainy one of the two.

Mary-Lou had been an angel child, the sweetest blessing. Beautiful, she'd won two baby competitions; she was also very intelligent, had started reading from a young age and loved the many books with matching cassette tapes that I'd bought her, and was able to amuse herself happily for hours drawing or playing with her toy ponies, dolls and soft toys. Always into girl stuff, she'd do my hair in various styles and rub my legs, arms and back with body lotion, or play with my make-up. Her school marks were always excellent, and being naturally academically inclined she didn't have to put in the effort Bert did. So good, loving and affectionate, I couldn't remember having to ever give her a smack or reprimand her as a child.

Teenage years are a difficult time in anyone's life. All the trials and tribulations of growing up – so many temptations, pimples, peer pressure, keeping up with the latest fashions, who's wearing what, who's going where, who's going out with who, there's nothing to watch on TV, too much homework, I hate washing dishes, can't I sleep longer – aw, Mum, can't I do it later, I'm busy now!

It's pretty tough at times, I acknowledged, remembering my own youth. My first year of schooling was as a boarder at a large, farm-type Kenyan school some distance from home, with Meg and my older brother. My dormitory had probably twenty beds, a metal locker beside each, and long high windows; it opened onto an exceptionally long, dark passage – with other dormitories coming off it on both sides – at the end of which was the only bathroom, with a high white ceiling that had a gaping black hole in it: an uncovered "trapdoor".

The previous old school mistress had died, and I remember well my early childhood experience with what I felt to be her ghost. Waking afraid one night, the eerie light of the moon shining into the dormitory, I'd distinctly felt someone sit on the end of my bed, where we had to keep our folded spare blanket – and was confronted with a white apparition. I could not make out if it was male or female, but it seemed female. What was peculiar was that although it seemed to be made of a kind of mist, it had a definite body weight. I just stared, too petrified to move or utter a sound. After a few seconds of sitting without conveying any form of threat to me, the white apparition simply disappeared into nothingness in the dormitory.

After this incident, I started having a terrifying nightmare, the same one repeatedly. Every time my mother was due to visit us at hostel in Kenya or left to return home to the farm after seeing us, the dream would come, over and over. She would be driving along the escarpment in Kenya, which was full of sharp curves and dangerous bends with a sheer drop of hundreds of metres on the one side of the dirt road. Placed at one of these very sharp bends, sticking out from the red-brown earth were all these spears, sharpened and glistening, waiting, in the hope that she wouldn't be able to slow down enough on the turn and her car would plough into the mountainside and she would become impaled on these jutting, killer metal spears. The dream always ended just before her car reached the bend.

My stomach would feel sick with anxiety every time I knew my mother was coming to visit us, and I remember having to walk down the long dormitory corridor at night to go and vomit in the bathroom. Then throughout my mother's visit, my stomach would be filled with the sick anxiety of her having to travel back home again, and I'd be in the bathroom once more to throw up after she'd left. But I don't recollect ever having told her about this dreadful nightmare – and I'm very pleased to say, it was just a nightmare. Perhaps it had something to do with what I'd obviously heard as a young child about the Mau-Mau War, I don't know, but until the age of thirteen I was terrified of the dark, to the extent that I could lie almost paralysed from fear in my bed at night.

The following year I started boarding school in the Eastern Cape, age eight, again with Meg and my older brother, Alex following a couple of years later. I can't say I was very unhappy at boarding school and I can't say I was happy. Love and affection is difficult to give to some hundred hostel children; we got this when we flew home to Kenya for three weeks in July and six weeks in December for the school holidays.

Our pocket money was fifty cents the first and last Saturday of term, when we'd walk into town "in crocodile", and another fifty cents for out-weekends, whether we had somewhere to go or not. I had a wonderful time with my fifty cents – a large Milky Bar slab of chocolate and a Choc-Nut Sundae with nuts sprinkled on top at the newly opened Wimpy Bar!

Hostel food was all right when you'd dug the worms out of your cabbage and porridge, and the discipline wasn't too bad. We got up to plenty of mischief, like sprinkling sugar on the stairs so we'd hear the old matron when she came to check if we were in bed or not, or have magical midnight feasts. Girls in the dorm would club in their saved pocket money, and we'd get one of the day scholars to buy fresh white bread, packets of crisps and a tin of condensed milk – and sometimes a can of sardines as well, if the money permitted. Someone usually had a torch. After lights-out, we'd huddle on the floor under the blankets with the torch on, in a tent between the beds, munching on delicious sandwiches: soft, dry white bread with crisps on top, with condensed milk drooled over it, and sometimes with sardines! We'd talk scary or ghost stuff – though by Standard Four or Five the ghosts and scary stuff were mostly replaced with consoling or encouraging each other about boyfriend matters, lots of oohs and aahs and giggling like mad.

I was often in trouble, whether I was guilty or not. It became the teachers' habit to punish me anyway as one of the "ringleaders" – which usually meant standing in a line waiting my turn for a good dose of Epsom Salts; I'd have to hold my nose otherwise I'd want to throw up. Never a popular child with lots of chums, I was more a loner with a few occasional friends.

Four days before the commencement of one particular June holiday, I was admitted to hospital with pneumonia, my left lung nearly collapsing. After that, the matron took me on the most wonderful shopping spree in the nearby city for warm winter clothing, as I was severely unprepared for the cold Cape winters. With my new pair of lace-up boots, I thought I looked really with-it and sexy!

The other two short holidays of the year were rather a problem, as we depended largely on the kindness of other children to offer us a place in their homes. I recall a couple of these short holidays or weekends being spent with my grandmother at her city flat. There were other entire short holidays, though, that I spent alone with the matron at the hostel. This was painful to my heart, watching other kids driving off home with their parents, returning with their tuck boxes packed to the brim with goodies like home-made biscuits, biltong, chips and rusks, or dried fruit – feeling the saliva rush to my mouth in longing as I silently watched them devour their tuck.

At the age of nine, my godmother sent me a stuffed toy koala bear, who became my dearest and greatest friend. I would pour out my troubles and worries to him, or cry from homesickness, clutching my little bear, burying my face in the pillow as I pulled the blankets over my head. My bear knew everything, always. I still have him today – severely worn now, being in his thirties – in a very special, safe resting place in my clothing cupboard.

My other toys in boarding school were a wooden top, a yo-yo, some jacks and marbles, an old pair of roller skates (handed down the line from my big brother) and a small cassette player which my parents bought me, and from which I gained many hours of musical pleasure. I also took classical piano lessons and had some guitar instruction.

I was not an exceptional academic pupil, but I always passed well. Sport was more my interest, swimming in particular. I achieved in athletics, tennis, diving and netball, obtained junior swimming colours, broke an under-eleven Border backstroke record and swam in the SA Schools Competition in Bloemfontein. Though my parents came from Kenya for one June holiday, they never saw me compete or achieve in school sport, which I found quite disheartening.

In high school I was at three different schools. In Standard Seven I constantly failed mathematics and science, dropping these subjects at the end of the year, while simultaneously being top in biology and English. Junior tennis champ, I continued with athletics, showing talent at discus, played first team hockey, obtained senior swimming colours and was girls' swimming captain – putting in hours and hours of daily training.

My first period arrived at the age of eleven during a December holiday. We'd been out all day, from before first light, on the back of a Land Rover driving through one of the game reserves in Kenya; I'd watched an elephant herd have a wonderful mud bath, and a group of giraffe with their long elegant necks nibble branches of thorn trees while their young remained cautiously at their sides. On my exhausted return home late that night, I was faced with this sudden change to womanhood. My mother gave me a brief discussion about menstruation while seated on the closed toilet lid, with me sitting on the side of the bath – seriously pointing out the delicate state of "sooner-than-expected maturity" I now found myself in. Under no circumstances were boys to venture too close, as I was now capable of having babies – my older brother would be instructed by my mother to keep his eyes peeled for any interested young males. My boarding school sex education, gleaned mostly from giggling female friends, left me in no doubt that children came from the male side of our species – from a willy inside a koekie – and not from the stork!

I left my mother's bathroom ensconced in a very large Dr. White's sanitary towel, held up by thin elastic linked through the loops around my waist. It was all very uncomfortable and looked, I thought, rather like an upside-down parachute – womanhood didn't seem too exciting to me at all!

There followed years of continuous extreme premenstrual tension and pain. I was born with my periods (bleeding from the vagina for a few days after birth) and mastitis (tender, swollen, painfully hard breasts) – as was my mother, as was Mary-Lou. After Mary-Lou's birth, the nurse on duty had never seen such a thing in her career and rushed to inform me that she was certain there was something wrong with my baby daughter. I assured her there wasn't anything wrong; this condition seems to run in the female side of our family.

At twelve, life improved somewhat. I received my first watch, a navy-blue strapped silver Timex with a large round face (which only conked in when I was twenty-four). My earlobes were pierced by an Indian gentleman in a tiny, rather dimly lit shop in the back-streets of the Kenyan coastal town – with me sitting on the edge of a single bed while my mother leant against the wall, watching. The fellow pulled out a large darning needle, lit a candle, dabbed my ear lobes with cotton wool moistened in disinfectant, held the sharp end of the needle in the candle flame for a few seconds, and then pushed it through my ear lobe! The first piercing seemed to go relatively smoothly, but by the second my mother had to sit on the chair because she felt faint. Of the two pierced ears, the second became infected, taking a couple of weeks to heal, after which my mother drove me to the port of Mombasa and bought me my first pair of good-quality earrings – natural white pearl studs, which I still have – and another pair of small gold sleepers to wear at school.

My first love, called Charlie, I met at age thirteen, in Standard Six. I thought he was really cute and we wrote each other plenty of letters with Holland (Hope Our Love Lasts And Never Dies) printed clearly on the back, or other young-love stuff. Well, Charlie came to visit me one Sunday afternoon during the hostel visitor's hour, and as we were saying goodbye at the hostel gate, he leaned forward and kissed me. It was a wonderful kiss, and I felt very pleased with myself – according to my boarding-school sexual instruction, it appeared that I'd just experienced the very seductive, advanced method of "French kissing"! I walked back to the prep room beaming, my heart dancing. But it didn't last long – I'd been seen in this embrace by the matron and was immediately sent to the Headmistress' office, where I was severely reprimanded, standing with my hands behind my back. "Young ladies do not behave in this manner!" My punishment was being banned from swimming for an entire season, and no more visitors either. It was like a death sentence to me, living out the months without being able to swim, watching other youngsters going to the pool – and Charlie and I drifted apart. I still had my priorities right at that stage.

Fourteen coincided with my body getting some rather strange, but decidedly pleasant tinglings in personal places and I started wondering quite often about sex. I had my first experience with a nineteen-year-old lad who'd joined the South African Army and who showed me love, affection and interest.

We were strolling back home through a park one evening when matters developed past the kissing stage and we landed up on the grass. I, unfortunately, can only report clutching at bits of turf during this, my first taste of the sexual act, and closing my eyes tight while enduring the lad's as-gentle-as-possible affections, using a "French letter". It was really a matter of skirt up, panties off and army pants down round ankles, and wasn't remotely as exciting or wonderful as any of my schoolgirl sex discussions had led me to anticipate! Added to which, it had been rather painful. Still, when I went to bed that night and found a tiny drop of blood in my knickers, I swooned, declared undying love, and fell asleep with a true Romeo and Juliet romance playing out in my heart and mind! The young lad seemed to lose interest quite soon after this – I think due to the fact that I wasn't a particularly responsive or educated sexual partner – and I suffered my first broken heart.

My second lover really broke my teenage heart, though I'm not sure one could exactly term him my "lover." Another young army lad – wow, but was he sexy! And he had a Mini as well! He took me for a drive one afternoon and my body felt on fire being anywhere next to him. Perhaps the Mini with its cramped interior space was partly to blame. Nevertheless, the windows were steaming up, crinkling papers which he dug out of his pocket assured me he was taking the necessary precautions – everything was going relatively smoothly, considering the lack of space for movement, when I was suddenly confronted with what I considered to be rather mammoth genitalia, which I felt absolutely certain my body could not accommodate. It seemed the young fellow hadn't only been building his body muscles during army training – he seemed to have been working on his "privates" as well! I was horrified, and squeaked and performed so much that he took me back home and dumped me immediately. Very heartsore, I felt he could have been a little more understanding and considerate, and that maybe in time I would have managed better. It was rather unfair, considering that the attempt had taken place in his tiny car!

I giggled in the early morning light at the memory of these "delicate" first sexual encounters, and I thought, cripes, have I come a long way since then – and I'm still learning about the sex stuff! Anyway, if I didn't sort out the stomach business and get more fibre in my diet, I'd have some other problems as well, like piles, which I could definitely do without – and which now reminded me of my longed-for trumpet!

Often I've wished I could sing well or master a musical instrument such as the trumpet, saxophone or violin. In 1976, the famous trumpeter Eddie Calvert, appearing in a show in South West Africa, had played this exquisite musical instrument directly in front of me. In my mind, he was playing to *me* and the impact was profound – from that day I wanted to play the trumpet.

So great was this yen of mine that in 1984, through my job as an assistant buyer, I tracked down just such a musical instrument in a pawnshop in a quaint town in the Orange Free State. My longed-for trumpet gleamed in the light of the shop window – with an external radiance of millions and millions of yellow sunflowers as a backdrop. The sight of these gigantic open blooms remains fixed in my memory – a carpet which stretched forever and ever, to the very edge of the world. Well, I just had to have that trumpet – surrounded safely by the yellow halo of peace and hope.

Six months later I'd paid it off. Finally, the great day dawned. My trumpet and I were to be a number at last; one, and together. The instrument, carefully packed inside a box tied securely with string, with MY name printed in bold letters across the top of the carton, together with "fragile", was finally placed before me. The driver of the cattle truck, under my strict and worried instructions, had perched the precious carton on the seat next to him on his long trip back to the cattle feedlot where my office was. When I got home that afternoon after work, Bert and Mary-Lou gathered round the box with me as with awe I lifted the long-awaited, magical musical instrument from its wrappings of tissue paper. I sighed with relief. Mum's got her trumpet at last! Oh boy – was I going to play up a storm with my trumpeting!

I fetched a soft cloth and gently polished the brass, noticing with some dismay a couple of dents, which I silently hoped wouldn't affect the sound this instrument could produce.

"Come on, Mum, play," Bert and Mary-Lou chorused eagerly, children's eyes gleaming in anticipation: their mother was now definitely going to be a famous trumpet player. Our financial problems were over – we'd never have another poor day in our lives again, with all the money I was going to make playing my famous trumpet!

Here goes, I thought. For dramatic effect, I put the instrument to my lips with slow deliberation, and blew. And blew, and blew. Nothing, not even a faint parp! I tried again. If this continues, I thought, perplexed and unwilling to give up, I'll need oxygen soon! Both lips were now tingly and numb from the blowing, cheeks were like a hamster's, and eyes were ready to pop. Maybe there's something stuck inside, I thought, turning my prized possession upside-down to gaze into its "trumpet". Close inspection proved it to be free of any possible blockages such as a mouse, a wasp's nest or a blob of cotton wool, or whatever likes to sometimes block up such an instrument. I really had no idea what could be the matter.

"Try again, Mummy," encouraged my enthusiastic little audience, in a sincere attempt to soothe my obvious disappointment and embarrassment. Very bravely, I did – with the same result. Children's patience only lasts so long, and I had to hand the trumpet over to their eager, outstretched hands.

Bert was first, then Mary-Lou. And there it was – sound from my beloved trumpet! Both my kids could get sound out of it!

"See, it's easy," they said giggling, and handed it back to me.

So I tried again – not even a parp!

After some days of deliberation and trying on the quiet, my trumpet would still not make so much as a muffled squeak, let alone a parp for me. This necessitated a telephone call to the local Afrikaans high school to enquire whether I could have lessons with the school band. Bearing in mind that we were one of a very few English families in a very Afrikaans environment, the school secretary was patient and listened attentively while I explained my predicament – but her final answer was a definite, gentle "no". Thereafter, my trumpet found pride of place in our home, hanging on the wall where everyone who visited could admire it – and they always asked if I could play. If I was alone I simply said "no", offering no further enlightenment. However, if Bert or Mary-Lou were around, they would relate, amidst much giggling, my efforts at becoming a famous trumpeter!

Sadly, I had to sell this, my prized trumpet of great sentimental value, when my husband's farming venture went bankrupt some years later, together with many other possessions of mine that I cherished – including the piano left to me by my grandmother.

Well, there were some nice things in life as well, thank heavens! Like the box of peach pink Kleenex tissues that I'd sometimes buy just as a treat for myself; or the odd shared pizza with lots of scrumptious olives and garlic on top – I could quite easily live entirely on pizza. And the feeling of Christmas – yes, it must be a really special day, I thought, if it got soldiers from opposing forces to stop fighting for a bit and get out of their trenches during the World Wars to wish each other well. It doesn't matter how much I age, I just love Christmas! And the Lord's Prayer, and my old leather St James Bible, and the Koran. Umm . . . and reading a good book. You know, in the early hours of the morning when you're exhausted and have to keep scrunching your eyes to focus properly because you can't put it down – what's going to happen next? – and you wake up with the book all higgledy-piggledy, and you as well, and you feel tired and refreshed all at the same time.

Anyway, I was feeling pretty tired now – less muddled, calmer – and grateful to my silent listeners: General, Dad and God.

"Well, I guess you aren't too mad yet," I said to God. "I mean, you haven't rained any frogs down on my head, no plagues of locusts either since I started this escort work. Don't you ever get mad?" Stupid question, I suppose, to put to God.

Silence. "Must be real busy, Your day: starving people, bombings, muggings, Aids, cancer, rapes. Tiring too! I guess You sometimes feel like I do – want to take Your brain out and put it on the chair, give Your head a rest. Maybe consider seeing a psychiatrist, take some Panado – perhaps even be tempted with a Brozam. Still, I know You don't miss a thing. I thought it was bad lacking sleep – can't imagine how it must feel never having any at all."

I could feel the effects of the Brozam now.

"Anyway, thanks for the money," I said. "I don't want to lose General and the kids – just keep us safe please."

I drifted into the beyond, General's head still on my chest. "No doubt," I thought, "I'll still be alive when I wake up at eleven in the morning."

Chapter Seven
The Guys

*S*o why do men visit such establishments – escort agencies? Lots of different reasons . . .

Getting divorced, or recently divorced. Wife died and he hasn't had sex for ages. Had a fight with the girlfriend, they've broken up and he's heart-sore. Been married twenty-four years, wife always has sex with the light off and gets dressed and undressed in the bathroom – wants to see what a fanny looks like! Friends had a bet with him. Wants to experience what it's like with a prostitute.

Other variations go like this: Nice atmosphere! Just passing by and stopped for a drink. She doesn't like sucking him. He can't do sexually what he really wants to do, with the mother of his children! She doesn't like oral sex at all – giving or receiving it. Wants to do it like in the porno books and blue movies. Married, but lonely. You'll play with yourself and let him watch, she won't. Doesn't have to remember your name or take you out for dinner, hoping to get you into the sack afterwards! Wife's in hospital, having an operation. You won't phone him afterwards to cry, or want to go out again, or get married. He doesn't have to pay you maintenance. Caught the wife in bed with his best friend. Doesn't want sex, just wants to talk! On holiday, or the missus is on holiday. Married, but they just don't get on. Wants to cash his salary cheque, have a drink, have a woman and get the change! Only wants to "muff". First time ever with a woman, he's a bit nervous. On a business trip and feeling in need of comforting. Wants "anal". Doesn't have to buy you something, or worry about being the one to take precautions. Likes uncomplicated sex – you owe him nothing and he owes you nothing.

And what are they like, these guys? Some are very intelligent men in prominent positions in society, others have ordinary jobs. There are blokes who scrape the money together or borrow it from their pals for "just this once". Regulars come back for the same girl, or for different ladies. Some guys have numerous escorts, one after the other, in the same night – I was once the third after two other girls (after soaping the client well in the shower first); the guy, in his early twenties, was pretty much broke, in both senses, after his strenuous and costly sexual escapades. Other blokes give cheques that bounce. Some men are listed as "bad clients", others told not to ever come back again. There are neat and clean fellows, others unkempt. Blokes with prostate or other problems. Very kind and gentle chaps, extremely shy guys too. Some talk a lot of shit, others you really enjoy chatting to. There are fellows who leave angry as hell, others who depart on cloud nine. Degrees of intoxication vary – arriving drunk, departing utterly plastered or completely sober, or arriving sober and leaving drunk.

The list is endless. Mechanics, lawyers, farmers, doctors, architects – I even had a crop-sprayer, as good at the sex as he seemed to be in his work! Some have dirty nails, scuffed or shiny shoes, and others with no shoes at all – after the rugby or cricket, still with cans of beer in their hands. For each man, the girl is comforter, giver of sexual favours and psychologist, all rolled into one.

Right in the beginning, one of my first clients was a cop. He was a big-built, strong guy with dark hair. We were finished before time was up and were chatting.

"What's that on the floor next to the table?" he asked.

I looked down and saw the gun poking out from under the tablecloth and nearly passed out from fright. He then kindly spent our remaining time together giving me advice on what to keep a look out for and how to protect myself.

"There's a strangler on the loose in Cape Town and he's preying on prostitutes," he advised me seriously. He was obviously genuinely concerned. "You've got to be more alert, Rachael. You should have noticed my gun and made me hand it in to management while we had our booking, but you didn't. I could have killed you."

"Yes," I answered, "I agree with you. I'll have to wake up, quite a lot I think. But then again, you don't need a gun to kill me. As you said, this guy out there is a strangler – I don't know if women are strong enough physically against guys like that, or really against any guy for that matter."

Just before he closed the door behind him on his way out, he looked at me and said softly, "Take care of yourself, okay?" I nodded.

Yes, I'd heard something about prostitutes being killed at the time. But it was only when I read an article in one of the local magazines, some time after this booking, that I realised there had indeed been a serial killer on the prowl. According to the article, the killer was still at large. Oh, lovely! What a pleasant job we all had – sitting painting our immaculately manicured fingernails bright red all day, doing our faces, curling our locks, strutting about in our heels, ample bosoms protruding sensually from our garments, drinking ginger squares from sunrise to sunrise! What a glorious life! Could anyone ask for more?

I remember Bob, the drunk, very well. Drunks are the worst. Apart from being pissed, they also behave badly and want to slobber all over you. Co-operation is zero with these guys.

"I want to come now," he says – hiccup – trying to straighten his spectacles.

"I know, my darling! But I think you've had too much brandy and coke tonight."

"Listen," Bob says, getting aggressive now, "I paid my money and I want to come now!" Two second pause. "Understand? Now!"

"Yes." Caress. Stroke. You stare at his drunken, flopping knob, pumped full of brandy and coke. Nothing will make this thing stand up, I think to myself. "Remember I said to you earlier that I think you should save your money and come back another night?"

"Don't tell me I'm drunk. I'll show you." Reaches for his glass on the table, concentrating now, finds it in his double-vision haze, has another swig, straightens specs again, turns and focuses on me. "Think I can't manage it?"

"No, darling, of course you can – when you haven't had so much brandy." Now you get the hairy-eyeball treatment and the really serious talk.

"I work hard for my money, you know – and you aren't doing your job properly. I want my money back, unless you make me come now." Hiccup; looks down at own flopping penis. "Why don't you play with it some more?" Takes it gently in hand. "Like this."

I pay attention. Still looks dead to me. Irritating drunken shit, I think. Look at my watch on the bedside table. Good, time's almost up – the only thing that is!

I hate it when the drunks challenge you. You know full well when they're past it. Bottom line: more mouth than money, and more money than dick.

Whenever I took off a pair of underpants, I'd think, "Lucky packet time!" Never knew what treats you were going to get. With dear, sweet, kind, polite, considerate Pensioner Paul, I got plenty. Said he hadn't had sex for six years, so I undressed him gently, fragile gentleman. Oh, holy moly! Endowed like some battleship gun turret he was! Not surprised he hadn't had sex for ages – probably frightened most women that got a look at it! Well, best get on with the job at hand, I thought.

"Come again," he says softly after a little while.

So you "do" – another faked sensual orgasm; gently arched back, delicate soft sigh, caressing your nipples to attention. Hope that does it, you think, in the following grateful silence.

Now he whisperingly asks, "Are you enjoying it?"

Nod your head, dreamy eyes gazing at his adorable face. Maybe the "you're a wonderful lover" eyelash flutter look will convince him – and remember to throw in the "I'm utterly satiated" look as well. Umm . . . silence, lower your lashes, pretend exquisite bliss, breathe sort of heavy and exhausted.

"I want you to come again," he now says!

Oh, you sweet, kind man, I'd rather strangle your knob – but you "do", putting a bit extra into the arched back and petal-soft sigh. Forget the nipples.

The fourth time he said, "I want you to come again," I sat up. Watch your

114

temper here girl, I thought. But I'd had enough of this faked coming shit. With all his pumping, my womb pressure was higher than that of the tyres on my little car parked outside. My vagina would fragment if I had to keep this up continuously!

"Now I've had enough," I said firmly. And he was sorry – really genuinely sorry: he just thought that probably the other guys didn't care if the escort came or not, and he wanted me to have a good time! He wanted to book me again, and one night sat with us girls until ten past four in the morning, lighting my cigarettes.

"Please," he whispered. I shook my head. "Please," he tried again.

"No," I said. I wasn't going to put up with his non-stop pumping again for another hour. Not bad though – the money part that is – for a pensioner. He's been a regular with some of the other girls since then.

One guy said I could "keep his socks" as a memento when he left – he was getting married the following Saturday. "Something to remember me by," were his words. Did he think I was going to frame the things? I dumped them in the condom bin.

I had a really sweet nineteen-year old, whose two pals waited patiently in the lounge. "Can I put it in you?" he asked.

And a guy in his early twenties who'd phoned in from Stellenbosch, and then came racing through to the agency. He was literally in and out in twenty-five minutes. After I'd showered and dressed again I went through to the lounge.

"What'd you do to that one, Granny?" Tammy asked, laughing.

"Nothing unusual," I answered. "Why?"

"Boy, did he have a grin on his face when he left," she said.

I remember a wonderful out booking with an engineer. Some of the other girls said he was crazy and weird, but I found him absolutely super. We zooted down the highway in his sports car, and he plonked his cell phone on my lap with a big grin and said, "If anyone calls, please take a message!"

I told him I didn't even know how to use a cell phone – he just laughed. He drove straight across the lawn and up to his front door. "How's that for service?" he said, then hopped out and opened my car door.

This client owned an amazing collection of CDs. I found he loved opera, as I did, singing out loud to the music and dancing. We drank bourbon, sang, danced and played chess together – all in the nude. And I didn't have to have sex with him. He just wanted to watch me touch myself while he touched himself – the hi-fi turned up, a hauntingly beautiful aria being the background for this intensely dramatic, visual sexual encounter.

One kind, elderly, very overweight farmer with a big paunch was so pleased with the time spent with me that he said he'd bring us all chops, ribs, dried sausage and biltong on his next trip to the city.

And I also remember having to push the driver's car after a booking, right outside a posh hotel I'd just walked out of! It hadn't been a nice booking. The guy had a "whopper of a chopper" and was very physical indeed – sex with him was thumping, thrashing, jarring movements in different positions, with hips rotating, deliberately slow then fast, up down, so he could observe his abilities. I felt pretty much mangled from his sexual antics, just managing to keep my body on the bed while I was on my back – but my neck and head were pushed over the edge of the mattress by his relentless thumping and I clutched at the sheets in desperation. I don't think he had a naturally aggressive character though, as we'd chatted pleasantly for a few minutes when I arrived, and he had a good and easy manner, although a rather quick way of speech and movement. I had a bath afterwards and dressed, feeling decidedly fragile, my legs wobbly and my insides like jelly. Then I had to try to walk sedately past the same receptionist on the way out of the hotel, wearing my white linen dress and maroon high heels – plus my hat!

What did I find waiting for me? Simon, in his conked-out car! He'd just fetched another girl from a booking. "Won't start," he said simply. "You two will have to push."

We girls must have looked a sight! By the time Simon got the car to fire, the two of us were huffing and puffing, hardly able to walk in our heeled shoes. Then he waited for us to catch up while he sat revving the engine.

Another booking at a hotel – this time with a psychiatrist from Port Elizabeth, who, according to him, had more degrees behind his name than a thermometer! Didn't want to have actual sex – felt guilty about his wife.

Instead he wanted to oil me all over and then masturbate as he sat on my stomach. I always carried baby oil with me, and he virtually finished the bottle – how the staff ever got it out of the bed sheets beats me.

First, I had to lie on my stomach and was oiled everywhere – it was even in my hair. Then I had to turn onto my back and was again oiled, from the neck down to my toes and wherever in-between! Then he sat on my stomach, penis on my chest between my breasts, captivated by his own well-oiled hard-on, absolutely loving his throbbing erection.

Well, I had to appear to be taking some interest in this as well, and patiently and fixedly watched the initial gentle, caressing movements of his hands around his penis. As his rhythm increased and his grip tightened, faster and faster, I concentrated more closely – then wham, he suddenly ejaculated, taking me by surprise; his semen shot straight in my face, some hitting me in the right eye. I'd never realised the stuff could sting like that, and had a red eye for about three days afterwards! Eye Gene was the cure.

I also, very distinctly and still with embarrassment, remember getting a case of the "fanny farts" during a booking with a very nice man. At the time,

I acted as though nothing was amiss – quite normal! I didn't even comment. Meanwhile, I was cringing. I have since read – and whether it's true or not I don't know – that fanny farts are caused by the pumping action of a penis which does not completely fit the vagina it is busy penetrating. Much like pumping a bicycle tube, this causes air to enter the vagina – which then forces the air out! I am relieved to say I have not had to endure the same embarrassment since.

One evening, one of the girls mentioned that her client had come (ejaculated) while they were in the shower – she didn't even have to go to the lounge after that, as her job was already done. She was relieved because it had been an easy booking; she simply got dressed after the shower and he was advised to do the same.

Well, I was like a stork after that for the next few nights – balancing on one leg, worried about my bare feet on the shower floor. I arrived at the agency the next night armed with a bottle of Jeyes Fluid to disinfect the tiles!

Luckily, in Puff's agency, the girls were allowed to say if they would do a particular booking or not. In some other agencies, I believe you have no choice and must go with whoever pays for you – or lose your job. However, I remember one time in the beginning when Puff said I had to do a booking.

It was about twenty-five to three in the morning when this guy came in, and all the other girls were out. I call him "my monster" – which is grossly unfair, because he was actually a kind, soft-spoken and honest man. Horrendous scars covered his face and body and he was very sensitive about his appearance. His request was straight and to the point, no time for games: "anal". I said I didn't do it. He didn't argue, paid the fee anyway – and had come and gone in twenty minutes. Due to his physical appearance, I was biased, and it's the only time I can remember taking the chance of closing my eyes tight.

Old Herman wanted to save me from my terrible life. Knee-high to a grasshopper he was, with a maroon Jag, electric gates and several Pekinese dogs – all beautifully groomed, with their pastel bows – shut in the spare room so they wouldn't bark and wake the neighbours. (I must admit he took wonderful care of his animals, and you could see he loved them; we even fed his Persian cat delicate kitty morsels on the kitchen counter). Anyway, Herman was drunk as a skunk, with his pants round his ankles – while I watched rugby on the television over his shoulder and held him up straight.

"I would never have sex with you on our first date," he tells me considerately. Serious matter this is. "I'm not that kind of man. I want to take you out to dinner first – and do it properly. You know what I mean?"

Smile at him sweetly and nod. Continue holding him up straight. Wonder who's playing in the rugby – try to see if it's the Boks over Herman's shoulder. Wonder how our team's doing anyway these days . . . Herman sips on his neat whisky, held precariously in one hand, as he leans heavily against me for support.

Must have been doing some really serious thinking, because he halts the odd pants-round-ankles shuffle-dance we're doing and says, "I'll set you up in your own place and you'll never have to work again in your life!"

Sure, I thought, just have to give you a poke when you want one, hey. Smile sweetly at Herman, steady him again, kick off my shoes – easier to dance and hold him up without my heels on.

Many men want to rescue girls from what they consider to be a shameful and dreadful existence. They make offers and promises of a far better life – the bed of roses kind (which probably would not last, as the girl's previous work would come between them emotionally; in arguments this would be thrown back at her). This kind of attachment, I think, men often confuse with love, although it usually revolves around sex. However, I have seen an honest and sincere affection develop between a man and a certain lady he often books. There are some cases where a female sex-worker and a male client do fall in love – I saw this happen once during my time with the girls. The lady left the escort agency, as her partner wouldn't allow her to continue such work – besides, he'd spent a fortune booking her continuously! Within a few months it was over and she was worse off than before – collecting tin cans for recycling to make ends meet, if I remember correctly.

I always gave a man his full time. If he paid for an hour, I gave him an hour. If he paid for two hours, I gave him the full two hours. But if he wanted to leave earlier, I didn't try to stop him.

Sometimes we had double bookings – two girls, two guys, sometimes three girls with three guys, and even two girls with four guys or more. These out bookings could be dangerous, but management first sussed out the clients to decide if they were all right. On these double or triple bookings we conducted our business in separate rooms; I never swapped partners.

I remember in particular a double with Shelley, where we went with four guys from Europe to their rented holiday duplex. The agreement was that only two of the guys would have sex. The other two were not included in the deal; they would sit in the lounge and watch television or something. However, Shelley – in my opinion – was either irresponsible or stupid, or perhaps hoping to get a large tip. Three of the men did her, one after the other, in the same bedroom with the door open, with no break in between: after the first one walked out, the second walked in, and then the third.

When we arrived at their flat, we two girls had gone to the bathroom to "powder our noses". I offered Shelley condoms, as I always had an abundant supply, but she declined. (This was the girl who later came out in sores all over her body.) I managed to get the guy I was with to come on my thigh, so my job was done.

On another triple booking at a client's business premises, the young fellow who was supposed to be my partner said he didn't go with prostitutes and that he'd told his boss this, so even if I was paid for he wouldn't be doing anything. I didn't push him about it and sat at the bar chatting while he played barman. In this business, that's what you call "easy money". I'm not sure what made him eventually become amorous; the time was running out when he suddenly decided to get started!

Nice-looking young guy, maybe twenty-three years old, good physique. On the bar counter was where he wanted it, but we were interrupted by someone wanting another drink, so he rushed me to another room. Again we were interrupted. I think his boss was checking to see if he was "doing it", despite his initial protests. Desperate now, he took me through to the kitchen and lifted me onto the top of the chest freezer.

By this stage it was sunrise and the driver was yelling his head off about "time up" and "you're going to be fined, Rachael, for being late!"

Poor chap, he never got finished. I was, by now, being yelled at by everyone that they were going back to the agency. The fellow was going "just wait, just wait a bit!" with only his shirt on, desperately trying to get matters to come to a head with me atop the chest freezer, green dress pulled up, knickers off, condom on, spares next to me on the freezer lid.

"Rachael!" Christina's voice shrilled through the offices, "You can jolly well find your own way home if you don't come now! We're not waiting any longer. And you're going to get fined!"

Sorry hunk, gotta go – and quick! Off with the condom, grab knickers, trousers and basket. We ran for the front door – him zipping his pants, me still naturally wet – and he stood outside waving goodbye, looking somewhat dejected. I took a lot of flack from the others on the trip back, but managed to get off the fine. I thought about it later and had a good laugh; we'd been interrupted three times, and I remembered several condoms I'd forgotten on the chest freezer by mistake – one used! Wonder what the cleaning staff thought when they arrived.

Almost sounds as if it could be fun, this type of employment, doesn't it? You do have the occasional high time, but let me assure you, generally it's nerve-wracking; and the number of men who want to have sex – vaginal, anal or blow job – without a condom is staggering. They look at you and say, "I'm safe. I haven't been with anyone else," or you get the "I'll give you something extra" line.

One guy said to me, "Come on, I'll give you a tip!"

"And just how much would that tip be?" I asked. How much extra would he pay me to expose myself to the risk of Aids?

"Fifty rand," he replied seriously. Oh boy, the last of the big spenders!

I looked at him straight and said, "My life's worth more than fifty rand, so either you agree to use a condom, or you can choose another lady who might be willing to oblige your request." He didn't argue, so it was condom on and no extra cash tip – well, at least the tip I got was protected!

Sometimes the condom breaks, sometimes it comes off, sometimes he keeps pulling it off and you land up getting mad. These unprotected times are pretty scary. A regular medical check-up is a must in this business – but you need to get a booking in order to make the money to afford the check-up!

Do you always fake orgasms, or do you sometimes have real ones?

With Frans, my very first client, I reached exquisite orgasms. But that was because we shared a natural, magnetic attraction. Also because he loved my body, loved to caress me slowly and sensually, watch my reactions, look into my eyes, show his appreciation of being with me. Frans made love to me, he didn't just book me for a poke – as in "get undressed babe, time's ticking by, this is costing me and I need to get my rocks off."

Frans booked me numerous evenings before he left to go back to Johannesburg; on each occasion we felt the same mutual chemistry. The fact that he was fourteen years younger than myself made no difference – and I honestly admit that I'd rather do a booking with a man that I found attractive, than with one I did not. Frans treated me each time with the utmost respect, and his manners were impeccable. I was by then armed with longer condoms supplied by the agency, and we didn't have any further problems in this regard!

I think Frans developed a certain emotional attachment to me, as is often the case in "the racket": men first find a lady sexually compatible, and then find themselves becoming emotionally attached as well. He wanted a more permanent arrangement for us; he tried every avenue of questioning to get my home telephone number, and wanted to see me privately, and to take me and my children out for the weekend – which was a strictly "not allowed" agency rule. However, firstly, I had a boyfriend, and secondly, I felt the age difference would in time become a problem in our relationship. This young man, I was sure, would one day find another woman closer to his own age with whom he would be happy, and he'd make a wonderful, considerate, caring father and husband – apart from the fact that his partner was assured of a magical sex life! I was in the business purely on a temporary basis to support my family. I had enough troubles already.

On a few occasions when I couldn't psych myself properly for the work, and the client wasn't friendly or was too physical, I'd deliberately turn the situation around and use him to satisfy myself. For two reasons – first, to take my mind off having to be with him and having his penis penetrate my body. Second, because the client – men being such visual creatures – then

120

thought he was turning me on. So much so, that he'd soon ejaculate and I could get the matter over and done with faster, remove the condom and talk a while instead, then dress him and send him on his way to wherever.

One thing I found all the men liked, without exception, was when I made them lie on their stomachs, totally relaxed, head to one side, arms bent upwards flat on the bed, eyes closed. Then I'd put some baby oil on their backs, remove my G-string and sit astride them, rubbing myself sensually and slowly, up and down, breasts and nipples on their shoulders and upper backs. And then arouse myself – to a certain extent – by concentrating on rhythmically making love to a little area of their bodies that is very susceptible to arousal: just where their bums start and you get the little V in the middle. The smoothness of the oil, the warmth and gentle, sensual movement created the sensation, for the men, that I was climaxing on their backs. That was it. Their bums were up, because the pecker beneath on the bed was hard, hot and ready. In my normal or real life, when I put this work aside, I love to climax in this way, on a man's back. I find it highly erotic, and have two orgasms to his one – a rather pleasant change!

Some guys, with a little encouragement – eyes still closed, speech hushed, sometimes faltering, sometimes halting for seconds, unable to concentrate properly – would oblige and divulge their "ultimate fantasies" to me whilst I rubbed myself on them in this way. They knew their fantasies were our secret. And fantasies are so magically perfect – just the way you want the encounter to be. If tried in real life, they often don't turn out the way you'd hoped and wished for.

The guys also found showering together very sensual. Before going to shower, I'd undress them completely myself, an item of clothing at a time, carefully and neatly – including their shoes and socks! I'd hang up their shirts and trousers and show them that I was hiding their car keys, wallets and any other valuables under the bedside table for safety while we were showering. I had quite a few positive comments on this little procedure. The men found this unusually submissive gesture of care and attention to be peculiarly pleasurable, almost as if I was performing an ancient rite to which men are entitled.

In the shower I'd stand behind them and lather their arms, backs, bums, between their buttocks and their legs, and lather my front. Then I'd stand against their soapy skin, put my arms around them and lather their fronts, from the neck down, including underarms, paying careful and slow attention to the washing of their genitals. That was it. The pecker, abundantly covered in soapsuds and receiving so much loving attention, was ready to fire on all cylinders! But we had to rinse bodies first. Then I washed their hands, wrapped their towels around them – often with some difficulty because of the protruding pecker – and back to the cubicle we went.

The new outfits I'd bought on sale were worth the expense: I knew I looked good in them, and felt more confident about myself. One dress was truly stunning – white linen with a patterned bodice cut low in the front; wearing this frock I never failed to get bookings. Another was a halter-neck silver dress flared from the waist, with an open back. Mary-Lou even lent me one of her dresses – green, not my colour, but it looked super too. High heels always seem to improve a woman's legs, but stilettos were out for me – I would have felt like a stork in spiky high heels at my age; besides, since my back operation in early 1988 to remove a crushed disc, I probably would have fallen over in stilettos. My maroon suede shoes had chunky heels of a comfortable height and looked smashing, even if I say so myself. Apart from these, I'd also found a very smart pair of evening shoes, sale items as well, covered in a slightly shiny black fabric. Despite Christina telling me not to wear my long hair up, I found I got more bookings with it up than down.

Despite trying to focus on a financial goal rather than on the client, I was never able "to see the money only"– even after playing Tina Turner's "Private Dancer" continuously. I made mental and sometimes written lists of "reasons for target", but could not think only of those during bookings; I couldn't cut off my emotions sufficiently. The majority of the other girls could, and focused far better. I'd keep seeing the face and the body and then feeling it inside me or touching me. A distanced repulsion or irritation would grow within my being, even a sense of quiet mockery; sometimes I seemed to be watching myself from somewhere else.

Christina's advice had been correct: very soon you lose the desire to kiss or do all the things that are natural when you make love. Even if the guy was handsome or had a good body or whatever, I felt a chasm of quiet dis-taste within my soul. I experienced an inner fight – one part of me knowing this kind of lovemaking to be dramatically lacking and unnatural, the other asking for endurance and temporary acceptance.

Physically, I seemed to have shrunk to being only a mortar, my vagina just a convenient object a man ground away in, and him the cold threshing pestle. But to get the money I had to do it. An occasional booking with a man that sparked a mutual chemistry was therefore almost a blessing (though my rules still applied) – it was a relief to find that physiologically, mentally and emotionally I could still respond normally and spontaneously, with a warmth within my heart and a tingling within my body. In a way, one could term this a kind of temporary healing; perhaps one day I would be able to return to my normal sexual self.

I showered by myself after each booking and put on clean underwear. Sometimes I would change into a different outfit, as I usually had a spare one in my car. Check make-up again, brush hair, clean teeth, check condom supply, put powder in my shoes, etc. etc. – over and over, again and again, the same routine.

Peak agency times, I found, were from about eleven thirty at night, with another busy spell from one thirty in the morning onwards. Sometimes I only got home at eight-thirty in the morning, by which stage I'd be in total over-drive, unable to sleep. That's when my mind didn't stop. It made no differ-ence then if the men had been kind or not, or whether the bookings had been good or bad. Their faces would go round and round in my head – and the bodies, and the attached penises. And I'd get sick in my stomach, and my soul just shrivelled within me, and the mere thought of sex made my skin crawl.

I'd reach for my Brozam then, thankfully swallow a sizeable dose, and wait for it to take effect. General was always there for me, his compassion reflect-ed in his gentle brown eyes, little paw in my hand as he lay beside me. When sleep came, it was a sleep to wipe out what had been – and to prepare for what was to come. I was grateful to get home alive, to be able to pay the bills, provide for my kids, buy General and Bart their dog food, feed the two cats, and stable Copper Band.

Afterwards you don't remember them all – the men. I think you only re-member certain ones for certain reasons. James remembers them better than I do.

Sometimes the escorting would turn my mind back down the corridors of time and I'd remember other sexual encounters in my life.

Let's face it, guys, there's a time and a place to get your rocks off. And on the public trains isn't one. It was in 1991 – this particular evening, I'd worked late at my secretarial job on the foreshore, and it was about seven fifteen when the train pulled out of Cape Town station; I'd be getting off at Wyn-berg. Across the aisle, against the window and facing the same way as my-self, sat a nurse completely engrossed in her paperback. A young white chap, very pale face, early twenties, blonde greasy hair to his shoulders, came and sat down opposite the nurse. He was wearing a blue button-up shirt with rolled-up sleeves, jeans and brown boots; his eyes bloodshot, face unshaven, strange look to the eyes. The nurse never moved an inch, twitched a muscle or shifted in her seat. I regularly checked him out the corner of my eye, whilst reading my own book.

With total calm, he pulled down his zip, took out his penis and proceeded to sit there and masturbate. I was dumbstruck; book open, now on my lap. Once finished, he simply wiped the semen from his hand onto his jeans, put his penis inside his trousers and pulled up the zip – which was when the conductor happened to walk into the carriage. The youngster immediately left for another coach, and I informed the conductor of the incident – leaving out the part that the wanker's penis had been as pale as his face. And the nurse was now decidedly less interested in her book, and more aware of her surroundings!

Sometimes, after a booking with a guy who was too "physical", I'd think of the boyfriend I'd had in 1980 after my divorce from Bert's father. We'd had a relationship and sex, but I have no recollection of the sexual act itself anymore. He was an attorney, outwardly loving and affectionate. However, he would suddenly change character, from an enticing, gentle lover to a monster of aggression. I could never figure out what I had done to set off this erratic, terrifying behaviour. I used to be dragged around by the hair or have my hair pulled out, be beaten and thrown around the house against the walls and furniture. It was literally a fight for my life. I shudder to think what would or could have happened if I hadn't attempted to defend myself on these occasions. He tried to strangle me several times, and twice attempted to push me out of the passenger door of the moving car. The second time I decided that falling out of the car and rolling across the ground was safer than remaining in the vehicle with him.

Ending a relationship with someone like this proved well nigh impossible. He simply would not allow us to split up; even mentioning it would set him off in a crazed rage again. I went to work at my secretarial job many times with a scarf around my neck to hide the bruises. I phoned my mother and told her what I was going through, and she in turn told my father. My dad then phoned my boyfriend and told him he'd give him a beating he wouldn't forget if he didn't stop hitting his daughter. I was given a severe bashing when that particular telephone conversation ended. And I didn't dare phone my parents about it again.

The end to this terrifying ordeal was that I found he'd suddenly been thrown in jail, literally, one afternoon, for theft of quite a tidy sum of money from the firm's trust fund. Whilst I didn't like him being in jail, I was extremely grateful that he was out of my life – and little Bert's life too.

Eventually, in this kind of relationship, you don't know who you are any more. Each time he'll say he's sorry and that he won't do it again, that he loves you and needs you – and you'll forgive him. But it'll happen again, and again. Psychologically, you begin to think you must be the cause, and the vicious circle continues. Eventually, your confidence is destroyed because your life is a constant waiting terror. You're afraid to try and change the situation, afraid of him. You know if you report him, find a job, move out, file for divorce, whatever, he'll follow you and beat you when he finds you. Worst of all is that, in utter despair, some women accept this as their lot in life and think they deserve the monster. Help is out there though, for any woman who finds herself in this unfortunate and miserable existence and wishes to change the circumstances of her life.

James's "tom cat" behaviour continued relentlessly and unabated from day one of my escorting, and utterly drained me. Both of us were caught in a financially inspired, traumatic sexual drama.

Sam, it turned out, hadn't had such a great holiday after all. Apparently he'd wrecked his car, a total write-off I believe, and now lay in hospital with a cracked collarbone recovering. Saved me some bother though, I thought, as I'd entertained the idea of cracking the thing myself. Sam's recuperation would, I was now informed by his secretary, keep him out of the office for even longer. Give the guy his due – he could certainly come up with unusual contingency plans to avoid paying me my commissions!

So James suggested that we move into his home in the southern suburbs. He applied for an additional bond to build on a small office at the front of his house, which was presently the front stoop, and have the en-suite bathroom tiled. Well, it made sense, he said. In my "normal" life I was in the same line of work as he was. Why not join forces and build the business together? I'd be happy and more secure and could stop escorting. And furthermore, I wouldn't need to take my tranquillisers any longer: "You can stop taking those pills now, they're not good for you – and you know I don't believe in taking tablets."

Yes, I'd certainly learnt many lessons in "the racket", but I was grateful for the opportunity to stop and be normal again. Or try to be normal again. James and I could return to "us" and heal our wounds. He'd been my teacher; he'd taught me to love myself and had brought out my inner sensuality. I was relieved to be able to return to just him, with no other men in my body. And I was relieved that he could give up the "tom cat" business.

I gave notice to my landlord, found new tenants for our house and began packing, in between work and "work". Forget about money coming from hospitalised Sam – I reckoned it'd be a long wait. Even when he recovered, it'd be an ongoing battle.

Mary-Lou would need a new school near James's house and Copper Band would also need new stabling close by – the horse would have to be trucked across the mountains to take up residence in new pastures. Coping with all these costs would be difficult, I knew, but we'd just have to work it out somehow.

Mary-Lou's birthday was in March; she wanted a fish tank, but the tanks I'd seen were large and I thought would be rather expensive. The gentleman in the pet shop was most helpful: a small tank, complete with air filter, plants and a few fish was one hundred and twenty rand. That was fine, and I felt pleased to be able to get her what she wanted. It was arranged to have the tank delivered to our house, an unexpected surprise for Mary-Lou.

Within a week, however, Mary-Lou said she'd rather have new roller blades like her friend Estelle; they wanted to roller blade together. And could she have them by the weekend?

Yes, she'd had a tough time with me escorting, I thought, and I wanted to be able to give her what she really wanted. I phoned Bert. There was no way I could afford these expensive items alone, on top of the fish tank, but with Bert's help it could be managed. Her brother agreed to put half the money in my bank account. I kept the goldfish tank for myself, and Mary-Lou was chuffed to bits about her new roller blades and went off with Estelle to have fun together. So it ended well – we were all happy with our new acquisitions and Bert, being a working man, was so pleased with himself to be able to buy his sister a birthday gift she really wanted – out of his very own pay!

Matthew's leg was out of plaster after his accident, and he was back riding his motorbike. He had his driver's licence and had been a big help, taking Mary-Lou to school most mornings in our little car so that I could sleep when I got home in the early hours. I'd started buying the daily newspaper and encouraged him to look for work. Eventually I nagged, checked the employment column myself, circled the appropriate positions and told him I'd be like shit under a shoe until he faced the fact that he'd only find work if he actively looked for it! And he did look – and with relief, found a suitable position.

Plans were progressing quite smoothly, all in all. I continued at the escort agency until the last week of March 1996, earning my final money in "the racket".

The night I bid Puff and the others goodbye, I didn't have to pay for one drink. Puff and some of the girls – Tammy, Amy, Christina and Cindy – kindly picked up the tab for me. At about quarter past twelve, Christina crossed to the hi-fi. There was a lull in clients just then.

"Hey, Rachael, how's about a last dance together?" she said, grinning.

"Yeah, I'm in the mood," piped up Cindy, kicking off her shoes and standing up. "Up, up, Granny," she said to me, taking both my hands and pulling me off the couch. "Amy, come on, you as well."

Puff took over the desk and the phones so that Tammy could join us. Christina hit the hi-fi volume control and Vaya Con Dios belted from the speakers:

> "I got on the phone and called the girls, said
> Meet me down at Curly Pearls, for a
> Ney, Nah Neh Nah
> In my high-heeled shoes and fancy fads . . ."

It felt good to dance with the girls one last time – to laugh and play the fool – but we only managed the one song together. A car pulled up outside and Puff reached for the volume control, yelling "shoes!" I felt quite heartsore, thinking I wouldn't be seeing these women again, except to visit on occasion.

I said goodbye to Puff and the girls at about ten past four in the morning.

"Now you can put your cast-iron frying pan away again," Tammy said laughingly as she hugged me at my car in the cool morning.

"Yeah," said Christina putting her hand on my shoulder. "I've seen a lot of stuff in this business, but I've never seen an escort walking around with a frying pan, until you, Rachael. Take care and visit, okay?"

"I will," I said, getting behind the wheel of my little car. "You take care as well, and keep in touch. And thanks for everything."

I drove home feeling a mixture of happiness and sadness. I could thankfully leave escorting behind me at last, but they had to stay on. But there really wasn't anything I could do about it – except think of them every day, understand their pain and hope and wish they'd one day find an easier way of earning a living.

Matthew had thankfully found another place to live, close to his work, and had left our home during the last week of March – so I had less responsibility for his well-being.

I remember so well the early morning of the day we finally moved to James's house. Bert was given a few days off from his job to help us with the removals, and it was glorious to have my son back home and to hear his laughter again after almost three months.

The last thing I packed and the first thing I unpacked was my hi-fi – I don't function properly without music.

Mary-Lou walked into the lounge at about six-thirty in the morning. "Mum," she said, "Bert says to tell you to please turn the music up – it doesn't matter if we wake the neighbours, we're leaving here today."

I turned up the volume and heard Bert join in, singing in his happy waking voice from down the passage. Next thing, Mary-Lou walks back into the lounge.

"Mum, Bert says to tell you, you're the best mother in the whole world!"

The love and joy of children, I thought with a smile, as I reached for another cardboard box to pack some last things in.

Yeah, so what did it really matter if the builders had taken longer than scheduled? That James's house was now covered in fine red dust and that I'd be cleaning like crazy again on that side – after scrubbing this side to the complete satisfaction of the landlord, for his new tenants? Or that James's garden was an utter mess from all the rubble and that the "professional" tiling man had professionally grouted the toilet lid closed as well? This was a new start!

I was also making a real effort to please James and had stopped taking my tranquillisers, which I'd been dependent on for almost five years; the dosage had increased considerably during my eight weeks or so of sex-working.

Finished – no more, none, not even one. I flushed the last of my tablets down the toilet. Cold turkey.

Bert took the canopy off our little bakkie and drove backwards and forwards the entire day, a seventy-five-kilometre round-trip each time, moving our possessions. The last members of the family to get packed were the most recent additions: the goldfish in their glass tank, with a bit less water than usual.

My little canine pal, General, had a new start ahead of him too, with two female companions, James's dogs, to keep him occupied. He was certainly in love and certainly very busy, and left in James's car with his paws on the dashboard, peering through the front window. It made no difference to him that his two new mates were spayed, for being the fellow he is, General was full of joy and hope – and a certain part of him was now full of life!

As I headed for James's house and our new life, in my mind I said goodbye forever to Rachael and her little frying pan.

It was all over now, thank heavens. It hadn't been easy – for any of us – but it had certainly got my family through a bad patch. We'd come out safe, that's what counted. I breathed a sigh of gratitude from deep within my soul.

Never in my wildest dreams could I have imagined that Rachael would be back with the girls, along with her basket and cast-iron frying pan, for a second stint of escorting later that same year.

Chapter Eight
Cold Turkey Cocktail

On a night in the middle of April 1996, I trudged to our house in the cool evening air on my way back from the shops, wearing my heels and normal work clothes. The escorting days were over and I was back to working from home only, this time with James.

In one hand I was carrying a couple of packets of groceries, and in the other a bag filled with what felt like one hundred kilograms of builder's sand. I'd found it in a pile on the street corner near the local shop; perfect for Petal's pee box, I thought.

One of Mary-Lou's few household chores was to regularly empty the cat-litter and replace it with fresh soil from the garden. Her other chores were to take her mugs and glasses to the kitchen, make her bed, keep her own room and cupboard tidy, help with washing dishes on occasion and lastly to keep her riding gear in suitable condition. We had no char. I did the housework and James has always been very good about dishwashing – disciplined from his youth.

James was out this particular evening seeing business clients, and I was relieved to have space again as we'd had visitors from Johannesburg who'd stayed for about ten days. What with the house move and all the cleaning after the builders had finished, finding a new school for Mary-Lou, plus sorting out new stabling for Copper Band, I was thankful the guests had gone back home.

I had been feeling strangely light-headed for some days, and put it down to not having taken a single tranquilliser since the day we moved to James's at the end of March – about two weeks now cold turkey. Compared to being on the tablets, I felt almost "high". I'd phoned our local pharmacist two days before about this and was told that I should not have stopped the tranquillisers so abruptly, as sudden withdrawal from long-term use of benzodiazepines was known to often have adverse effects, including convulsions – sometimes even fatal. However, seeing that I was coping and only feeling light-headed, things would probably be all right and I'd manage without the tablets. I was doing okay so far, I thought. Who knows, perhaps I'd manage to kick the pill-popping habit without too much difficulty after all.

It's strange how the smallest thing in life can become the straw that breaks the camel's back.

I opened the front garden gate, my shoulders feeling as if they'd popped out of their sockets from the weight of the bags that I'd lugged for blocks back to our house – whereupon my beady eyes beheld the dog basket, left outside, the bedding now damp from the evening air. I'd asked Mary-Lou to take it in and she'd said she would. Was it really so much to ask of a fourteen-year-old, to bring in a small dog basket? After all, she'd ample strength to ride her horse! Here was me, lugging sand for the cat-litter box. Why was it that it was always me that had to do everything? Hey, I'm not Wonderwoman, I get tired as well you know, I thought, irritated.

Mary-Lou was in her bedroom listening to music. I knocked on her door and asked her why she hadn't brought the basket in.

"Sorry," she said, appearing momentarily around the door with a vaguely apologetic look on her face, "I forgot," and went back to listening to her music.

I changed into a pair of James's white cotton boxer shorts (I often wore his shorts at home; they felt most comfortable), my blue T-shirt and beige winter fluffy-dog slippers with the dark brown floppy ears – all the while simmering inside with annoyance. I went through to the kitchen and opened an inexpensive bottle of red wine, poured myself a glass and took a few generous sips. Feeling pretty agitated, I reckoned a couple of glasses of vino should do the trick: I'd be ready to fall into bed and sleep. And a Brozam tablet would sure be welcome right now, I thought, as I busied myself in the kitchen. Not much chance of that though – I'd flushed the last pills down the toilet the day we'd moved.

So began the Cold Turkey Cocktail. I do not remember everything that happened that night. Of course it wasn't about the dog basket alone, but that's what sparked if off. I really felt tired – not only in body and mind, but tired in my soul; just sick and tired of everything. I'd had enough of everyone's shit, enough of it always being me who'd got the bull by the tits!

Fuck the lot, the whole fucking lot – everything, all of it, I thought, having another sip of wine. Forget about trying to please anyone some of the time, let alone all of the time. When would it ever be enough, I wondered. When would I ever have tried or done enough, continuously picked up after other people enough, given up or sold enough? Quite obviously, never! How long are you expected to never get annoyed or angry, how much manipulation are you expected to put up with before you reach your limit? Well, right now I felt as though I'd reached mine – I'd had it up to my neck and down to my toes!

My mind now began systematically digging up the past as I reached, repeatedly, for the glass of wine on the kitchen counter.

First salute was to Sam – with his never-ending monthly crap about my commissions. Yeah, at the age of thirty-eight you'd think a person would have built up some financial security and not be so dependent on a monthly income, hey? Be able to get a bond on a house, have a bit of money in a savings account perhaps. Life's not quite like that, is it? Not my life anyway, I thought. Stability? Not worth mentioning!

And as for the builders and all the mess they'd left behind! Never mind – woman not only has an earning job of work to do, I thought sarcastically, she also stands before, behind and after you. She'll clean up, won't she? And some "professional" tiler – my arse, didn't even notice he'd grouted the toilet lid closed! Lucky woman walks behind you to check, hey?

I topped up the wine in the glass and had another sip.

Next on the list in my simmering annoyance came the four husbands who'd taken every damn thing I ever had – yes, that's right, four! Really need my head read on that score, I thought vehemently. Given up the lot for them: my piano, my beloved trumpet, almost all my jewellery, even down to my little Wedgwood dish, plus the policies I'd taken out as security for my kids. And don't even ask me about shame, I thought – shame and humiliation; many a time I'd wished I could be an ostrich and bury my head in the sand, preferably forever!

Four marriages, but no engagement ring – for my third marriage I traded both my previous nine-carat gold wedding bands in for two new silver ones. And as for a honeymoon – what's that? Miss Idiot marries for love: gets married on Friday or Saturday and back to work I go on Monday – four times! Talk about blind repetition – when would I ever learn? Never been unfaithful, ever, and I'd never had to get married because of a pregnancy either – no, just this pathetic love shit I always had in my head, utterly ridiculous really.

Where had my sister Meg and I gone wrong? Was my unsuccessful married life due to the fact that I'd been at boarding school, an all-girls' school in another country, from such a young age? Seen my parents only twice a year, and had insufficient ability to judge men? Was this why I kept messing up good and proper? Was it the loneliness of my youth and the yearning to be loved that so pushed me towards the "happy house and babies" notion of wedded bliss? Beats me, I thought, taking another swig of wine.

Husband number one, Jack, I'd married at eighteen in Windhoek, against my parents' advice. He was seventeen years older than me. Wife number two I was, Bert his only child. Drove a green Chevrolet, voted second-best-dressed man in the city, fancy furniture, lovely hi-fi. Starry-eyed bliss didn't last long, did it? Three months later I found myself facing life with a late-home-again, been-to-the-pub-after-work drunk – an alcoholic. I'd hardly understood the proper meaning of the word at that age. I thought it only happened to other people, not me – it was a nasty shock.

I hardly ever went anywhere after Bert's birth – "Like a prisoner in your own home," my dad would often say when he visited us. I wasn't allowed to get my driver's licence or play sport, and Jack even did all the shopping. Twenty rand a month pocket money was my allowance from the time I stopped working, a month before Bert's birth. Bert was not only my baby – he became my dearest little friend as well.

One day a man arrived from the OK Bazaars to take the hi-fi as Mister hadn't been paying the instalments. What a surprise – I'd thought Jack owned the hi-fi! Well, out came my little nest egg from my job before Bert's birth; that's what saved the hi-fi.

On a day in early January 1979, Jack left – just left, walked out with his clothes in suitcases and went to live with his friend who'd sent us a "With Sympathy" card for our wedding, and never came back. Never once did he phone to see if we had money for food – or consider how a twenty-one-year-old, jobless housewife with a small child would manage to pay the rent, water and electricity.

Lucky for Bert and me, my ex-boss gave me a job as a receptionist – and I then had to almost immediately ask for time off to have an abortion. Yes, I'd managed to fall pregnant. Boxing Day 1978, about a week before Jack walked out, had been one of those rare and lucky occasions for me, about once every three to four months, when there was any sex in our marriage! What covered the cost of that sweet little procedure? Simple really – the two thousand three hundred rand my grandmother had left each of her four grandchildren. Mine paid my flight to Holland and the clinic. Jack not only claimed the baby wasn't his but also refused to put even ten rand towards the cost.

Our divorce, which my father paid for – paid for the wedding as well – took seven months to finalise. Why? Because I asked for one hundred rand a month as maintenance for Bert. Eventually Jack agreed to seventy-five rand for his son – which he didn't bother to pay for the next sixteen and a half years anyway, despite all my efforts. Apart from that, my first divorce settlement consisted of some furniture and the hi-fi.

After this I found a better paid job, a secretarial position at the coast, and little Bert and I made our way to our new life on the back of an uncovered lorry, surrounded by our belongings. A family friend who owned a farm had most kindly given us the use of this truck, together with three workers, for the six-hundred-kilometre trip to the coast.

Bert and I lay on the bed on the back with my enormous elephant-ear pot plant shading us from the harsh Namibian sun – cars travelling behind us found the sight quite amusing. On the long journey, the driver made a detour through one of the townships, stocking up on the local brewed beer; by eleven o'clock that night our three helpers were in good-spirited inebriation, and while carrying our possessions up the outside staircase to the top of the block of flats, the washing machine and one of the speakers of the hi-fi took a pretty much expected fall. Still, we'd got to where we needed to be and it'd been quite an interesting adventure. Despite the local brew, they were good blokes, cheerful, polite and very helpful. I was grateful.

In 1991, I spent three hundred rand on a private detective to find Jack when he vanished a second time. He was arrested, pleaded poverty before the magistrate, and then just vanished again for the third time – until we found him once more, four years later, when he coincidentally decided to live in the same town that Bert went to school in. Then the no-good so-and-so died in 1995 – too much drinking over the years – and I was expected to sort out his final resting-place!

Ultimately, I was owed about thirty thousand rand by Bert's father. And if you don't continue regularly fighting for your child support, the Maintenance Court takes this to mean that you don't need the financial assistance anyway – never mind the fact that to attend hearings, a working mother has to repeatedly request time off from her job, which is what keeps her and her kids alive.

Sorry, Mother, best get on with bringing up the children without financial assistance from me. Tired, Mother? Too bad, perhaps you should lie down and rest a while – you'll be as good as new after a bit of rejuvenating sleep. No money, Mother? Well, make a plan – you always make a plan. Perhaps you should sell something again. Besides, if I pay you maintenance you'll just spend it on yourself, won't you? Depressed, Mother, having a hard time? Oh, shame, well I do think of you occasionally – and you know, you've done a marvellous job really without any money from me. Sorry, I can't help. I need the bucks for my booze, or my gambling, or my night out with the guys, or my new wheels, or to spend on another woman.

Which brought me to the next husband. Number two, called Bobby, was in the teaching profession. My mother warned me against this marriage too – said he and his kids would be a stone around my neck! (He had custody of his children from his previous marriage.) Smashingly good-looking, macho physique; coached the local ladies hockey team, which is how I met him. The women loved this one, flocked like bees round a honey pot to the charm and good looks – I was really flattered when he fancied me, out of all his admirers.

Bobby didn't own a car when I met him. My dad had bought me a little Austin car for my twenty-first birthday present. He felt Bert and I should have our own wheels, be independent and able to get about. Pretty soon after meeting Bobby I was told by him to sell my car, and did, to the school secretary – after all, it wasn't big enough for him, his two children, Bert and me!

Dad then gave Bobby our family's VW kombi, which had been driven out of Angola on the back of our lorry when my family escaped with the last escorted convoy in 1975. Well, that seemed big enough. Bobby later sold the kombi and bought two second-hand Minis instead.

Soon, the various married women started appearing in our married life. Pregnant, I'd walk back from my full day's work at the office, first stopping off at the doctor on the way for an injection to "hold" Mary-Lou because I was "spotting". Next, I had to buy some groceries that I carried home – only to find Bobby and Miss Hotpants colleague-teacher-married-admirer enjoying a cosy record-playing session together on our brown lounge carpet. Not once either! Then they had ongoing cosy little tête-à-têtes at our front gate or outside in her parked car – because I told him I didn't want this woman in my home again when I wasn't there.

Now appeared the two married women from the ladies' hockey team who pitched up at our home on several occasions in the evening. I'd answer the door, holding my baby daughter on my hip – and they'd ask my husband if he'd go out with them, as their own husbands were home babysitting their children! Sorry, but he couldn't, he'd say – I'd told him this crap had to stop.

My mother arrived unexpectedly one afternoon to visit, to find me extremely depressed – there was no money for food – and gave me a hundred rand for groceries. Despite finances being tight, however, Mister felt that he really needed to go on a cricket tour with his buddies, forked out a tidy sum of money – first buying himself some new cricket gear – and then had a grand time with his cricket mates while I stayed home and looked after the children. He also found the money to buy a brand-new, out-of-the-box, really fancy, powerful motorbike. Couldn't afford a car – and you can't fit much family on even a big new Honda!

Finally came one of the local doctors' wives – after the married teacher-admirer. Doctor-wife was the cherry on the top for me. Oh, the sweet little love-letters Bobby wrote her – "I have kissed on this spot!"

Let me tell you a little thing about love notes. If you're going to write them, remember this for future reference – don't use a note pad with thin or flimsy paper, particularly airmail paper, and don't press hard when you write or use a sharp pencil or fine hard-nibbed pen. While you may have torn off the top page and delivered your clandestine love note to your admirer, it only takes a suspecting wife to pick up a pencil and shade the underlying page to reveal exactly what you've written! Perhaps I should've been a detective, I thought – oh, I was utterly impressed with my genius!

At six o'clock one morning, standing on our front balcony, having just fed and changed Mary-Lou, I watched Doctor-wife drop Bobby off in her VW Kombi at our gate, after they'd spent the entire night together. Bobby had gone to the "Round Table meeting" the previous evening on his motorbike; now he was carrying his crash helmet in his hand, and had to fetch his motorbike later from "somewhere else"! Umm, Bobby . . . "charity work" keeps you out the entire night with another man's wife while your own wife is home looking after your four children, the youngest still bottle-fed – not very charitable, that, is it?

Bert has a distinct memory of running out of the house at about the age of five, and trying to climb up on top of the garden wall to get away from another of Bobby's rather heavy-handed hidings. After all, his kids were as good as gold! By that stage, Bobby was the second man, who wasn't Bert's own father, to have hit the child as punishment in his young life.

I had it out with the doctor's wife in our kitchen one day – this after the kissy love-notes and the entire night they'd spent together. She begged me not to tell her husband, said his health wasn't good.

The final straw was when my best friend, a teacher, asked me to go round to her house as she had something to tell me. During the break in the evening school meeting, she'd gone back to her classroom to collect something – and lo and behold, who did she find in one of the passages? None other than the doctor's wife and Bobby in a rather warm embrace. Perhaps he was comforting her?

Well, I wasn't prepared to face further married life with the good-looking womaniser, and left him. That was a blow to his ego. He told people he'd no idea where I'd gone – I'd simply up and left him! Quite odd, seeing as he had personally seen Mary-Lou, Bert and I off on the train, with the kids waving out the open window, on our way to my parents.

My dad then paid for us to fly to the Orange Free State, to friends of mine who assured me there was work for me there, to start our lives over again.

I had to pay half the divorce costs, and in the settlement I got one of the Minis, a hundred and fifty rand a month maintenance for Mary-Lou, and my furniture – two items of which Bobby quite happily kept when the removals truck arrived to collect my belongings: my beige bean bag I'd bought before I even met him and my very large, round grass mat. During the period of finalising the divorce, Bobby wrote me a letter saying he was considering becoming a priest – pity I never kept it! He was married again before I was, and fathered in total four children by three wives.

Bobby never missed a maintenance payment, give the guy his due. Just because he'd a fancy for other women is no reason to imply he wasn't a nice person – he was enormously liked and respected by his colleagues, popular with everyone, the centre of attention, and exceptionally intelligent and charming with sweeping long lashes shading alluring eyes, a lovely smile and good teeth. He wasn't aggressive, had good manners, hardly drank and didn't smoke, studied diligently to improve his qualifications, and also went to church regularly. Mary-Lou inherited her intelligence and looks from Bobby. Looking at it logically, a man can't help it if he's irresistible to the opposite sex – the difference is whether he encourages them or not.

Who gives a sausage anyway? After all, I'd become a prostitute many years later, at thirty-eight – now that's something to get the tongues wagging! Look at her, that'll teach her a lesson. Hey, but I can tell you, it paid the bills for me and my kids all those years later – which is something you four husbands didn't always get right!

Now, no need to get snotty and smug, I thought, sipping merrily on the cheap cabernet, or was it a sauvignon?

I managed to rent a house with an old stove with two plates that worked, paid off a second-hand fridge over three months – until then the milk had kept fresh in cold water in the sink – and bought two beds on hire purchase, a tiny black and white TV and eventually a cheap two-seater couch (before we'd had to sit on a camping mattress – my bean bag would've been appreciated). The Free State winters were freezing, and the house had no carpeting. I managed to afford two two-bar heaters, one a month. I'd hang the children's bath towels over a chair, and we'd sit on the mat in front of the heaters, reading bedtime stories. Later I managed to afford a loose carpet – my woven grass mat sure would've helped! While I worked fourteen kilometres away from home, my children, thank God, were cared for by the kindest woman I've ever met in my life, an African lady named Tiny. It was during this already difficult time that I bled two litres of blood through the stomach from having my wisdom teeth removed, and almost died.

Anyway, it worked out okay, the kids and I survived. We were happier after our move from Bobby, and Mary-Lou hardly remembered him.

I remembered an occasion after this second marriage, sitting at the round kitchen table in Namibia with my dad one evening.

"My girl," he said looking at me, "I don't know how you stay sane, you've been through already what most people live in a lifetime."

Hey, and we were only halfway there! Dad kept forking out for my multiple wedding celebrations – nothing quite like hope is there? Perhaps I took after my grandfather, I thought – he'd had three wives! Difference was that they all died natural deaths, there were no divorces, and Grandfather made a success of his life, as opposed to my continuous mess.

Next, we get to number three, I thought, raising my glass in mock salute. Both my parents had liked Terry and I'd reckoned he was a good guy at heart, the best of the lot.

Terry was a fairly good-looking, tall, very strong man with a degree in agriculture, a hard worker, two years younger than myself. I was his first and only wife. When we met he was having some pretty severe emotional problems adjusting to civilian life, after his horrendous experiences while fighting in one of the elite South African forces on the Angolan border for two years. He buried his problems in drinking bouts, during which he wanted to harm himself with a knife. He particularly adored Mary-Lou, who loved him, and I helped him resolve the drinking problem, which he handled well for some time. Family life proved most therapeutic, and settled his sometimes aggressive and unpredictable behaviour, but it wouldn't last indefinitely.

I remember many happy, fun times with Terry. He later adopted Mary-Lou; Bobby was then no longer required to pay maintenance for her. Bert didn't want to be adopted and we didn't push him.

Terry's unpredictable character was a big problem – he once swapped our car over the garden fence with the neighbour, for a really beat-up vehicle, without discussing the matter with me. And that was after I'd had to sell my little Mini! He also had a quick and sometimes nasty temper.

Bert took some pretty bad hidings from Terry – now the third man to hit my young son. My mothering heart and soul were sometimes awash in a silent desperation, witnessing this enormously strong adult man dish out physical punishment to Bert, who lay cowering in fear on his bed as the blows rained down. At moments like these in my life I've felt so ashamed of myself, and wished I'd the physical strength to give these men a taste of their own medicine. There was only one occasion that Terry raised his hand in anger to hit me. I was holding Mary-Lou at the time, and perhaps this is what saved me, because he managed to control his temper, lowering his arm. I don't remember him ever hitting Mary-Lou.

Terry changed jobs six times, necessitating nine house moves between South Africa, Namibia and the Transkei, ending up in the Eastern Cape. His two brilliant jobs in Namibia were acquired through my father's connections. In northern Namibia we were so happy and financially secure. I worked and was due for promotion, Terry was relaxed and his drinking and temper were controlled. But he wanted his own farm, the stepping stone to that being a return to South Africa – although I advised him against this move. He was fired from his next job, in the Free State, after some months. Arriving home one afternoon, I found him sitting at the kitchen table with his final pay. It was during this time that I had to undergo my back operation, which, thankfully, my dad paid for.

There hadn't been any work for me in the small town where we lived. Luckily, I was able to keep us going financially by working in the Greek corner café, selling one "zol" (cigarette) at a time, packets of Boxer tobacco and fish and chips, standing on my feet for hours while Terry went to the Transkei in search of work. This was when I had to sell my piano and the first of my policies was surrendered.

The fifth job was brilliant, a lucky break with good money in the Transkei, doing what Terry liked – working a dairy herd. We lived well and were very happy once more, though Bert and Mary-Lou had to go to boarding school in the Cape, which necessitated plenty of trips to and fro. But Terry ultimately wanted to be his own boss and threw this job in as well, finally buying his dream farm.

Despite sound advice from my father with regard to farming, Terry managed to notch up a couple of hundred thousand rand debt by the time he finally packed this venture in as well – or so I believe. I'd strictly not been permitted to be involved in the financial aspects of this farming business.

During this time the last of my possessions of any value had to be sold to get us through financially. I remember well trudging to the pawnshop to sell my two beautiful necklaces, which were very old and had been handed down to me by my mother, and which I've never seen the likes of again – I felt so ashamed. Then it was my little diamond ring for eighty rand, and so on.

Terry's first poor farming decision was to sell live chickens, on credit, in rural areas of the Transkei – needless to say, this resulted in an immediate and considerable financial loss. Although he didn't get his money back on the second trip, it was still several weeks before he was put off the idea. While he was out on the Transkei chicken run, I was left in a farmhouse that stank of rat piss – I had to rip up all the carpets – with an unreliable gas geyser and a back door that couldn't be locked. Considering that there'd been some unpleasant incidents in the area, my nerves felt pretty raw.

Some of the farm labourers' children had scabies, and one of my first priorities was to have a two-year-old hospitalised and the severe scabies brought under control before it infected my own family.

I dug the garden and vegetable garden, my back taking strain. I repeatedly had to pull Terry's tractor out of a large hole (the same hole!) in one of the fields, using our bakkie, or I'd have to try to tow him backwards up the hill when his lorry wouldn't start – he'd keep parking it at the bottom of the slope! I also helped to drive calves, which he'd bought for fattening, from the Transkei.

One Easter Saturday I was left to drive to town with Bert and Mary-Lou, with no spare tyre and a slow puncture. Needless to say, the kids and I landed up stranded on the side of a dirt road, and hitched a lift into town with a passing taxi. That turned out to be quite fun – the occupants were a lot more considerate and helpful than my husband!

Terry's drinking started once more in earnest – out cold on the bedroom floor after vomiting into the flower beds – and his temper got worse. Financially, matters became precarious. This wasn't helped by him deciding to make a fire break around the house one windy day. I said that I didn't feel it was a suitable day; plus it was a Saturday, and the farm staff had gone home around noon.

"Why don't you stick to being a wife and let me stick to being the farmer," he said. "I now what I'm doing!"

"Well, I'm a farmer's daughter you know, and not for nothing," I replied, exasperated. "It might be only a gentle breeze now, but what if it picks up?"

Irritated with his nagging, interfering wife, off Terry went. I watched through the house windows with Mary-Lou, feeling extremely anxious about the large electrical box, with danger signs stuck all over it, a few metres from the front gate. The neighbouring farmer's trailer, which Terry had borrowed and not yet returned, was parked not far away.

It was a lovely wind that picked up that afternoon, and a lovely fire, Terry – yes, you deserve ten out of ten for that one!

The flames crackled and popped excitedly, heading straight for the trailer, then the electrical box. Terry rushed frantically for the front garden hose-pipe, which wasn't quite long enough; then he tried the green plastic rake, which only took a couple of minutes to melt into a mangled shape. Next came the sacks to beat out the fire. Mary-Lou and I ran up the hill to call the house girl and her children. Luckily she had several kids and was home at the time. Well, by the time that fire was put out there was fine black ash all over our home, and the brand-new fencing, which had eventually been completed on Friday afternoon at a considerable cost, was burnt!

Now I was told to find work in the small town, which I did, a miserable job selling spare parts in a gloomy, dismal and cold lower-floor workshop. Depression was getting to me. I started lying on my bed whenever I could, curled up in a ball. Mary-Lou was suffering immensely from the chilblains on her fingers and toes.

My godmother in England sent me a gift of British currency to help me and my children, and I decided to do a computer course to further my employment opportunities. Fetching me the afternoon I completed my training, Terry told me that I was to leave, move out, the following week by the latest – he felt sure someone would be along soon to take my possessions in lieu of some of his debts. He also asked me to lend him a substantial amount of money to buy more calves, which he intended to fatten for resale.

"I'll double your investment in a few months," he assured me. "You'll see, you'll get it all back, plus."

"No way," I answered. "I've taken enough losses already."

That was the beginning of the end of our marriage. I found a house for myself and the children in a nearby city, paid the deposit and rent, bought a little second-hand car for us (Terry kept our bakkie, apart from other things), moved, set my kids up in school, paid the water, electricity, groceries – everything.

We survived this ordeal solely thanks to my godmother and to the fact that I did temp secretarial work – thirteen different positions – until I found a permanent job. I later moved to this firm's Cape Town offices, which offered a higher salary and promotion.

Terry paid our 1989 divorce costs: I said I wasn't spending another cent of my money. My settlement was two hundred and fifty rand maintenance for Mary-Lou, and she and Bert went to him for the short school holidays. None of my three divorces so far had given me any money, or medical costs, clothing or schooling for my children; just straight child maintenance.

Before he finally gave up on his farming venture, Terry sold Mary-Lou's horse – and unbeknown to us, also stopped paying his two life policies, on which she was beneficiary. He then found other work.

On two occasions Terry phoned me to say he'd had severe car accidents and felt there was an unseen hand guarding over him, as he should've been dead. I said it was perhaps time he slowed down his driving and stopped tempting fate. The third car accident in early 1992 killed him, though I believe he was a passenger at the time. Apparently the driver was under-age, unlicensed or a learner. This ended Terry's maintenance payments for Mary-Lou, with no pay-out from his policies, though he did manage to leave a small amount of money in trust for her.

Oh fuck, what a life, I thought, topping up my wine glass again. Can't complain about it being boring though, can you, woman? No, I never knew what the next man would bring, parcelled up quietly for me to deal with, and then have to grab my kids, pack up and start over again. Most times, when I thought of the husbands, it felt like just the house that changed. I actually felt sick from the filth other people kept putting in my life – and shook my head, amazed at the memories that flooded back in this systematic digging up of the past.

God, please grant me the ability to find some sense one day, I thought wryly. The level of the wine bottle had dropped considerably by this stage and I still wasn't feeling sleepy; neither was it seeming to ease my agitation. Actually, quite the contrary, I was feeling pretty wound up with all the reminiscing. Mary-Lou was still in her bedroom, listening to her music.

Men have so many rights, I thought. And they get away with plenty shit too! Bar brawls and punch-ups, rape, murder, a couple or several wives at a time! Cripes, not that I'd want more than one husband at a time – no thank you.

Another of my unhappy associations with men came back to mind then. My parents were tobacco farming in Angola at the time. I was sixteen, in the middle of my year at secretarial college in Rhodesia, and fell pregnant. My steady boyfriend, a German in his twenties, told me he sure as hell wasn't going to marry me, and I'd better get rid of the baby. He'd heard you could have an abortion done in Beira, in neighbouring Mozambique; boyfriend paid for us to fly there. While he lay on the beach sunning himself, I had to get a taxi driver to take me to the place, a large block of flats in a filthy area of the city, where a nursing sister (or so I was given to believe) who only spoke Portuguese performed the procedure.

For three days I underwent the most horrendous back-street abortion – my legs in stirrups, a round plastic bowl under my buttocks, with a female interpreter holding my hand, begging me not to pass out as I was scraped and stuffed during this barbaric ordeal. I was not even allowed an aspirin for the pain – the interpreter explained it was essential that I receive no medication, and that I did not pass out at any time during these treatments. The procedure was illegal, and calling a doctor if anything went wrong was out of the question.

I clearly remember sitting on the hotel bed after the first day, clutching the pillow to my abdomen and rocking back and forth for hours from the pain – and there were still two more days of treatment to survive. My abdomen was horrendously swollen from the tubing and cotton wool that had been stuffed inside my vagina while I bled. Boyfriend, however, continued sunning himself on the beach – after all, as he pointed out, he was there on holiday, and I wasn't!

By the time we boarded the plane to fly back to Rhodesia, I was unable to walk up straight and sought medical treatment from a doctor on arrival. The infection was severe – and every day of my pregnancy with Bert, I was terrified my child would be born deformed.

I gave birth to Mary-Lou at the age of twenty-four, a planned pregnancy – in fact, I'd struggled to fall pregnant as I was having trouble with my periods. And every day of being pregnant with her as well, I wondered if my second child would be normal. God blessed me, though, with a beautiful little girl.

When Mary-Lou was about ten months old I requested to be sterilised. After my experiences with men, I definitely didn't want another pregnancy, and asked my doctor to make sure he didn't just tie my tubes: "Cut them so nothing can find its way in," I asked him. I had six metal clips. I think it's one of the few wise decisions I've ever made in my life – but I still had some wisdom teeth at that stage!

I couldn't tell you exactly what I was doing in the kitchen while my mind dug up all this old shit from my past – I was on a roll of angry, unhappy memories. I knew our dogs needed their supper, the kitchen needed tidying and there were business files to work on as well. Perhaps I went through to the office, which was next to the lounge. What I remember most distinctly was drinking the bottle of wine and becoming more and more agitated about the men I'd encountered in my life.

The case of the snogging dentist popped to mind now. Had his dental surgery in Gardens, Cape Town – really nice man, I was assured, good in his work, very thorough, considerate and gentle. Umm . . . I've always been terrified of dentists – don't really know why. Something about the noise of that tiny whizzing drill makes the hair on my neck stand up; I imagine it could drill right through my jaw and up into my head or down into my neck!

Well, husband number four put my mind at ease – you won't feel one bit anxious with my dentist, he said. So off I went for a check-up and a new bite plate, telling the man how anxious I felt. Not to worry dear, feel quite relaxed, I'll give you some gas, you won't feel a thing. Never had gas before at a dentist's – okay, I'll try it. Went smooth as butter – didn't need any fillings, come back next week and we'll fit your bite plate. Bliss! Why didn't any dentist think of this before for me?

So, back I went a week later. We did the gas thing again (to fit a bite plate?!), yes, he turned the gas right up, how are you feeling? I couldn't get my hands to co-operate one bit with my brain, they sort of floated about near me somewhere. That seems about right, the dentist said, you'll be perfectly relaxed. Dental assistant left the room, dentist sort of whizzed up and down next to me on his little round-wheely chair, fetching my new bite plate and fitted it – spot-on first time, not the slightest bit of adjustment needed, now wasn't that easy and painless? I'm so blessed having found such a kind, considerate dentist after all these years, thank you – yes, one of these days I'm going to have the most attractive teeth on the planet!

Next thing I know I've got his hands all over me, down my dress on my breasts, up under my petticoat, fiddling in my knickers – my hands grab the air wildly, I can't move properly, I'm attached to gas equipment, maybe it'll explode, I can't walk, God this man isn't "well", I think . . . then he lifts the gas mask off my face for a moment, gives me a quick snog and puts it back, now he's taken my right hand and is rubbing it all over its hard penis as it sits on its little wheely chair next to me!

Good grief! Relax, dear, he says, gas makes you feel wonderful doesn't it, like having too much bubbly champagne, you're all light and free, oh it's an amazing feeling – rub, rub.

Suddenly, dental assistant comes back into the room. All finished here, the dentist says, quickly taking the gas mask off me – you just lie there a minute dear, I'll give you a hand up just now. No, I'm fine thanks, I mumble, getting out of the dental chair with some effort. Careful you don't fall dear. Cross unsteadily to the basin, wash my hands. Piece of pus, I think – and what really winds me up is that I have to pay you as well!

"Give Margaret a nice cup of sweet tea," the dentist shouts to his receptionist as I begin to walk slowly to the waiting room, feeling the wall as I go along, clutching my new bite plate.

"There now, that wasn't so bad was it, you're not anxious anymore now that you've had the gas twice, see how much easier it is?" the kindly elderly receptionist says. "You really shouldn't try driving your car just yet, give it another ten minutes or so."

Sip the sweet tea, don't like tea anyway and hate sugar in it in the first place. Sit quiet a while then pluck up some courage. "Is doctor married?"

I get a strange look from the receptionist. "Yes."

Married or not, this was a middle-aged man, highly qualified with a successful business; if I'd ever tried to report that incident, who would've believed me, an oft-married woman? They'd have said I was vindictive, sexually desperate or psychologically sub-standard, trying to ruin his good reputation – something in that vein anyway, I'm sure. I had as much hope of anyone believing my story as General has of getting his leg over a cow elephant!

Some years later, with James at my side, I got a new bite plate – from a different dentist, who never even suggested gas!

Well, we're not finished yet with men experiences – not till we get past the job interview rape at seventeen in Rhodesia. Shit, the amount of emotional baggage women have to drag around inside themselves, it can start to weigh you down after a time, particularly if other shit is dumped on top of it, over and over.

The wine bottle was beginning to look as though I'd soon be squeezing the thing – can still get a couple more drops out of that . . . wish I could sleep though.

I'd spoken little of this rape experience and first addressed the matter openly, which took some considerable amount of courage, when I was married to Bobby. It came as a shock to hear that he found it disgusting that I had "agreed" to sexual intercourse. Some men have a peculiar way of viewing rape – the woman must have, in some way, encouraged the perpetrator, and therefore be partly if not entirely responsible. Hearing his biased male opinion, I kept quiet about it in later years, carrying it silently within myself.

In my first job at seventeen as secretary to an accountant, I spent my entire day alone in a room typing figures for hours on end. While pleased to have a job and be supporting myself, I found the work totally without stimulation and felt that I should look for another position. An advert in the local paper requested written applications together with a full curriculum vitae. I sent mine off.

A secretary contacted me and set up a late afternoon appointment. That way I could go straight home afterwards, instead of having to return to work.

On the second floor of the brown brick building, the secretary asked me to wait in the reception area. She would advise the gentleman who was going to interview me of my arrival, she said, indicating his presence in an office behind hers. Open vertical blinds covered the glass door and windows between the two rooms.

After a few minutes, the secretary came to tell me that unfortunately Mr

So-and-so had some unexpected, urgent matter to attend to, would I mind waiting a bit longer? I said that was fine, I'd wait, and paged through a magazine, occasionally glancing up to see her on the phone or typing, busying herself in her office. Time was ticking by, but I didn't want to appear rude so decided to keep quiet and look through my CV and the certificates that I'd brought with me. I noticed the secretary go through to the inner office and speak to the interviewer.

She returned to me, apologised on the interviewer's behalf for keeping me waiting so long. Would it be inconvenient to ask me to wait a little bit longer, otherwise we'd have to reschedule the appointment? He would be most appreciative if I could wait, as the position needed to be filled soon. It was getting late, almost time for the staff to go home, but the gentleman would gladly give me a lift to my place of residence after my interview, having kept me waiting so long. I didn't sense anything untoward about that. I'd have to request time off work again if I didn't do the interview that afternoon, so I said that would be fine.

Some minutes later I watched her pack up her desk, as did other staff in the office area down the passage. She popped her head through the office door behind her, then coming to me with her handbag, said that Mr So-and-so would call me himself in a minute or two and was sorry, again, for the unexpected delay. I watched the employees walk past me on their way home, down the few stairs to the lift; the place became very quiet.

Ah, at last! Here he came: well-ironed, plain blue long-sleeved shirt, dark trousers, tie, neat light-brown hair, polished shoes – he seemed about as old as my dad, and at seventeen my forty-five-year-old father seemed quite old.

My gentleman interviewer seemed friendly enough, smiled, shook my hand and apologised for keeping me waiting so long. I followed him into his office. He closed the door and told me to sit in front of his desk, indicating a wooden chair – my back to the closed door.

Sorry there wasn't any tea to offer me, the staff had unfortunately gone home now. I said that was fine. And not to worry, he'd give me a lift home. I said thank you. His desk was neat. The office furnishings weren't smart, simple and practical really – wooden desk, some shelves against the wall, reddish-brown carpeting.

He had a copy of my CV on his desk, and referred to it as he interviewed me, seeming to find my background most interesting: born in Kenya, schooled in South Africa, living in Salisbury, parents now in Angola farming tobacco – so no close family members nearby.

I'm not a closed type of person, never have been, and answered questions about my background quite innocently and fully. I was very young to be working, but my qualifications were rather impressive, why did I want to leave my present job? Had I my own flat, living alone? Yes.

144

Through the long window behind his chair, I could see it was becoming dark outside. During the questioning he'd stood up from his desk, switching his office light on, and I saw him now raise his hand in a wave to someone behind me. Turning, I saw the security guard holding the door handle, the glass office door open.

"Everything alright here?" the security guard asked.

"Yes," he answered, smiling, "just interviewing the young lady. I was unfortunately a bit late and kept her waiting so we're running past schedule."

"Okay," the security guard said, "let me know if you need any help. I'll be downstairs, just doing my round checks."

"We'll be finished just now," my interviewer advised. "It's getting late so I'll give the lady a lift home – I'll let you know when we leave, Reg."

"Okey dokey," the guard said and nodded at me, and I smiled. He closed the door behind him and went off, no need for concern – he was on first-name terms with my interviewer, there were other more worrying things in Rhodesia than a seventeen-year-old having a late job interview with someone easily as old as her father. I was in good hands.

My interviewer then got up from his chair and moved slightly to my left, seemingly in thought, looking out through the window.

"Do you have a boyfriend?" he asked, back turned to me.

The question made me feel uncomfortable. I hesitated a moment; I didn't understand what this had to do with my proposed job and didn't know if I should be answering something like that. Why should he want to know anyway?

"Well, do you?" he asked again. "Have a boyfriend."

I've been known to be pretty direct in my life, and have landed in a bit of trouble on several occasions for what others have considered to be stubborn attitude.

"Why do you want to know that?" I asked.

"It's only a question," he answered, turning, "and not a difficult one at that."

"But what's my having a boyfriend got to do with me and this job?"

I kept quiet then, looking down, fiddling with my hands – I just wasn't feeling quite right in my stomach. Everything had been fine so far, but now there was a distinct change in the tone of his voice.

Crossing behind me, he closed the blinds across the glass wall that divided his office from his secretary's, and said, "You suddenly seem to have a very defensive attitude to a simple question."

I continued looking down, fiddling with my fingers. "I don't mean to be like that, it's just that I don't know why you would want to know that."

In my stomach, I felt caught between fear of being disrespectful to someone older than myself who was interviewing me for a job, a man at that, and a distinct anxiety as to how to respond to the tone of his voice and his obvious reluctance to drop the issue.

The next moment I felt his hand from behind me, hard, around the sides and back of my neck, as he pulled me up from the chair and pushed me to the carpeted floor. "Down, get down."

I do not remember him having to undo his trousers – they were open already, though not pulled down. Still with his hand round my neck, the front of my neck now, he held me forcefully down on the carpeted floor. "Off, take them off – your panties – now."

I hesitated, wide- and wild-eyed. Keeping his one hand aggressively round my neck, he pulled up my loose skirt with his other hand and started tugging at my knickers.

"Now," he said harshly but quietly, "right now."

In a second my mind put the picture together. Shouting or hoping for help from the security guard was pointless; he was downstairs. At seventeen, I was being held forcefully on the floor of a now deserted office building, a few storeys up, in evening hour, by a man maybe thirty years older than myself with aggression in his voice and a tight painful grip on my neck. I didn't stand a chance.

I took my knickers off. He spread my legs with his free hand, pushed me down flat on the floor while still holding my neck, moved between my legs, pulled his underpants down, put his penis inside me and thrust heavily, quickly and forcefully. I lay completely still on the reddish-brown carpet. He then withdrew, stood up, zipped his trousers and crossed to his desk.

"Get dressed," he said, dialling a number on his phone.

I put my knickers on, still sitting on the floor, and heard him speak to someone, obviously the security guard, in a pleasant tone of voice, saying we were leaving – thanks, we'd be going out the back way to his car.

I stood up.

"Get your stuff." He put on his jacket, feeling in the pocket.

I picked up my handbag and the envelope containing my CV.

Today, I still cannot remember walking from that office to his car. I remember the drive to my flat – I didn't speak; I remember the jacaranda trees of Salisbury in the early night lights, yet I cannot properly remember exactly where he dropped me off – it doesn't seem to have been directly outside my block of flats.

I never told anyone and went to work the next day. I'd never have found another job if I'd reported the rape – who'd believe a seventeen-year-old girl anyway? I later received a telephone call from the secretary saying that I unfortunately did not fit the position, but thanking me for my time.

I never told my mother about this – she would definitely have told my father; they'd had a bad enough year in Angola already.

After a few more weeks of drudgery, I decided to again try for other work and was lucky to land the first interview I had – with a woman. I would be working for a very senior executive nearing retirement, a Mr Goldman. He turned out to be a gentle, quiet man, and for some reason was always very kind to me.

The job-interview rape affected every other job interview I've ever had, and I've had many because I've had to move so often. Most particularly it affected me with male interviewers. I'd become extremely anxious and unable to relax, I would sweat and my heart would pound. A woman interviewer in 1989 told me I should try to smile more, as I came across as being distant, quite cold and extremely tense. Not really surprising, is it?

And it's just another reason why I depended so heavily on tranquillisers to give me enough courage to walk into a room and have paid sex with unknown men when I became a sex-worker all those years later.

The bottle of red wine was now past squeezing, but I still had a bit left in my glass. And there was one more to go – one more husband, that is, number four; this was where I finally earned my place in the Psychiatric Hall of Fame, I thought, if there was such a place. Some seriously diminished brain cells resided between my ears. I've only one word to describe my experience with Frank, and it's "humiliation". My blood started to boil thinking about him.

I was his fifth wife. He had three children from his first marriage, all grown up and working, and two children from another wife, then in their final years of schooling. He always paid his maintenance – plus school fees, clothes and other incidentals. Never did I bemoan these payments, in fact quite the opposite, having battled without child support myself so many years.

Shortly after I met him, my godmother from England sent me my second and final gift of British pounds. With this money I bought a better quality car: Bert and Mary-Lou were at boarding school in the country, and safety was a priority with all the travelling I did to get them to and from hostel. It was a second-hand old-model BMW, a 520i in good condition, and I paid twelve thousand rand cash for it in a private deal. Six thousand rand I loaned to Frank, leaving me two thousand.

A few people made silly comments about me driving a better car than Frank's new model Ford, so within about six weeks he traded his car in on a second-hand BMW 728i!

My dad then gave us one of his two boats, all the boating gear and the trailer –which ultimately was to go to Bert. We had a lot of fun with this sailing boat, including Frank's two younger children when they were with us.

What with my car and the boat, let alone his seven-series BMW, one day the Sheriff arrived at our house: two of Frank's ex-wives (including the mother of these two children) were suing him, and the Sheriff had come to collect some of his possessions to pay his debt.

Well, husband wasn't at home at the time. Pay up or I take the stuff, the Sheriff advised. If there's one thing my dad taught me it was always to keep your name clean with creditors. I got on the phone to my bank manager and wrote up that debt, on my name, to the tune of just under six thousand rand. The Sheriff left clutching my cheque and his papers marked "Paid". "That settles that nicely," he said. I hope so, I thought; the wives should be pleased – they've got their money, no drama either.

But that wasn't enough, was it? Now the ex-wife decides to subpoena me – yes, me – to the Supreme Court because she wants an increase in maintenance for her two children and reckons I'm the reason she doesn't get enough money out of Frank!

The attorney had a lot of fun shredding me – firstly about my surname and then particularly about my second-hand, old-model BMW. It didn't make any difference that Frank hadn't paid one cent towards the cost of my car, or that I worked full-time in our business.

I don't know how a learned person can spend time arguing at length about how many bottles of shampoo each person in a household uses per month, or how many packets of washing powder, fabric softener, dishwasher, tubes of toothpaste – the entire list of toiletries, even down to the toilet paper! This subject was harped on in depth for a considerable amount of time. My insides felt pretty bust that day after court.

On one of our visits to my parents in Namibia in 1993, my dad warned Frank not to continually speak to me in a derogatory manner, and Bert was instructed by his grandfather to keep an eye on future developments at home, which I think he took literally, because a short while later – in Standard Eight, sixteen years old – Bert had suddenly had enough shit from the husbands that passed through my life and gave Frank a hiding; yes, he lost his rag and punched him. Husband said he went to the doctor for cracked ribs, also said he'd get a restraining order against Bert. I was called into Frank's office and given the choice, him or Bert. I chose Bert, and was given a week to get out and find another house to live in.

My six thousand rand was returned. Frank also paid my deposit and first month's rent on the small house I found, and bought me a dilapidated fridge.

My nerves were finished. I almost had a breakdown after a few weeks and begged him to take me back. Two of the conditions for my return were that Bert's home visits be limited, and that I had to give away my little dog that I'd had for two years and loved, bought with the money from my godmother.

Life was pretty much a mess after that. Frank packed his suitcase one day and walked casually down the path as Mary-Lou and I watched from the window, put the case in the back of his BMW and drove to a flat he'd rented not far from our house, where he spent an entire week with another woman. After which he simply came back, stopped at the front of our house, took his suitcase out the boot of his car and walked up the front path to the door again. Certain of our local clients got to hear of his escapade – news travels fast – and the love-nest he'd rented for the week also just happened to be owned by a woman with connections to where we stabled Mary-Lou's horse. I felt so humiliated.

I eventually left Frank just before Christmas 1994, with a cheque for four hundred and fifty rand for my "secretarial services"! My fridge was an orange cooler box holding a couple of packets of ice. By six o'clock on the evening of the day we moved out, the new woman's car was parked at the house. Nothing quite like keeping all your options open!

The children and I survived this re-start mostly with financial assistance from my mother. We shared a house with her after my dad's death until she met her second husband a while later. And I walked, like a homing missile, from Frank straight into Sam, starting work with him in January 1995 – and we know that story already!

My fourth divorce settlement was five thousand rand – one thousand went to pay my attorney's fees. Things were so tough financially after Frank that by mid-1995, I had to trade in my old second-hand BMW on a smaller car, the little bakkie, because I couldn't afford the repairs or petrol on the safe old BMW.

Before we leave husband number four, I thought mockingly, care to tell the secret of how you met him? Why not cringe again – after all, you should be getting used to it by now! It was a short while after Meg's death. Full of heartache and loneliness, I decided to answer one of those newspaper adverts. Later I learned that this was the same way Frank found a couple of his other wives – the lonely hearts column! Yes, you can occasionally do some nutty things when you're having a tough time in life, I consoled myself.

Well, that about rounds up why I've had a pretty "broke" life, I thought in disgust and dismay. I've often heard about divorces where the wife takes the husband to the cleaners – well, that certainly hadn't been me. It was the other way around in my case, all four times!

My children and I have eaten more cheap fish fingers and bony fish-packs than I care to remember. On several occasions in our lives of struggle Bert would say dejectedly, "Mummy, I hate being poor."

And Mary-Lou would boldly reply, "It's not that bad really, it's quite fun!"

My anger was now near boiling point. In my mind, I could hear a conversation James and I had had when I moved into his house at the end of March – we'd been discussing our insurance needs.

"Well, your computer's only worth about five hundred rand," he'd said in a matter-of-fact tone of voice.

"How come it's only worth five hundred rand now?" I answered indignantly, trying to comprehend such an enormous depreciation in value. "I had to buy it from Frank for two thousand eight hundred when we split up, even though it'd been bought by the business during our working life together." He hadn't even owned a computer when I met him – and been left with the better one and the laser printer!

This is the point in my trip down memory lane when the volcano inside me blew, and the molten larva spewed forth.

Fuck the whole crock of shit, I thought. That's exactly the reason that women like me – like the girls, good women – are out there selling their bodies to get by from month to month. If this so-called micro-chipped computer was now only worth five hundred rand, after all the crap I'd lived through and all the money I'd had to pay for it, then I didn't need it! I could easily buy myself another one – after all, lying on my back or being burned with a lit cigarette for 3.125 fucks would buy me a brand new computer, wouldn't it? My mind flipped.

Systematically, I took each part of my computer equipment – hard drive, monitor, keyboard and finally the printer, one at a time – and threw them with all my might against the garden wall, over and over, until every last piece was smashed and broken to smithereens.

Each part of my computer equalled one ex-husband and all his crap.

Even with its considerable weight, the hard drive sailed through the night air like a missile, directly on target, and dissolved in a resounding crash with my first outburst of pent-up anger. I examined the site of impact carefully. Umm . . . should've been in the amphibious armoured division, with my perfect shelling abilities, I thought, quite impressed. The motherboard hung limply from the shattered box by a single, sorry green wire.

I know how you feel, I thought – finished – and gave it a gentle prod with the right toe of my doggie slippers. Good. Time for your hard-earned rest!

Next was the monitor. I judged the distance from the wall for a good swing. It flew through the air like a jet fighter and the screen, as if ambushed, imploded in a haze of glass bullets. In the second after it hit the concrete wall, the infinitesimal tinkle of shattered glass was like music to my ears. Definitely missed my vocation in life, I thought! Good, but not good enough.

Next was the keyboard. That was lightweight – I could stand a nice distance from the wall with this one. Bit like bowling overhand, I thought: full arm-swing possible here. Perhaps I should've been the one to go on cricket tour instead? Smack!

Keys from the keyboard flew in every direction, like splitting-hot, bouncing popcorn.

Last, but not least, we have the pleasure of the printer, I thought gleeful-ly. Bit heavier and a more difficult sort of shape to handle, this one. Pity my female biceps only allow a waist-height, ninety degree swing with this weight, my mind flashed, as I corrected my stance. Goodbye. Off you go . . . smash!

Any reasonably large, unbroken computer bits I then proceeded to re-aim at the garden wall until all were thoroughly demolished – if you're going to do something, then you may as well do it properly. In the chill night air, the outside light illuminated the shattered remnants of my anger.

I was on a roll now, pouring out years of pent-up emotional pain. The volcano wasn't ready to stop yet, and went through to the kitchen.

For all the shit you lot put me through, I thought, I'm not surprised I landed up feeling depressed and suicidal from trying to get through life – doesn't require a rocket scientist to figure that out, does it?

That's when I started on my crockery – none of James's crockery, just my own. I stood at the dining room table and threw the plates, one at a time, in slow motion – rather like throwing a Frisbee on a gentle day at the beach. I watched each plate as it sailed through the air, gracefully and with ease, and then shattered to smithereens on the kitchen floor.

Perhaps if I'd been Greek no one would have minded how many plates I broke that night.

It was about now on this night in April 1996, during my plate-throwing exer-cise, that James arrived back home, to be met with glass and broken china, some flying, some lying smashed and broken, all over the dining room and kitchen. He did the only thing he could think of – he walked up to me and hit me hard in the face. I don't think he meant to hit me across the eyes, but that's where, in desperation and shock, the blow landed.

I was standing near the lounge door, which had two glass panes in it. For a split second I wanted to see if it was really like you see it in the movies, where you get all cut up and bleed to death. I just put my fist straight through the top pane of glass and remember looking at my right arm afterwards, dis-appointed at the lack of expected horrendous cuts. There were cuts all right and I was bleeding, but not the death bleeding I'd been hoping for.

Between James and Mary-Lou they decided that the only way to stop me breaking more stuff and hurting myself further would be to tie me up. This they proceeded to do, with the extension lead and washing line – my hands tied tight together behind my back, then my feet tied together. Under the circumstances, it was the only thing they could do.

I went crazy trying to get loose. Apart from the fact that the cords were so tight my wrists and ankles were hurting badly, I desperately wanted to wee; neither James nor Mary-Lou would untie me, so I eventually just weed in my pants. I was so filled with terror at being tied up that I started hitting into the walls and furniture in a desperate attempt to get loose, so they decided to untie me.

James phoned the local medical centre and asked that the doctor on duty be called out to our house, and then phoned my aunt Myrl.

After the phone calls, James and Mary-Lou stood outside in the garden and waited for the doctor to arrive. They felt it was better to let me carry on breaking my plates and not antagonise me any further.

I don't remember the doctor's arrival. I remember him being quite short and small. He wasn't my normal doctor and knew nothing about me; I didn't want him near me. He wouldn't tell me what he wanted to inject me with and I swore at him plenty because I'd quit my pills and wanted to know if the injection was the same kind of medication. The short doctor seemed to vanish for a while then. (I was later told that he'd hidden in the garden, behind the cactus plant.)

Two policemen then arrived and grabbed me forcefully by the arms. That blew it. I fought them with all my might from the moment they laid their hands on my body.

"Listen, lady . . ." their voices echoed as they clenched my upper arms as if in a vice grip. I know the "listen lady" line well enough, thank you, my mind screamed in fear.

Between the two policemen and James they got me to the main bedroom and held me down on the double bed while the doctor gave me an injection.

"It'll take about three to five minutes to work properly," the doctor said.

I attacked him verbally again for refusing to tell me what he was injecting me with. The policemen, doctor, James and Mary-Lou just watched my anger while the injection was supposed to have its desired effect.

There apparently was no change after ten minutes, so the doctor decided to call the ambulance and have me removed to a psychiatric institution – the loony bin!

James, however, would not allow this and asked the doctor to "just please knock me out". He'd take care of me. "Whatever it takes to knock her out, just give it to her."

So we went through the same procedure again, me being held down by the two policemen and James, and the doctor refilled his syringe with another dose of medication to calm me or, even better, completely put me out. James says it was enough to knock out an ox. This, I believe, was around four o'clock in the morning on Friday. The second injection flattened me, much to everyone's relief. The volcano finally subsided in a couple of minutes, and James felt safe enough to guide me as I staggered, trying to walk, still chewing on hours-old Beechies gum.

I was woken twenty-nine hours later with some effort by James. He'd made an appointment for me to see a psychiatrist, Dr Marten. I was in the bed in the spare room, chewing gum stuck to the sheet and my T-shirt, dried blood all over the place. My eyes were purple-yellow, swollen and I could just see through the slits. Apart from the fact that I was still pretty heavily sedated and not too steady on my feet, I had massive dark bruises all over my body, cuts on my wrist and arm from the glass pane that I'd put my fist through – and looked like shit.

Mary-Lou seemed fine, though understandably very quiet. She'd had a bad time that night with me doing my bananas; I imagined she must have felt afraid. It most definitely wasn't a pleasant experience for her to have to go through, or James for that matter. He'd looked after her while I'd been out from the injection – he was always good about cooking; even if it was just stew or fried eggs on toast I knew she and the animals would've been fed. Little was said as I tried, unsteadily, to get dressed to go and see Dr Marten with James. Mary-Lou said she'd stay home.

The house seemed remarkably clean and tidy, as if nothing had happened – there wasn't any sign of broken plates and glass. Retrieved parts of my smashed computer were in a pile outside the office door. I had a distinct sense of guarded calmness from James and Mary-Lou; their apprehension was obvious. I knew they were worried about saying something which might upset me and set me off again, so the three of us spoke little.

James sat next to me in Dr Marten's office, the Saturday morning after my Cold Turkey Cocktail episode. I had my hat on, pulled down low, and my sunglasses on to hide my swollen, bruised eyes, and looked like a walking nightmare. After explaining the situation briefly, the psychiatrist was unsympathetic.

"You did this to yourself, Margaret," he said. "Aren't you ashamed of your appalling behaviour?"

"Yes, it was a big mess," I answered slowly, "breaking my stuff."

I took a breath and he remained quiet. James didn't say a word.

Dr Marten eyed my pathetic state aloofly. "You're very lucky the doctor didn't have you admitted and put away for good," he said, tapping his pen on his note pad, "with behaviour like that."

"I know it wasn't right," I said slowly, "but I have to admit, it was a sort of relief to me, getting my anger out."

The psychiatrist stared at me in disbelief, shaking his head.

Well, there really didn't seem any point in talking about anything to anyone, anymore. I didn't see Dr Marten after this – quite frankly, General understood me better.

Mixed with my relief at having gotten rid of my pent-up emotions was a sense of quiet shame and awed amazement at how long I'd had this "fit", and the amount of pain that had spewed forth from inside me. I was truly grateful that the little doctor who'd taken refuge amongst the cactuses had found it within himself to listen to James and inject me a second time.

On the way home after seeing Dr Marten that Saturday, I refilled my prescription of tranquillisers; sure as shit, I wasn't ever going to stop them without correct medical supervision again.

I was sitting working in my office at home one afternoon about a week later, after fetching Mary-Lou from school. I still had bruises, but the cuts were healing nicely, and being back on my pills, I was thankfully feeling quite normal once again – no strange light-headedness. Mary-Lou quietly came and sat in the afternoon sun on the spare chair near the front door, her hands under her bum, kicking her feet – and started giggling.

"Yeah, what's so funny?" I asked my teenage daughter, looking up from the file I was working on.

"You," she replied.

"Me – funny? Funny in what way?" I asked carefully and evenly.

"Well . . ." she said hesitantly, "you sure gave the doctor and the policemen a hard time, and you sure told them what you thought of them." She kept quiet a few seconds. "And it was, well, funny, you know."

"If it was so funny, then how come everyone's walking around me so quietly and carefully?" I asked. "Why hasn't anyone said anything about my fit?" She kept quiet, fidgeting about on the chair. "Or are you all perhaps afraid to mention it, in case it sets me off again?"

"Yes – we thought we'd just keep quiet about it for a while." I waited. "Bert phoned though, and told James that the worst thing he could have done was to hit you – anything else, but not to have hit you."

"Well, I don't suppose he knew what else to do right then," I answered.

"You know what, Mum," Mary-Lou said, smiling and seeming more at ease now, "it's the first time I've ever listened to you properly. When you asked me to make you some rooibos tea, I went straight to the kitchen and did it – even though I had to get the brush and dustpan and sweep a path to the kettle first."

I must have looked at her blankly. "Don't you remember asking me to make you some rooibos tea?" she asked, somewhat amazed.

"No," I answered thoughtfully. "It's a pretty drastic way of getting you to listen to me, isn't it? Anyway – what's that mark next to your eye?"

"It's a small cut I got from the glass flying around," she answered. "But it's okay," she said, touching her face next to her eye. "It's got a scab now so it's nearly gone."

"I'm sorry," I said. "Cripes, I sure made a terrible mess, didn't I? Who cleaned up?"

"I helped James a bit, then he said I must go to bed and he cleaned up the rest. It took him quite a long time, a few hours, I think."

"I bet it did. Anyway, you can stop worrying now because I'm back on my Brozams – and I'll never just stop them like that again." Growing up is pretty difficult, I thought, especially when you're supposed to be grown up already! I sighed. "It was a really stupid thing to do," I said, looking at Mary-Lou sitting on the chair, "stopping my pills. I should have known better after nearly five years, and gradually lowered the dosage with a doctor's help." She kept quiet. "I didn't properly consider the stress I'd been under, either; I thought I could just quit and cope. But we only learn one way, don't we – the hard way, hey?"

Mary-Lou smiled and nodded. The ice was broken and we could try to live normally again, the two of us and James.

Shortly thereafter, Mary-Lou started nagging me daily, wanting to go back to her old boarding school in the country, where she'd been with Bert some years earlier.

"But you hated boarding school, Mary-Lou," I said. "You nagged me to bring you back home, and I did."

"Yes, I know, but that's when I was younger. I'd like to go back now though, all my old friends are there."

Obviously I wasn't looking too entranced by this proposal.

"Look how well Bert did at that school, he passed Matric with exemption," she said convincingly.

I didn't utter a word.

"I can't stand the school I'm in here – there's no discipline, the kids throw stuff around during class, the teachers don't have any control and you can't get any work done." I remained quiet, in thought. "Please . . . please, Mum?" she begged.

"Mary-Lou, changing school a third time in the first half of the year is a bit much for anyone," I answered. "You haven't even had time to settle properly in this one yet. Apart from that," I added, taking a sip of my cold coffee, "it's a big expense - three uniforms in half a year, plus kitting you out for hostel again. I don't know – I just can't keep up, I'm battling enough to pay for Copper as well."

I then went to the bank for a loan and kitted Mary-Lou out for boarding school again, just as she'd wanted. She seemed very happy amongst her old pals in familiar school surroundings and I breathed a sigh of relief. Perhaps it had been the best thing after all.

155

Chapter Nine
Welcome Again, Kind Sir

*F*inancially, things had gotten really tough. James and I were struggling to survive; we couldn't afford the breakdown of our business as well.

With Bert's permission, I sold my father's boat to try to ease finances – the boat, two outboard motors, all the gear and the trailer for a meagre four thousand rand. That was the last possession I had of any cash value. I didn't feel good about doing it, but I knew my dad would forgive me – he'd know the decision wasn't made lightly. Somehow, some time in my life, I'd try to make it up to Bert.

Sitting at the dining-room table one afternoon, I stared dejectedly at the pile of work files around me, and my gaze came to rest on my favourite velvet hat – hanging next to my hi-fi on the CD stand.

There was, however, a way of earning money that sure would be of help to us. The clients would ask no questions; they didn't need to know anything about my personal life. I didn't have to go out and look for business, did I? The business came to me. And I could still carry on in the meantime working with James.

Sure as shit I can still do my best to help my little family and our small business!

I went to my old hi-fi set and put a CD into the player, selecting a brilliant number by the very talented Mr Joe Cocker, and most appropriate the track was too:

> "Baby take off your coat – real slow
> Take off your shoes – I'll take off your shoes
> Baby take off your dress – yes, yes, yes
> You can leave your hat on . . ."

Yes, there was reason to try. I phoned Puff at the agency – it was good to hear his voice again.

"Sure, Rachael, you can have your job back," he said, sounding genuinely pleased. "Come in whenever you're ready – you know the drill."

James wasn't ecstatic about the matter when I discussed it with him later – that other stress would be back; but we could do with the financial help.

I pulled out my little cast-iron frying pan and packed my work basket again.

There's some life in this old bird yet, I thought.

Being back with the girls was strangely soothing. During the day I worked in our investment business with James, at night I became Rachael or Granny again, with my hat on – making and drinking copious mugs of the agency coffee and sharing my home-made sandwiches.

The girls understand only too well the hardship of life and getting through a day – all they want is to make enough money to to go home at the end of a shift able to feed and support their families. Whilst the work isn't what one really wants to be doing in life, some is better than none and beggars can't be choosers.

The girls don't question you intently about your home life; if you divulge any information, they also don't make snotty remarks or put you down. If they want to know more, they seem to have an inbred sense of when and how much to ask – and how to be gentle about it. I never once felt wary of their interest when I spoke about my problems. I never felt worried that they'd be off telling the planet about my personal life, or that they'd cook up some kind of further shit for me.

With the girls, work's work, pay is pay, a bad day's one that will pass – have a drink on me, tomorrow will be better, you'll see; laughing soothes and heals the tired soul, so come on Rachael, join in. The other stuff that comes with the job – yeah, that's not too great is it, but it's not forever. It's work to eat, or go without and cry more. We're friends, we care and we're fun to be with.

I am grateful to the girls and Puff for this second period of honest friendship and undivided support in a very difficult and emotionally traumatic time of my life.

I think it was a Sunday night when I fell asleep in the bath from the "Brozam coffee" overdose. James was sitting in front of the television in the lounge, asleep – I could hear his snores quite clearly from the bathroom. Both of us were permanently exhausted.

I'd been sitting in my Nymphae Soak, reflecting on my life. The feared cloud of deep depression came down on me suddenly again, like a demonic black raven swooping to get me. It seemed to fall from the bathroom ceiling and fly into my mind – settling in my inner sanctuary, unequivocally home to nest – and stare at me with its sharp beady black eyes.

I couldn't take it any more; I didn't even bother to try and fight it – I simply got out of the bath, fetched my vial of tranquillisers, poured the lot into my mug of coffee on the side of the bath and stirred the contents with my toothbrush. Without any emotion whatsoever, I drank the now shocking pink coffee, lay back in the bath and went to sleep.

I awoke groggily in the freezing cold bath water. James was still asleep in the lounge, still snoring – I tried calling him, but when there was no response

I stood up unsteadily to get my towel, turned the wrong way in my dazed tranquillised state and fell heavily against the side of the bath.

By the Tuesday, I was sure I'd cracked some ribs – the pain was excruciating – and wound three bandages from our medicine cabinet round my chest. That didn't help, and by Friday I decided it would be best to see my doctor and made an appointment at the local medical centre. Each breath I took was utter hell – If I could've breathed through my ears, I would have!

The receptionist informed me on arrival that my doctor was unavailable and that a Doctor Cohen would tend to me. I had eased myself into the reception chair, my favourite hat on as usual, hardly daring to move for the pain and breathing very shallowly, when a short man walked up and stood in front of me. I looked up and he extended his hand, which I shook rather feebly.

"Hello, I'm Doctor Cohen," he said. "Please follow me."

I stood up slowly. The doctor seemed to be studying me.

"I've met you before," he said.

"I don't think so," I answered, pulling my hat down more. Cripes, I thought, has this guy been to the agency and I don't recognise him? Oh, shit.

"Yes, I'm definitely sure we've met," Dr Cohen said. "For the moment I can't remember where, but I know I've met you before."

Sorry, I thought, but I don't remember seeing you before in my life. He gave me a smile and I followed him through to his consulting room, where he indicated that I should sit in the chair next to his desk.

"Yes, Margaret," he said, opening my folder, "what can I do for you today?"

I told him I thought I'd cracked my ribs. Dr Cohen examined me and then sent me for x-rays immediately, to the radiologist down the passage. I returned with the large brown envelope, my hat still pulled well down, handed him the envelope and sat down slowly in the chair again.

Suddenly the penny dropped. "I was called to your house earlier this year to inject you! I knew I was right about having met you," Dr Cohen said.

The penny dropped for me then as well. "Oh, hell," I said sheepishly. "So you're the doctor I half scared to death when I had my fit in April. I'm told you ran outside and took cover behind the garden cactus till the police arrived! I'm sorry about that – I just lost it that night."

Dr Cohen smiled gently. "Okay, let's have a look at those x-rays," he said. He went to the light at the window, held the X-rays up and studied my rib cage, pictured from various angles.

"Yes, I can see two, possibly three cracks on the right side – you must remove those bandages immediately." He returned to his desk and sat down. "Basically there's nothing you can do; they'll heal by themselves in about six weeks. I know it's very painful – you'll just have to take it easy and rest up a bit. Take some tablets for pain."

"Thanks," I said, and then added, "I guess you're sitting a little easier in your chair right now, hey – considering I've got cracked ribs, and in too much pain to give you a hard time again!"

He gave me a broad grin then – I suppose patients can be quite interesting. We had a lengthy chat after that about the night in April, and a good laugh. Thank heavens he was forgiving, and I filled him in on matters since then.

From then on, he became our family doctor – Bert and James would see him as well. By now, Dr Cohen knows all there is to know about me, including the escorting and my tranquilliser addiction. I've prescribed tablets for Dr Cohen's headaches, and a holiday for his stress, but he won't listen! He's very kind, understanding, a thorough and good doctor, with a wonderful sense of humour – it's just as well I cracked the ribs otherwise we may never have met again.

Being back in escorting, I needed medical check-ups apart from other aches and pains.

"Hello, it's your neighbourhood psychotic come to visit you again," I'd say when I saw him; he'd just laugh. He promised that while I was in his medical care, he wouldn't let anyone take me away – he'd got to know me better by then. Sometimes James would go with me and tell Dr Cohen a few jokes to brighten up his day – the English sense of humour!

I remember one of my visits to him when he said, as usual, "So, how are you today, Margaret?"

We're conditioned to ask this question; we're also conditioned to answer, "Fine, thank you" – which seems a bit ridiculous, as I probably wouldn't be seeing the doctor if I was fine.

So, on this occasion I gave it some thought and answered slowly, "Let's see how I am today. Well, I haven't had to go to the morgue, or bury anyone, or have a condom break on me – so I guess I could rightly say that, yes, I'm fine, apart from a little medical problem!"

Dr Cohen leant back in his chair and laughed. "You're a good tonic to my day, Margaret."

"Well, in that case," I replied, "I'll have to send you a bill for entertaining you on my visits!"

And I'd joke with him when I had a pap smear done – how I hate those things! There was always a nurse present during this procedure, but the humour remained between doctor and patient. No point in frightening staff unnecessarily with stories of garden cacti – but the occasional strange look from the nurse was understandable, I had to admit.

"Oh," I'd say in the pre-proverbial-"just-relax" position on the bed, "I see you've wised up and got some personal protection now!"

Dr Cohen laughed. "Pass me the KY please, Sister."

"I'd have brought my own if I'd known you used it," I'd answer.

"Okay, Margaret, just relax now," Doctor Cohen would say reassuringly, concentrating as he gently inserted the cold steel instrument to expand my much-used vagina for the joyous feminine "cell-check". At least he didn't say "open sesame!"

"Now, where've I heard that phrase before?" I'd answer, breathing slowly, spread-eagled, tense as a rubber band. Cripes, you'd think I'd be used to this position by now!

"With you around, Margaret," replied Dr Cohen easily, holding the little wooden swab stick, checking then scraping it against the small glass slide, "I don't need headache tablets!"

Chapter Ten
Madame Sophie

*M*adam Sophie is a psychic and clairvoyant. I was given her phone number by my friend Vieve, who'd consulted Sophie for "readings" on her past, present and future, and was most impressed with her abilities.

I felt compelled to see Madam Sophie when I awoke one morning, and was relieved when she answered my telephone call personally, instead of my having to leave a message on an answering machine.

If Madam Sophie was as good as Vieve said, perhaps she could tell me when the escorting would end.

Following her directions, I arrived at ten minutes past twelve; immediately I noticed how neat and pretty the garden of this home was. An enormous jacaranda tree stood like a gigantic umbrella over hundreds of violets, their leaves massed together in a circle in the shade beneath.

A rainbow lorikeet squawked and chatted, shuffling up and down the perch of his open birdcage amongst the violets, and I stopped to admire the brilliant colours of his feathers, particularly his rich purple plumage. The bird seemed unperturbed my by inquisitive presence, perfectly happy in this lush green environment – as content, I felt sure, as he would have been in his natural habitat.

I was met at the locked security gate by two barking, plump, shorthaired brown dachshunds, their tails wagging like mad.

A voice from inside the house said, "They're happy and welcoming you – that's because Scrump and Smidge immediately recognise an animal lover."

Madam Sophie was lovely, I thought: in her late fifties perhaps, the lady had style and taste. Her hazel eyes struck me immediately as being the most interesting feature of her warm, open face. Her make-up was just right – not too much, not too little and applied with care. She had auburn hair falling to her neck beneath a green and white scarf tied at the back of her head, and wore a soft, flowing, calf-length dark green skirt with a loosely fitting crocheted white top; the only jewellery I noticed was a pair of medium-sized hoop earrings. Her feet were clad in soft, black, silent dancing shoes. I liked her immediately.

"You're on time," she said, unlocking the security gate and smiling.

"I try to be – though sometimes things don't work out that way. I didn't want to be late to see you today."

161

"Come in, my dear," she said, standing aside for me to pass, and I waited while she re-locked the security gate.

"Let's go through, follow me." Her movements were fluid and youthful for her age, and I thought she must've had dancing lessons some time in her life. She ushered me into a room and pointed to a well-worn easy chair in front of a large old wooden desk.

"Make yourself comfortable, I'll be back in a minute."

I put my handbag down on the floor and removed my cotton jacket to hang over the back of the chair – and nearly jumped out of my skin with the sudden shriek of "fuck off!", which came from I didn't know where. I stood motionless for a few seconds.

"Naughty Pablo," replied Sophie's soothing voice.

I looked around slowly and warily – to see Madam Sophie walking quietly in her silent shoes towards a perch in the opposite corner of the room, talking to an African grey parrot.

"Naughty Pablo," the bird repeated, in exactly the same voice, and Sophie and I both laughed. The African grey then laughed as well, imitating Sophie perfectly, and I heaved a sigh of relief and plonked down in the chair, on the camel-coloured shawl that was draped across the worn blue upholstery.

Sophie scratched Pablo's head and then his tummy, and he lifted one foot onto her hand as if to position himself better. I watched human and parrot, quite relaxed from my seat on the chair, and it was obvious the exquisite bird loved a tummy tickle: his feathers all ruffled and his black eyes dancing as he eyed his mistress intently. Then Sophie leaned forward and gently kissed her feathered friend on his curved black beak, and the parrot gave her a little nibble on the lip in return.

"Sexy, sexy," Pablo said, quite enraptured with Sophie's attentions.

"Sexy Pablo," was Sophie's response.

I smiled at these two – an unusual set of lovebirds they were indeed.

"Sorry about that, about the profanity," Sophie volunteered, her back still turned to me as she fed the parrot a few green peas. "A dear friend of mine taught him these useful words on a lazy Sunday afternoon, over and over, after we'd had a good lunch and some expensive cognac, and I've been struggling ever since – not to get Pablo to stop swearing, but to get him to be more careful with his timing. And as you heard, I haven't succeeded yet."

"Oh, it's quite okay," I answered, "I just got a bit of a fright – I didn't know where it was coming from or why! I say the word myself."

"I say the word too, dear – but that's between us, isn't it?" Sophie said, giving the bird another pea. "Actually, Pablo speaks real French as well," she said turning and giving me a wink.

"Real French – as in French French, like *je' taime* or *si vous plais*?" I asked, astounded.

"Quite so," Sophie smiled proudly, giving Pablo a gentle scratch under the chin. "His previous owner was French – he natters away in it, though I hardly understand a word myself. And now he seems to have acquired a different form of the language as well, doesn't he?"

"Amazing," I answered thoughtfully, "but African greys are known for their intelligence. We also had one in our family when I was young, a female, and she knew a few words in Swahili as well as English."

"An absolute pleasure he is, my Pablo," Sophie divulged, "except when he imitates the ringing of the telephone and I'm outside in the garden!" She adjusted the bird toys on the perch and then crossed to her desk, sitting down in the old brown chair.

"Right, shuffle the cards, dear," she said, holding a pack out to me, "until you feel you've handled them enough. It's important to put your energy into them."

I shuffled – and a shuffle it was, as I've never had the knack of handling a deck of cards.

"I wouldn't take up gambling if I were you," she said, smiling, "but it doesn't matter for this exercise, just as long as you handle the cards. When you're ready, place them on the table and split the pack in two." Sophie lit a cigarette and watched me shuffle.

I placed the pack of cards in front of her on the wooden desk and split it in two, to her left.

Madam Sophie then laid the cards out in neat rows, face up, in front of her on the desk. I immediately noticed that only one did not have a sword on its face, and all but one were dark-coloured and oppressive. One picture really stood out from the rest: a silent, screaming soul, tied up, unable to move.

"Tell me, my dear," she said, concentrating, "what are your silent screams?"

I must have seemed hesitant because she continued immediately, leaning forward and looking directly into my eyes.

"I believe what I see before me in the cards. No matter how hard you try, you cannot save the world from pain, so why do you burden yourself with everyone's baggage? What else do you scream for?"

I kept quiet for a few seconds, looked down at my hands and swallowed – there was a lump in my throat.

"What's your name again, dear?"

"Margaret," I answered, half looking up.

"Margaret, you can confide in me," Sophie said gently. "It'll remain between us, but I can't interpret the cards before me correctly unless I have some help from you." She lit another cigarette and sat back in her chair.

And then it spilled out of me, all of it, about the tranquillisers, the depression, the finances, the escorting. Sophie sat and listened intently, waiting with all the time in the world for me to finish and regain some self-control.

While I related my anxieties, she reached into one of the desk drawers, took out some tissues and passed the box across the desk to me.

"A very dear friend of mine died from an opium overdose in her late twenties," Sophie said sadly, inhaling on the cigarette in her hand, her mind meandering through the corridors of sad memories. "Like you, she was in the sex business, trying to support her family; she lost both her children to the authorities of those days."

I listened quietly, not wanting to interrupt her train of thought.

"She and I spent many, many hours talking about the hardships of the racket, so I understand only too well what you're telling me. And in those days there weren't even condoms or agencies where the girls could have some form of protection." Sophie took another puff on her cigarette and continued.

"From Hillbrow at its meanest, to the ships in Cape Town harbour, this dear friend of mine experienced it all, and let me tell you – because I know – some of the girls never came back from those ships. But we'll talk more about it later. Let's finish your reading first."

She put her cigarette out in the ashtray on the corner of her desk, read the remainder of the cards, and then read both my hands.

"The left hand is the life you're given, and the right is what you do with it. You will live to well into your eighties."

"If it's going to be anything like what's passed, and what's happening at present, then I don't want to live to fifty," I answered with a sigh, wiping my nose and dabbing my eyes with her tissues.

"I know, but you must stop wanting and trying to end your life, because you'll never succeed. It's not your time yet."

How did she pick up all this stuff?

Sophie looked up from studying my hand, saying firmly but gently, "No matter what you do to try and crush your pain forever, you'll just find yourself back in this world – and quite possibly as a cabbage. I mean that, Margaret."

I looked down momentarily, and Sophie continued: "We are each given a specific span of time to live – and you haven't lived yours yet. We also all have certain lessons to learn during our life on earth. It may sound odd, but personal trauma is sometimes sent to us, not only as a lesson for ourselves, but also very definitely to awaken the qualities of compassion and responsibility within others as well. Do you understand, Margaret?"

"I'm not sure," I answered.

"In time you will. Trauma is also growth."

"I don't feel that I'm growing from this, I feel as though I'm dying inside instead," I answered flatly.

"You like reading don't you, Margaret? I noticed you taking an interest in my bookshelves."

"Yes," I nodded.

"Sometimes when we're in pain and confusion, we move away from the divine belief centre which resides within each of us. Perhaps it would be good for you to have some guidance in this regard – try reading works by Chopra or the Dalai Lama for example. Go to the library – move towards spiritual nourishment perhaps. There are many books available."

"The friend who gave me your phone number is keen on the I Ching," I answered, "and she does t'ai chi meditation every day. I love the reading, but I don't know if I'm into that mind stuff right now."

"Time, Margaret – everything in its own time. Patience – true patience, Margaret, you must still learn, still practise within yourself." Sophie gave me a gentle smile from across her desk. "Now let's have a cup of tea, dear – come along."

I followed her through to her kitchen and she put the kettle on. We chatted easily for about another hour after the reading – about life, religion, her animals, her garden. I felt completely comfortable in her presence and found her enormously interesting, warm-hearted and honest.

As I stood up to leave for home, Sophie deliberately said, "Fuck off!"; her beloved African grey parrot answered, "I love you, Pablo!" and we both laughed as we walked towards her front door.

"See what I mean," she said, giving me a wink. "As with the majority of males, even the bird's timing's fucked – isn't it just a joy being a woman!"

I wiped the tears of laughter from the corners of my eyes as she unlocked the front security gate, then straightened her scarf.

We made our way across the lush lawn towards the gate, stopping a moment to chat to Sophie's lorikeet – quite relaxed and still nattering away in the violets.

"Beautiful Congo!" she said, leaning forward and gently stroking his head.

"Indeed he is," I agreed, quite in awe of Sophie's exotic companion.

"Take care, my dear," Sophie said, closing the garden gate behind me. "Come and see me again whenever you feel the need – and remember what I said about becoming a cabbage. I meant it." She stood at the gate and waited while I started the engine and drove off, giving me a wave good-bye as I turned the corner.

What a lovely woman, I thought as I drove home. I felt so much better for chatting to someone who understood – and for the laughter.

In time I would visit this lady often, not only for card readings, but socially as well. Not a wealthy woman by any stretch of the imagination, her kindness and love of animals took precedence over her financial concerns, and this unselfish quality of caring was perhaps what initially drew me to her most. I would learn the intricacies of Sophie's daily schedule as she juggled clients and family needs, her personal relaxation only becoming a priority well after dark.

Every evening her two chickens, Nelly and Dodger, would hop up the back steps to the kitchen door and cluck on the glass pane, reminding their mistress that feeding time had drawn nigh. Sophie would fill her orange bucket with grain and the two fowls would scramble down the steps in single file at her heels, out onto the grass in the back garden, where she'd scatter handfuls of seed in a wide circle on the lush carpet of lawn. The pigeons would literally drop out of nowhere in answer to Sophie's familiar call, at times feeding from her outstretched hand. Even guinea fowl appeared. It was a family affair – with Scrump and Smidge keeping order among the sometimes squabbling birds, Sophie's ginger cat lazing on the outside rocker unperturbed, and her toy pom lying on the back steps as he watched the merriment in a somewhat absentminded manner, rather like an ongoing television series.

Sometimes I would sit on the steps of Sophie's home and watch the scene of happy feeding-time, glad to witness this ritual, not often seen in city life. I never tired of the reruns and always left Sophie's home more at peace with myself.

Sophie would acquire further family as the months passed – another parrot, various budgies and cockatiels, a duckling and a goose. Hamsters that rolled around inside special balls with air holes for exercise became a familiar sight. More canine companions followed too.

Sophie's garden was another great comfort and joy in her life. Anyone could see her "green fingers" in the established and carefully manicured beds of diverse and abundant foliage, intermingled with bursts of brilliant colour dotted along the fence. Nelly and Dodger would wander around in the sun scratching amongst the shrubs and plants as they whiled away the day until afternoon feeding time.

There were occasions when the front garden was a carpet of mauve petals from the massive jacaranda, and Congo's plumage was accentuated against this backdrop as he chatted away happily in his garden paradise, oblivious to the passing world. But my favourite time was when the masses and masses of deep purple violets burst their buds in splendour – I'd just have to stand still to imprint this magnificent picture in my mind.

Sophie's unusual hobby of making "grass pictures" gave her mind total relaxation from her oft-sought telepathic abilities. An assortment of indigenous bushveld grasses would be collected; these were first dried, then dyed in a multitude of colours, then pressed flat by placing them within a book –

which Sophie would sit on at her desk! The grasses were then painstakingly stuck onto whatever outline Sophie was working on, the finished product being quite remarkable – at first glance one gained the impression that the pictures were finely painted.

Sophie's hands were never idle. In spare moments out would come the wool and crochet hook, and in all the colours of the rainbow she'd crochet bed covers, large and small, sewing each square together with the patience and care of a surgeon. Her talents, abilities and energy seemed without end.

Sophie became a good and true friend, and we spent many hours chatting about "the racket" and laughing till our sides ached about all the hysterically funny things that happen in the business of being a sex-worker. Laughing with Sophie about it felt good, like a cleansing – a douche for the mind!

"It's essential to have a sense of humour when you're in the racket," she'd say.

Over the next six years, I would become eternally grateful – to Sophie, and to my friend, Vieve, who'd given me Sophie's telephone number. Vieve, with her natural red hair and love of dancing, who shares my Aquarian nature, with the ruling planet of Uranus.

James never misses the opportunity for a bit of English humour: "That's why you've had so much upheaval in your life – you're ruled by Ur-anus!" And he may well have a point!

Sophie predicts that the manuscript that has become *Rachael – Woman of The Night* will one day be published.

"Oh, I don't know, I'm not sure about its acceptability or what has been referred to as my credibility – or my own fears. Still so many fears, Sophie," I tell her doubtfully.

"Margaret," she says with a sigh, "a perceived inferior quality of character in others, today or yesterday, does not necessarily mean a same inferior quality of character tomorrow. People often make this mistake when judging one another."

I nod my head solemnly, consoled.

"Did you get that?" Sophie asks, "Or do I have to repeat it?"

"No, it's okay – I got it. Thanks."

"And anyway," she adds with a smile as she takes a sip of tea from her mug on the desk, "what have I told you, again and again, my dear? Time – everything in its own time. And patience, Margaret, practise patience."

Chapter Eleven
Mikayla's Beautiful, Different Loving

*I*t was some time in my second period of escorting, during the healing of my cracked ribs, that I awoke one day with the overwhelming feeling that I needed gentleness – and instinctively knew I'd find it in the touch and loving of another woman.

I seemed stuck in a world of callous, conceited, unfeeling people. Most particularly, having had to start escorting again, I couldn't stand the cold baseness of men – so much of their lives seemed to revolve around their genitals. I couldn't stand any more the clinical, unemotional sexual intercourse with them. All the rules. I couldn't stand the penises: the sight of them, the feel of them, whether they were in me, on my body, or if I had to touch or even look at them. Never-ending condoms – would it break or come off, would he try to pull it off? Asking the men please not to lie or put any weight on the right side of my chest, because of the pain of my cracked ribs; checking their bodies for the smallest unusual mark; the continual stress of bookings; adrenaline always at a maximum. My life being worth just a fuck.

Everything was measured by a fuck again. A conflict waged within me: whilst I needed the money, I couldn't take any more the apathy that went with money changing hands for a woman's body. And I missed being able to kiss – lingering, sensual kissing.

The trauma of escorting again made me ache for gentleness. I yearned for it. My soul demanded it.

The only obvious physical pain, though, was from my cracked ribs.

I just wanted softness. And I wanted it from someone I didn't know – who couldn't hurt me, couldn't take from me, who didn't owe me anything. Someone who didn't pity me or care about me or love me – and who wouldn't need to say, "I'll phone you back." Someone I didn't owe anything to, someone I didn't love, who wouldn't say things they didn't mean. Someone unattached from me, who wouldn't check on my every move, who understood just a part of my agony – if only the escorting; who I wouldn't have to explain a thing to.

James couldn't fill this need. Only a woman could.

So I searched for and found her – Mikayla – through an escort agency advert in the Cape Argus, and phoned from a public call box one evening, outside the well-lit post office, at about eight o'clock. A lady answered the call.

I said, "Hello, my name's Rachael. I've got a rather unusual request – I'd like to book a lady for an hour. Not for a man, for myself."

There was a pause on the other end of the line, and then, "Just hold please, I'll call the Manageress."

Another lady came on the line. "Good evening, can I help you?"

I repeated my particular request.

"I'm not sure if we have anyone prepared to do that."

"I know it's rather unusual," I answered, "but I'm in the same business and it's getting to me a bit – I'm so tired of men. Do you think you could discuss it with your ladies? And I'll phone you back in about five minutes."

"Okay," she said. "What are you like?"

"I'm thirty-eight, five foot six, fifty-five kilograms, dark hair to my shoulders, bust size 36B." I was used to this – us girls were continually described to clients at Puff's agency so it didn't bother me in the slightest; it was rather like a stuck gramophone record.

"So you want someone a bit like yourself?" she asked cautiously.

"Yes, that's fine. I'd appreciate it," I answered. I wasn't actually particularly concerned about that – only that I would be with a woman.

"All right – phone me back in five minutes and I'll chat to the ladies in the meantime."

I waited the allotted five minutes. Was I nervous? Yes, a bit. I lit a smoke and dialled the number again after exactly five minutes.

"Hello," a voice said. "Mikayla speaking, can I help you?"

"I hope so," I answered. "It's Rachael here – I phoned earlier."

"Oh, yes," she said. "Dot told me about your request and I'm quite happy to spend an hour with you."

We discussed the fees and she gave me directions. I said I'd be there within half an hour, but got a bit lost trying to find the place at night. It was down a side alley, off the main road in the Claremont area. The house was set well back on the property and surrounded by enormous blue-gum trees. I arrived about ten minutes late, but she'd waited.

Mikayla was a bit younger than me and about the same height, dressed neatly in a short black mini-skirt, black stockings and good quality, closed, medium-heel shoes. Heavier than me, with shapely legs, she wore a white blouse stretched across her ample bust – considerably bigger than mine. Her smile and face were friendly and I liked her immediately. I also found her attractive. She spoke nicely and was well mannered – from her accent I felt she was fluent in both English and Afrikaans. Her hair was long, straight and blonde and her make-up heavier than mine, her eyes accentuated by black eyeliner and mascara.

She took my arm and gently guided me to a room at the front of the house.

It was very sparsely furnished, with only a massage bed covered by a clean white sheet. On the wall in front of the massage bed was a large mirror.

"Thanks for agreeing to do this," I said a bit shyly and nervously, as I put my small handbag on the bed and took out my purse.

"Oh, that's okay, just relax," she answered – and we both giggled.

"Famous words, aren't they, in this business," I said, handing the notes to her.

"You're right about that," she smiled, taking the money without counting it. "Would you like a drink?"

I said I'd have a double whisky on the rocks and that she should get herself something as well. "I'll be back in a minute then. I think we should go to another room – the bed in here isn't very comfortable. I'll find out if we can use the room next door instead." She squeezed my arm and left, closing the door quietly behind her. I hopped up onto the massage bed and lit a smoke.

In a couple of minutes Mikayla was back with our drinks. "Here, double whisky on the rocks. Cheers."

"Cheers," I replied as we touched glasses together and took sips of our drinks – she was having a brandy and coke.

"Okay, we can use the next room, so let's go through, shall we?" Mikayla said, smiling at me over the rim of her glass.

"Could we shower together?" I asked.

"Sure, the shower's down the passage. I'll fetch some towels for us."

I jumped down from the bed, picked up my bag and followed her through. This room was definitely better – cosier and more relaxed, less austere. Three-quarter bed covered in a patterned quilt in various shades of brown, matching curtains, bedside table and lamp, built-in cupboards – like a bedroom in any ordinary house. We put our drinks on the table and I sat down on the bed.

"Back in a jiffy," Mikayla said, giving me a wink, "just fetching our towels." In seconds she was back, closed and locked the door behind her, came across to the bed and sat down close to me, so that our bodies touched. Without a word, she first put the towels at the end of the bed, then lit a smoke and took a drag. Looking at me shyly she said, "You must tell me what you want to do, okay?"

"I'm not terribly sure," I answered, looking at her. "And I don't know how to really explain it either. I've just had enough of men – this business starts getting to you after a while." I paused, feeling our mutual attraction for each other through the softness of our bare arms. She waited for me to continue. "I just need the gentleness of a feminine touch. Sometimes I think men don't know how to touch a woman properly. I suppose you could say I'm pretty confused." I took another sip of my whisky and reached for my smokes.

170

"Your head gets stuffed in this work," Mikayla agreed gently. "I know how you feel. Everything's so cold. Sometimes I get mixed up myself. That's why I agreed to spend the hour with you when Dot asked us."

"Mustn't forget the time then, hey?" I said, smiling and deliberately pointing to my watch.

"Don't worry about it," she answered. "This time's different. We won't even watch the clock. Business is quiet tonight." She took a sip of her drink and added, "Who cares anyway?" and put her arm around my shoulders.

I sensed from this gesture that she also wanted to make love with a woman, but was as shy as I was, and not quite sure how to begin. She kept her arm around my shoulders and I leant my head against hers.

"When we've finished our smokes, shall we go and have that shower together?" I suggested.

"Okay," she replied, putting her lit Chesterfield in the large ceramic ashtray, and then immediately took off her shoes, crossed to the cupboard, took out two hangers and started to undress, hanging up her clothes.

I followed her lead, hanging my own clothes up next to hers. It felt a bit strange – us two women undressing next to each other like this. I didn't rush, but I think she felt it was best to get this initial phase over as quickly as possible. She lay down on the bed naked, on her back atop the quilt, her head propped against the headboard, smoke in hand. "Do you like a back tickle?" she asked with a soft smile.

"Oh yes, I love having my back tickled," I replied, removing my G-string and standing a moment. "I've always said if I was rich I'd employ someone just to tickle my back." My eyes were drawn to her new nakedness, noticing her ample, rounded breasts and finding with some astonishment – and pleasure – that I really did want to touch them.

"Good," she said, patting the mattress. "Then come and lie next to me and I'll give you a bit of a back tickle before we shower."

I put my G-string on the chair and crossed to the bed, also naked, and lay down next to her, wincing as I turned onto my stomach, putting my weight on my elbows. "I can't lie flat on my stomach – I'm recovering from cracked ribs and I can't take any pressure on the right side of my chest."

"How the hell did you crack your ribs?" Mikayla asked with concern, looking into my eyes and putting her hand through my hair.

"I fell in the bath some weeks ago, but it's a lot better now than it was. In the beginning each breath was pure hell." Mikayla continued playing with my hair and kept quiet. I sensed she was waiting for me to continue. "My doctor says it'll take about six weeks to heal, and there's nothing you can do to ease it." I smiled at her and had another sip of my whisky.

Mikayla held my gaze for a moment then said, "We'll go easy on the right side then, won't we?" Leaning over me to put out her smoke she whispered, smiling, "Right now though, it's back tickle time." She sat up next to me and tickled my shoulders, down my back and over my bottom. Up and down, round and round, from one side to the other with her one hand while with the other she played with my hair. "You've got lovely thick hair," she said softly.

"Thanks," I said. "It's the famous wash-'n-dry-by-itself style. I'm too lazy for the blow-drying drama – too much bother."

"You're lucky, mine's fine and dead straight. I have to blow-dry it every day to give it some body and style, otherwise it just hangs like a curtain."

There followed a few seconds of silence in which I felt her lean gently against me, lingeringly, her breasts on my back, not sure what to do next. "Shall we go and have that shower?" she whispered hesitantly, leaning forward and touching my shoulder.

I nodded and she climbed over me carefully, picked up the towels and held out one, which I took and wrapped around my chest. She did the same. "Come on, then," she encouraged, taking my hand to follow her.

We went through to the en-suite bathroom, where she did a wee, then took her towel off and hung it on the rail. The bathroom light remained off, the only light coming from the main bedroom – the effect was soft and shadowed, and gently erotic.

"I'll get the water right first," she said, stepping into the shower and pulling the curtain.

I also did a wee, hung my towel on the rail and joined her. Nothing of any significance happened in the shower, except the accidental-on-purpose bumping into each other as we soaped ourselves and rinsed in turn under the water, and giggled about being women and trying to get the soap out of nooks and crannies in the spray – a bath being so much easier. I sensed, though, that she definitely wanted things to happen between us that night, but that I'd have to take the initiative. I felt certain it was her first time with a woman too.

We seesawed between fleeting moments of timid physical chemistry; almost a pretence of casual wanton touching – and then shyness again – neither of us openly studying the other's naked body as we shared the jet of warm spray. Her body glistened wet in the gently shadowed bathroom light and I found it difficult to avert my eyes as she lathered her full breasts and washed between her legs.

If I'd had the courage, I would have told Mikayla how very beautiful she was, how exquisite her female form seemed to my mind, how proud she should feel to be a woman. But I kept the thoughts to myself, shyness at the unexpected intrigue of her body prevailing – though I later wished I hadn't. I wished I'd voiced my appreciation of her natural naked beauty.

Back in the bedroom she took the damp bath towels and hung them over

172

the cupboard door. We crossed to the bed, and Mikayla lit a Chesterfield and lay back as she'd done before, on the side of the mattress against the wall. I felt more at ease now, inexplicably less shy to study her naked form closer, my eyes lingering on the contours of her body. I noticed she shaved; her light brown pubic hair was neat and trimmed. Her nipples were large, like mine, but lighter – a soft pink compared to my own dark brown.

"You relax and have your smoke," I said softly, tracing my finger down her tummy, from her neck to her navel. It was now or never, I thought.

"Okay," she whispered, watching me.

I leaned forward to her beautiful full breasts and gently kissed one nipple – then opened my mouth and teased the pink flesh with my tongue. Soft, soft, wet. I felt it harden and put my hand across to caress her other breast, and played with and kissed them lingeringly, in turn.

Mikayla put out her smoke in the ashtray and lay with her hands at her sides, relaxed, eyes closed. I traced my mouth and tongue all over her chest and stomach, around her navel – always going back to her erect nipples as she arched her body toward me, asking me without words to love her breasts again and again. And I did.

Then she sighed, opened her eyes and pulled me to her, forcefully but gently. I raised myself across her, looked into her eyes and slowly put my lips to hers. She responded without hesitation, our tongues searching – easy, tasting, feeling, slow – a whole new sensation to discover and savour; the wetness from our wombs building, the soft flesh of our breasts against each other, our nipples caressing. My fingers traced her lips, her open, wanting, kissing mouth. She took my hand and put it down to the soft brown hair between her thighs for a moment, then pushed my fingers gently between her legs, to feel and touch her wetness, just as I'd hoped and thought it should be – not the fake way we did it with the escorting men, but real and wanting.

I brought my fingers back to Mikayla's lips – inside her mouth, on our tongues – for us to share and taste her wetness together, as we kissed. She wanted me to touch the aching softness between her thighs again – her body told me this was what she wanted. But I wanted to linger and tease her a while longer, and moved gently down – then back to her erect nipples, pulling them between my fingers, harder, still harder. She took my hand again and put it between her legs, this time keeping it in her wetness with her own hand over mine, so that I understood her aching. Her back arched, she opened her legs slowly, then gently but firmly pushed my head down between her thighs to her moist, sweet wanting.

I'd sometimes wondered what it would be like – what another woman would taste like. Mikayla was clean, she smelled good. She tasted nice, so nice – so soft. It felt good, so good, to love her like this, and I took my time, my fingers and tongue arousing and lingering on and in her delicate softness, kissing, stroking, rubbing gently, knowing exactly, from my own body, where to find her special place. She sighed and moaned, her wetness against my face, her body moving rhythmically to her own wanton thrusting – unashamed now of this new sensation between us.

And I felt her yearning threshold through the pressure of her movement on my face; her inner quivering sexual desire, rising to ecstasy against my tongue. She came, trembling, abandoned – holding my head gently between her legs, her hands in my hair, and I tasted and loved her beautiful, natural pleasure, waiting for her breathing to soften. Then I turned her on her stomach and climaxed against the smooth softness of the skin on her back, rubbing my wetness against the exquisite contour of her naked form – drifting in her unashamed acceptance of my own need for fulfilment, her warmth beneath me flowing upwards in a culminating wave throughout my being.

Afterwards, we lay side by side for a while, not speaking – just tracing fingers against warm skin. She broke the silence.

"Want a shower?" she asked, then added, "Maybe a smoke first, then a shower?" and giggled softly, her head resting on my shoulder.

"That'd be nice," I said, "though rather a pity, the shower that is – to break the peace of lying with you like this right now." I sighed. "But I think I'm well over the one hour limit by now, aren't I?" I looked at her and she nodded, smiling like a shy, naughty girl once more.

After our shower I went through to the lounge and had a drink with Mikayla and the other girls in that agency. Their driver was there as well. No one treated me strangely. Everyone was friendly. There weren't any clients at the time and some of us, including myself, sat on the floor and just chatted.

When I left she saw me to the door. I gave her a hug and we kissed, normally, on the mouth.

"Thanks a lot, Mikayla, I appreciate it." I said honestly and sincerely.

"It was great – thank you," she answered softly, smiling, then gave me a wink and added, "Take care of the ribs."

I sat in my car for a while and lit a cigarette, the smoke curling through the top of the window into the cool night air. That our loving would be considered by some to be morally wrong was of no consequence. She was a good woman and I was grateful for her soft caress, and for her allowing me to love her. We never met again. I've never been with another woman after Mikayla – or before her – though I've thought of her sometimes. I still don't understand the void in my life which needed this particular fulfilment at that time. Whatever it was, she responded unselfishly, as I'd hoped, without questioning or pressure, even if it was only temporary. And, yes, I found making love to her to be highly erotic. Mikayla taught me another kind of very beautiful love – the love of a woman.

The following evening, when I checked my handbag before going to the agency, I found almost half of the money I'd given Mikayla hidden down the inside of my handbag. She'd obviously only taken enough to cover the agency's fee.

Chapter Twelve
Guys for Bucks

*S*o, Granny Rachael was back with the girls again at the agency, waiting for clients through the long nights, as we each faced our own personal targets.

There were a few new faces amongst the ladies, and some of the girls I'd worked with the first time round had left. Tammy was still there managing the front desk, as was Amy, with her soft heart for animals and her gentle advice, and Christina – sharp as ever, never missing a smidgin of the goings-on. Cindy continued raking in the money doing the work she enjoyed, her insatiable appetite for sex still smouldering – sometimes wriggling about on her chair to temporarily relieve her fired-up womb if she hadn't managed to land a booking with a client who turned her on, still faithfully doing her pencil exercises every day at home.

Otherwise things were the same – not much changes in the world of the sex-worker. Agency rules still had to be adhered to, drivers organised, the reception and lounges kept tidy, glasses and cups washed, an abundant supply of condoms kept in the reception desk drawer; pay-time for the girls remained at four in the morning.

Business hummed most nights. Puff was his usual protective self, a solid shoulder to lean on after a difficult booking. I was grateful to be able to work in his particular agency again, and we often chatted in his office during lulls in activity. The two drivers, Henry and Simon, still drove their cars like lunatics: the red VW Golf still sped round corners on two wheels, the metallic blue Opel still screeched to a halt outside the agency door.

The girls still faced the same stress levels; sometimes there were tears. Peckish bellies continued to munch on burgers and take-away foods at odd hours – but Dotty Dick had left the agency, so thankfully I no longer had to keep a watchful eye on my home-made sandwiches.

Despite being back to illicit paid sex, my aching heart was gladdened and my despairing spirit lifted as I shared, once again, in the honest, unaffected laughter of the girls. Why was their laughter so special to me? I think because they understood hardship, understood that many things in the normal outside world that people have petty squabbles over, just aren't worth it. Life in the racket instils a strange and new sense of freedom of laughter.

Each night that I escorted for additional income was an eighty-kilometre round trip to and from the agency, and James and I decided I should drive his car as it was nippier than my little Nissan and cheaper on petrol – but it had no heater. The nights were still cold, and on my way home in the early mornings my fingers felt quite numb on occasion, holding the steering in the chilly air.

So I now packed a tog bag containing leggings, knitted leg warmers, scarf, Beanie, my jersey with the big floppy collar, takkies and socks – all of which I left in the car, changing into this abominable snowman gear before I left for home, usually at quarter past four in the morning. My old jacket I'd put over my legs and knees, which made the drive home warmer, but it was not enough.

As before, the twinkling lights of the sleeping city of Cape Town heralded the end of my working night. I never tired of this magnificent early morning delight of silent electricity, whether I'd had a good shift or not at the agency. To say that a city has life is true, and this becomes more obvious and decidedly fascinating during the hours of darkness.

Table Mountain, without doubt because of her stability and central dominance, reminded me of the human heart – her soft lighting unobtrusively belying her position of supreme importance. Among the array of coloured city lights, the brighter, larger illuminations followed paths like arteries in the circulatory system, while the medium-strength lighting resembled veins, and lastly the soft lights seemed to spread in fine webs, like capillaries. Flashes of coloured neon light represented important nerve centres: pulsating destinations and onward transmission sites in the chain of continued life.

As I came over the hill on the N1 Highway, the static energy of this city, still asleep, throbbed – coiled like a spring of molecules, waiting to explode silently into the daylight to dance and fuse with the bustling, jostling human bodies that would pound the warming concrete and asphalt.

During the day I averaged about four hours' sleep, usually from seven in the morning till eleven, after which I worked from home with James. By about five-thirty in the afternoon it was time to prepare for my night life as Rachael, starting with the long soak in my water world.

Usually James would make my box of sandwiches; real nice they were compared to mine – tuna mayonnaise or cheese and tomato, slices cut round the edges, cheese grated, all with the precision and perfection of James's Virgo character. Me, I made the quickest sandwiches: peanut-butter, finished.

It became a regular question from the girls when I walked through the agency door: "What's on the sarnies tonight, Granny?"

The old routine. Except that this time I was living in the same house as James while I escorted, and that was a somewhat different trauma. Before I moved in with him, I'd been able to find some space and peace for the

Nymphae Soak, some time to cross from them to him in my mind before he wanted his share of sex as well. Now there was no space or peace. We tried, in our separate ways, to cope with this wounding emotional turmoil – some days were better, others painful; sometimes we found a quiet wavering acceptance.

The Nymphae Soak – be it before going to work at the agency in the evenings or on returning home in the early hours – was now usually watched closely by James. He used the en-suite bathroom as he preferred showering, while I used the other larger bathroom, which had the bath – plus there was sufficient space to accommodate my rocking chair, which was older than Bert. Perched on the toilet seat or reclining on the rocker as I soaked in the tub, James studied all preparations and cleansing routines most carefully.

"Why are you washing your hair again, you washed it last night?"

"Because I wash my hair every night doing this work – hygienic reasons, that's all."

Then he regularly started searching through the contents of my woven grass work basket.

"I thought I asked you not to wear this white G-string I gave you."

Out it would come, together with the others, and we'd go through a G-string rigmarole with them all laid out on the bed; what I could and could not wear.

I always washed my underwear by hand each day, so he'd see it on the washing line – more questions.

"How many G-strings do you wear in one night?"

And it didn't take long for the rest of the shit to follow. He knew how much money I made per booking, so when I got home he was waiting in the kitchen, kettle on the boil, sometimes pleasant, other times ready for a fight.

"How come you've got less money than you're supposed to have for two bookings?"

"Well, I bought a packet of smokes. I paid my bar bill as well."

"So how many drinks did you have?"

That would be calculated as well. Sometimes, I'd add that I'd bought a pie.

"But I make sandwiches for you," he said, annoyed.

"I know and they're very nice, but I share them with some of the girls. And sometimes I just feel like a pie, you know I love pies."

The pies caused more than a few arguments: James considered it quite unnecessary that I buy a pie when he made sandwiches, while I didn't see why I shouldn't be allowed something as simple as a pie if I was going to do this kind of work for extra money to help us.

"Well, what's the use of doing this work for extra money if you're just going to spend the extra money on pies?" he'd say.

Smoking caused more arguments than I care to remember. To James, any-one who smoked and didn't have a job to pay for their cigarettes shouldn't be smoking in the first place – he seemed to conveniently forget he'd once been a smoker himself.

And the men – like a stuck record James was. What was he like, good-looking, ugly, big chopper, how did we do it, did he like it, did I like it? Oh, fuck off, James, with all your nagging and shit, I'd think.

"Why are you late? I was just about going to look for you."

"You know very well that I drive slowly – I'm tired from being awake all night and can't afford to have an accident. Sometimes I drive slower, that's all."

"Did you stop off somewhere else on the way home, maybe to do a pri-vate booking?" he'd grill me, obvious mistrust in his voice, which irritated me intensely.

"Yes, James," I'd reply sarcastically – I'd learnt fast from his humour – "I stopped for a free quickie at the beachfront with someone. Why don't you just quit your shit? It's bad enough already. I'm tired and I still need to bath."

And after the early morning bath – yes, his pecker was up, doing the silent submarine periscope salute again, studying the bedroom furnishings all by itself while its owner sulked if it hadn't had its share of attention! Well, just as before, if I could do it with others, then James could have his share as well, when he wanted it – including when I had cracked ribs, and I'd have to remind him to please not lie on the right side of my chest. He was back to being his tom-cat self with a vengeance; there were times when I felt so off sex I could quite gladly have given his erect and sulking penis a smack on its head with my little cast-iron frying pan!

I still had to psych myself each evening, I still couldn't see the money only and I still couldn't do more than three bookings in any twenty-four hour pe-riod. Sometimes I'd sit all night at the agency till four in the morning and never have a booking – I couldn't figure out which was worse, no bookings or bookings.

By the end of November we decided to invest in a cell phone. That way all the money would be mine if I had any bookings, instead of losing a fair chunk to the agency – taking into account the cost of the petrol each night, and of course my smokes, drinks and occasional pie!

Puff kindly agreed that I could work alone using my cell phone, as well as working at the agency.

So it now became three jobs at once. Having advertised – where? In the local newspaper of course – it was now normal work at home, cell phone bookings at all hours of the day and night (always at the client's chosen premises), and if I didn't get enough bookings that way, the agency in the evening. Having the cell phone meant that I had to be ready to leave at any time if a call came in – a pecker whose owner had conjured up in his mind all kinds of sex simply didn't like waiting too long for the arranged Rachael to arrive to relieve his frustrations.

Some of the guys I went to on cell appointments wouldn't bath or shower first. Either they just wouldn't, or they said they'd showered already, or they didn't have the facilities and couldn't. However, I was always bathed, hair washed etc. when I arrived for an appointment. After phoning James (my "heavy"!) in front of the client to say I'd arrived and that all was fine, I'd switch the cell phone off. When I was safely in my car after an appointment, I'd switch the cell on again to tell James that I was on my way home. I had plenty of cell phone requests for threesomes, which I didn't do, and plenty of requests from men who wanted sex in their offices, especially on the desk!

Escorting from cell phone bookings meant further stress and higher anxiety levels; this was far more dangerous than working at the agency, where one could shout for help and where there were people in the vicinity to take note of the client and the time. On these appointments I would face unknown men alone, without any protection – only my little cast-iron frying pan within easy reach in my basket. I always left the telephone number and address of each and every cell phone booking I went on for James – it was vital he be able to trace me if I never arrived home.

Another disadvantage of working by phone appointments was that the client couldn't see me and I couldn't see him or the surroundings that I'd be in; I never knew whether there'd be more than one guy when I arrived or whether it was perhaps a set-up. Luckily, I never had any serious problems.

I worked out my "description and fees" speech, and James sometimes even answered the calls using the same speech – for some reason, he didn't mind doing this. I kept the same rates as the agency, with no additional charge for petrol. Using the cell phone for bookings meant I now had to become a map-reader as well!

On arrival at a phone appointment, if the client was happy with what he saw before him, I would first ask for the money – cash only as previously discussed, but never handled or counted it until after the sex. I would ask him to put my fee under a magazine or newspaper; only when the sexual act was completed and I was dressed to leave would I put the cash in my purse, leaving immediately. I also gave all prospective clients the run-down on my rules over the phone so there'd be no misunderstandings when I arrived.

On an evening cell phone appointment it wasn't possible to change into my warmer gear afterwards, so I used my jacket or a towel, sometimes both, wrapped around my legs for warmth.

If I went through to the agency, I would only switch off the cell once I'd phoned James to report arriving safely, and then switch on again when I left the agency to report being on my way home.

James's mental and emotional suffering at my having to resume this work became totally impossible to deal with: understandably jealous to begin with, he now became unhealthily jealous, over-possessive. I was interrogated relentlessly about everything. If I went to the mall to pay bills and then have a cup of coffee – just for a little peace and space from him, from the tension at home – then he'd phone me, up to nine times an hour! He made a mental note of every cent I earned. I never stashed any of this money away for myself, it was all used for business and household expenses – and it certainly helped, quite dramatically in fact.

A very dear friend of mine, Grace, whom I met when we were both working with Sam in '95, was currently unemployed. She knew the intricacies of the paperwork and calculations involved in our type of business, and I offered her work two or three mornings a week from nine to one in the afternoon, so that our home business telephone would be answered and necessary paperwork continued while James and I were out seeing our business clients.

Grace and I've always got along like a house on fire, both being Aquarians, though she is February and fourteen years older than me; she is perhaps the only person I've ever known who can understand me completely without me having to continually explain my feelings and emotions. Plus, she has a wonderful sense of humour and a very open mind – so apart from helping us to stay abreast of the work at home, Grace was an enormous emotional support for me during this difficult second phase of escorting.

The money I earned per hour from escorting far outweighed my petrol, cell phone and pie costs, as well as Grace's pay – we openly discussed my fee for escorting and agreed quite happily on her hourly rate. Considering the emotional and physical stress I was under and the effect it was having on my own work ability, it was financially more beneficial to employ Grace than to try to cope with the work myself. Grace, James and I worked well together; he trusted her one hundred percent, which was most important, and she became an emotional support for him as well.

So my sex work, in effect, provided employment and income for another member of the general public – I paid Grace cash every Friday without fail before she went home, from my personal earnings. Having worked with Grace in the employ of Sam, where we both experienced the stress of continually not being paid on time, I made it a priority that I'd never inflict this kind of abuse on her.

There were occasions when Grace went home with some spinach or carrots as well from James's vegetable patch in our back garden – the year had so far been too stressful to allow him to devote sufficient time to establishing a varied, substantial veggie patch, but every little bit extra counts.

My anxiety levels were phenomenal during this period in my life, my tranquillisers never far from reach. Every time I swallowed a Brozam tablet, I
was grateful for a temporary relief from the burning anxiety in my gut. Grace
commented in concern several times, hoping one day I'd be able to quit the
habit, but she never hounded me about it, understanding the emotional
stress I was under.

James is not a heavy drinker or even a daily drinker. At a party he sometimes makes up for lost time, though he doesn't become aggressive or verbally abusive; it's funny but can also get a bit ridiculous and look pretty fool-
ish – not uncommon when one is under the influence of alcohol. I've seen
it happen to others many a time and remember occasions in my younger
years when I became totally inebriated, making a fool of myself – the ghastly
hangover and embarrassment the following day cured me of wanting to
overindulge too often. By the end of an alcohol binge, James usually navigated a path to somewhere, threw up and went to bed to sleep it off; since
meeting him, I'd only seen him in a drinking, party mood twice.

I was bathing before going to the agency one night, sitting in the Nymphae
Soak going through my psyching process, when James somehow managed
to get himself totally sloshed, on what I don't know, in an extremely short
space of time – I think while he was in the kitchen, maybe making my sandwiches or doing some supper.

Everything just became too much for him – he staggered into the bathroom, plonked down in my rocking chair in a drunken stupor and started
crying. Eventually, after trying to discuss matters sensibly and compassionately with him, which is pretty difficult when someone is so intoxicated, I
had to really shout, swear and scream to get him to quit his behaviour and
go to bed to sleep off the effects of whatever he'd had – he wasn't capable of
doing anything else, particularly not work on business files.

"I'd do the work for you if I could," he sobbed, blowing his nose on some
toilet paper.

"Yes, I know you would," I answered. "We've been over all that before.
Fact is you can't do it though – as the woman and the younger of us, I make
the most money from the sex work, while you're more qualified to make
most of the income from our other business work."

"But I feel so bad," he sniffed, wiping his tired, tearful eyes, dumping the
soggy loo paper under the toilet lid as he reached for the one-ply roll again.
"I hate it when you have to go there, to other men, I just hate it."

"I hate it too, and you don't make it any easier with all your crap and
checking and questioning and digging around in my basket. You're driving
me mad with your shit!"

James folded in the rocking chair, a sobbing wreck. I felt his pain, understood that as a man it seemed to him as though he'd let me down, not

182

being able to support us the way he wanted to, but right then there was no other way. Life isn't easy. When I left that night for work at the agency James was in bed asleep, the dogs curled up next to him as they comforted him with their gentle presence. He'd sobered up by morning.

In early January 1997, James's sister and her husband came to stay with us for a few days' holiday. I'd never met either of them before, and we invited a few couples around for a braai at our home on the Sunday so that our friends could meet them as well. As I sat down next to one of our female guests to eat my lunch, the lady started a conversation with me about prostitution. How or why this came about, I've no idea, but I never forgot her fixed, uninformed and what I felt to be prejudiced viewpoint.

"I really don't see why women turn to prostitution, I'm sure there must be other available work for them to do instead of selling their bodies. Perhaps if they looked hard enough, they'd find work instead of resorting to such means."

I nearly choked on my food, her opening statement so took me by surprise. If she only knew that the very food on the plate on her lap, had been part bought and paid for by my prostitution, I wondered what her reaction would've been.

"Life can be tough," I answered, trying to make light of the matter and divert her thoughts to some other topic, "especially when you've a family to feed, bills to settle and no income. I'm sure they've all got their valid reasons – jobs are pretty scarce these days."

This wasn't the time or the place for me to answer her the way I would've liked to, and to avoid any further comment from her on the subject, said I needed to check on something in the kitchen and excused myself rather hurriedly.

Before James's sister left on her return trip home, he told her what I did for additional income – she and I had a chat about it sitting on the double bed. I was so relieved and touched that she never behaved any differently towards me afterwards, and has never, in any way, made me feel uncomfortable; and neither has anyone else in James's family.

And so, here are some of the guys for you, from this second period of escorting in 1996:

"I give my maid twenty rand to wank me off twice a week in the kitchen," this repulsive white man said to me.

This booking I consider to be, over all, the second-worst I ever had – the first being the client who terrorised me with the lit cigarette. This was a wealthy man in his forties, in some smart job, living in a mansion on the side of the mountain in one of the pricey suburbs of Cape Town. His wife was away.

You sick shit, I thought. I wanted to throw up. That's what I call really taking unfair advantage of another person. You don't even have the decency to pay her the proper fee for wanking you off. Why? Could it be because she's not white like you? I wish someone would take your filthy sick dick and shove it in your own gob. I couldn't get out of this house fast enough – the one hour seemed to take forever.

"I love legs, I can come just looking at legs," he'd said on the cell phone. "Make sure you wear fishnet stockings and high heels."

He was standing on the front step waiting for me to arrive, wearing a pair of blue boxer shorts, when I stopped my car outside his house around six-thirty one evening. He watched every move I made from my car to the front door, eyes fixed on my fishnet stockings, and ushered me through the front door with a lewd expression, locking first the security gate and then the front door behind us and deliberately removing the keys. There was no way out of this man's house – the windows were barred as well.

Perhaps three steps from the front door was the TV lounge, the room littered with porno magazines, lying open, haphazardly all over the place – on the chairs, coffee table and floor; a really gross blue movie was playing on the TV. He indicated my fee lying on the coffee table and I placed a magazine over the notes.

No wasting time here. I was immediately instructed to put my basket down on the lounge carpet and remain standing in front of him, to the side of the television screen, so that he could look at my legs and the blue movie at the same time. Then he pulled down his blue boxer shorts, leaned back on the sofa and proceeded to masturbate while I watched him, moaning and groaning and slobbering at the delights all around him.

I was then instructed to undress in front of him. I put two condoms on the coffee table. Then I was told to lie down on the carpet with my legs open – once again in front of the television set – and touch myself while he masturbated again, sitting on the couch.

Thereafter, he stood up, took a condom from the coffee table, rolled it down over his once again erect penis, lay on me on the carpet and watched the blue movie on the screen as he thrust away inside me. I could've just as easily been a pomegranate with a hole in it – just any hole, whether it be hard or soft, to stick his penis into would have been enough; he seemed without sensitivity of soul – in a lusting live sexual trance. When he finished, he pulled off the sodden condom, dumped it on the coffee table and sat down on the couch again. I've never encountered another client so coldly glassy-eyed concerning sex; it was pure enraptured filth fulfilment.

I asked to use the bathroom to dress and he grudgingly agreed, accompanying me down the passage. The house was enormous, the furnishings quality, and from a security point of view the place was as tight as a duck's arse. As I was about to leave I put the cash fee, still under the magazine on the coffee table, in my purse.

It was at this point that he informed me, with a lewd smirk, of his sexual abuse of his maid. I made no comment. I felt sure she'd lose her job if she refused his repulsive request. As he unlocked the front door and security gate, he said he'd give me a call again. I nodded acknowledgement, said goodbye and walked to my car. A few weeks later he phoned me again on the cell.

"Do you remember me?" he asked. "Can we make a time – in the late afternoon, like last time?"

"Yes, I remember you well," I answered slowly. "And thank you," I paused, "but no thank you, you'll never have enough money to ever get me back to your house."

I didn't say goodbye, just cut the call off. "Goodbye" was far too respectful for this so-called stable, acceptable member of society. This man turned my stomach.

Another cell booking, this time at what is considered to be Cape Town's second most smart, expensive hotel. A top executive of an import/export company in Cape Town for meetings and photos with certain Government Ministers – fed up because he'd lost money that day betting on the horses! Fed up? I wouldn't know why really – he kept bragging about his job, houses, overseas trips and holidays, boats, money etc. His expensive running shoes he showed to me with pride, picking them up off the carpet, holding them for me to admire, to prove his dedication and determination to remain in tip-top physical condition for his very senior management position.

"I work out regularly to keep fit," he informed me, clutching his expensive brand-name trainers.

"That's sensible," I answered evenly. "There's a tremendous amount of pressure and responsibility in a high-powered job."

I nodded in mock appreciation – and was then requested to first sit and read him sections of the local newspaper. Deliberately, I chose to read him his horoscope as well, to see if things would improve in his sorry life.

After that I asked him what he wanted to do sexually, during our time together. I was sitting next to him on the couch and he was touching and stroking my hair.

"You've got such beautiful hair," he said quietly, and paused a moment. "I've always wanted to come in a woman's hair – baby, just let me come in your hair!"

I crossed to the double bed in the sumptuously furnished hotel room, undressed to my G-string only, put two condoms on the bedside table and lay down on the white bed linen. He removed all his clothing, crossed to the bed, took off my G-string, then caressed and studied my body for some time.

It was most peculiar, but I obliged his particular request – better than having him inside me. All I did was lie still. Then on his knees – one hand rhythmically stimulating his penis, the other hand holding and rubbing my long dark hair all over his genitals – he shook and moaned as he built to climax.

"Oh baby, you've got such beautiful hair," he moaned as he ejaculated, rubbing his semen around in my hair. I lay still. Then he got off the bed, put his underpants and trousers on again, informing me I should leave immediately as he wanted to sleep, he faced a busy day in the morning and it was important that he get a good night's rest. I was given time only to put my head quickly into the bathroom basin, under the tap, then dress again and leave.

Luckily I wear hats and always carried my favourite with me – the soft, reversible velvet was now firmly ensconced atop my head, stuck down with inadequately washed-off semen! I stopped off at the agency on my way home just to say hello to the girls, and one of the clients walked up to me – a good-looking guy in his thirties.

"Hats really don't suit you," he said in a mocking tone of voice as he tapped me on the shoulder to get my attention. "I'd take it off if I were you, if I hoped to make any money."

If you knew what was under this hat, I thought with a sweet smile, I'd bet you'd rather I kept it on!

When I arrived home after the cum-in-my-hair booking, it was the usual bath routine for me – plus hair wash in the early hours! And my poor hat took a long soak in a bucket with the necessary detergents.

Another cell phone booking, a pretty magic one this time – with a senior executive whose office premises were in the Waterfront area. The security guards on duty seemed to have been informed of my arrival, and I was shown straight inside the building without any trouble and accompanied to the very plush boardroom, where my client was waiting.

Once we were alone, he locked the door behind us, shook my hand politely, thanked me for keeping the appointment and introduced himself.

"Can I pour you a drink?" he asked, his hand on my upper arm in a friendly and relaxed manner.

"Yes," I said, "a double whisky on the rocks would be nice please, if you have."

"Good choice," he answered with a nod of approval, smiling. "I'll join you in a whisky as well," he said as he crossed the room to a very beautiful wooden corner cabinet, which turned out to be a well-stocked bar with a bar fridge. I put my basket down on one of the chairs and leaned against the boardroom table, studying him as he poured our drinks and put some music on – good choice, the "Texas, Southside," CD.

"Your two-hour fee is here, under the ice bucket," he said, looking across at me. His tone of voice carried no inference of contempt towards me for the work that I did. I nodded acknowledgement.

In his late forties I'd say: good-looking with greying, distinguished, not-too-short hair; neat, polite, well-mannered and friendly; a smart dresser without being flashy; polished shoes and clean, well-cut fingernails. I found him very attractive, smoulderingly sensuous to be exact, perhaps a mixture of Jeremy Irons and Micky Rourke – two men I consider utterly stunning – and didn't think I'd be needing the KY Jelly with this exquisite example of masculinity!

We said cheers, clinked glasses and had sips of our whiskies. This sensuous man didn't waste too much time in casual chat, but he didn't rush matters either. I sensed that he found me equally attractive and we had an instant, natural and simultaneous explosion of body chemistry when our skin touched. I had two hours of exceptionally wonderful sex with this guy – mostly on the beautiful polished wood boardroom table, which had a few marks on it when we were finished – perhaps from the ice cubes? We used condoms, and I relaxed one of my rules with him and allowed kissing. He was an emotional, perfected lover – one of those rare occasions when the work became pleasure.

Another call on the cell – the guy wanted to do it "Greek style". I said it was one of my rules, I didn't do it. He was most persistent. "Couldn't I change my mind? He loved it, I probably would too if I'd just try it, he'd do it slowly and carefully." I was adamant in my decision, but he nagged and nagged on the other end of the line. If you love it so much, I thought, exasperated at this guy's reluctance to accept no for an answer, maybe you've got rancid feta on the end of your knob! I cut the call off on my Siemens.

Working from the cell phone, I also made a regular client – a Muslim gentleman who treated me like gold, and who was exceptionally polite and well-mannered. He'd book into a hotel room for a few hours only; money was no problem. We had many chats about lots of things in life. I have a very special regard and love for the writings contained in the Koran, having had an English translation myself (which I'd leant to Mary-Lou; I never managed to find another copy), and he explained many things about the Koran, and even took time to show me basic letters of the Arabic alphabet. Although he called me Rachael, in all our time together I only ever addressed him as Mr Ebrahim.

Christina and I went on a booking to one of the hotels in the northern suburbs with about six rugby guys, on tour in Cape Town at the time. The deal was that only two of the guys would be doing something as only they'd paid; however, these six guys were sharing hotel rooms. Christina and I were in separate bedrooms with our separate clients. I completed my job

187

and went into the en-suite bathroom – the other guys had sneaked in while I was in the bath and stolen my underwear. What a drama! And quite pathetic really, running around the hotel passages sniffing and throwing my G-string and bra around. Well, I had plenty of spare underwear in my basket, but that wasn't the point; this behaviour had to stop – and I wanted my lingerie back. My partner was very supportive in his efforts to retrieve my underwear from his rugby mates. However, it took a call to the agency to send the driver to sort them out before I was given my G-string and bra back! I then found out that Christina had hidden in the bedroom cupboard while I was busy in the other room, as her partner couldn't get the other guys out of the bedroom!

A twenty-eight-year-old yuppie, in his smart Daniel Hechter suit and snazzy tie, sat enthralled before me on a bar stool – wow, a conversation about sex with a real, live escort: this was serious stuff!

"Do you deep throat?"

"Well, not too deep, it kinda makes you want to throw up."

"But do you do it?"

You could almost hear his thoughts ticking over – broad grin, eyes never leaving my face. Not bad looking though, nice build.

"Do you multiple orgasm?"

This was too much for me right then, I just laughed and laughed! I was in a good mood that night and didn't give a shit. I'd a couple of questions of my own for him though – actually, a four-part question, seeing he was so into sexual interrogation!

"If your body had been designed in such a way that your mouth could reach your penis," I said to him and paused a moment, "would you be prepared to give yourself a blow-job?"

"Yeah, sure, definitely," he replied enthusiastically with a grin.

"At any given time, as well?" I added.

"Sure," he said.

"So," I continued, "I take it that includes in the height of summer when you've been in your office clothes for fourteen hours – or when you've been jogging and you're very sweaty, particularly inside your underjocks."

"Hell no, not then," he said, suddenly more serious, pondering the matter more carefully now.

"And why would that be?" I asked. "You said you would for sure, at any given time."

"Well, what I meant was that at any given time, when I'd had a shower first."

"Quite an interesting thought process isn't it? But the question isn't finished yet, here's the next part. Ready?" He nodded, waiting for me to continue. I took a sip of my drink.

"Okay, so we've established that you'd be prepared to give yourself a blow-job, but only if your penis was clean, as in showered or bathed. So, with a clean penis, would you be prepared to ejaculate in your own mouth?"

He thought for a few seconds and seemed undecided. "I'll have to give that one a bit more thought. Is that the end of the question?"

"No," I answered. "Here's the last part. When you've decided if you'd be prepared to ejaculate in your own mouth or not, would you be prepared to swallow your own cum?"

"Hell," he said, taking a healthy swig on his beer, "I've never thought about it that way at all before. Actually, I haven't thought about it at all, never entered my head before, to look at it from that perspective." He gave me a somewhat embarrassed, shy grin.

I smiled in amusement. "Well, that's what guys expect us to do for them," I said. "If I reverse the question and put it to myself, I would answer that I'd definitely go down on myself, but only if I was clean as well. Makes for an interesting discussion though, doesn't it?" I paused a moment. "You'd be amazed at some of the answers people give. Anyway, enough of that for now hey, so relax, where were we before my long question?"

He was eager to continue our chat and now assured me that he was really well endowed. Perhaps I didn't look believing or interested, because he now took my hand and placed it on the bulge in his trousers to prove it. I couldn't stop laughing. As if to prove his sincerity, he then offered me a job as his assistant, outlining the basic employment conditions – that he'd be entitled to sex at the office whenever he wanted it. I could fly to Durban and Johannesburg with him on his business trips, and I'd be assured of eight thousand rand per month take-home pay!

Do they really think we believe this crap? What a scream. I couldn't stop laughing, and we agreed to take a rain check for some other time!

Sometimes men make you laugh, sometimes they make you want to cry.

"Do you know about the virgin thing?" Amy once asked me. "Some people believe that having sex with a virgin will cure them of Aids or that it will prevent HIV infection."

"Good grief, I'm shocked," I answered, utterly amazed.

"Yeah, but it doesn't end there I'm afraid," Amy countered. "The virgin thing even extends as far as animals as well."

"I'm not with you," I said, somewhat confused.

"I'm told that people also have sex with animals to "cure" HIV. Animals as small as toy-poms or as large as donkeys and horses – I've even heard camels as well."

"Crikey Moses," I replied in disbelief. "You'd have to get a ladder or a table or something to stand on to have sex with an animal like that – and what if it kicked you?"

"It's simple really – the animal is first tied to a gate post or a fence or something and then its legs are also tied together."

"Well, I never . . ." I responded in horror. "I feel angry inside when I hear about stuff like this," I said taking a swig on my coffee.

"What you feeling angry about now, Rachael?" Christina piped in as she plonked down on the couch next to Amy.

"She's wound up about the virgin and sex with animals thing," Amy replied.

"Didn't you know about that?" Christina asked casually. "My, my – life sure is teaching you some lessons isn't it, Rachael?"

I shook my head. "I think I'll get another drink," I answered, "I need one after hearing shit like that."

"Reality sucks doesn't it, all the double standards," Christina offered evenly, opening a large packet of Simba crisps. "And people think what we do for a living is bad – we're flipping saints in comparison to some. Anyway, want some chips?" She held out the packet to Amy and then to myself.

"Thanks, but I'll get the whisky instead," I answered, standing up. "I'm a bit off eating right now."

Another booking with a policeman I remember well. It was about a quarter to eleven one night and I was busy collecting mugs and glasses for washing, when the front door bell went and Tammy let three guys in. I said good evening and went to the kitchen.

Tammy came to me some minutes later while I was washing up.

"Leave that now, Rachael, you're on a booking," she informed me. "Only one guy has booked and he's on a reduced rate."

"What does that mean?" I asked, turning from the sink and looking at her.

"He's a cop – Murder and Robbery. Sometimes cops get a reduced rate – could be a pal of Puff's, or maybe he owes the guy a favour."

"So, how much am I going to make then?" I asked, irritated.

"You'll get your normal fee, don't worry, just the agency will get less. The other two will wait for him and have a drink. And treat him real nice, okay? That's a personal message for you from Puff – real nice, Rachael."

"Okay. Has he got a gun on him?" I asked, remembering my other policeman from before.

"He's handed it in to me already – I'll give it back when you've finished."

He was a nice guy, that policeman: not much taller than myself, good looking, with a nice body; very clean and well spoken. I was extra careful and extra attentive during my time with him. Treat him real nice, Tammy had said. I wasn't sure what "real nice" meant, so I bent one of my rules for this client and allowed kissing – I didn't want any reports getting back to Puff that I hadn't done my job properly.

The policeman seemed quite satisfied and content with his money spent. He didn't ask to do anal or anything in particular; he seemed quite happy to leave it to me, enjoyed kissing and fondling me and never queried the use of the condom. He was a pretty intense guy, and a good lover.

Afterwards, I asked him about the strangler – was he still out there, uncaught? Yes.

The night I met with what I call the bum bloke, I thought Puff's eyes were going to pop out of their sockets from rage. I'd given this client the run-down on my rules prior to going into the cubicle lounge with him, one of which (as you are aware by now) was that I did not do anal. A lot of men request sex doggie style – I think it's a base instinct for them of combined lust, force, power and control – and I did not suspect the client would try anything else when he requested this position.

I sat on the toilet seat afterwards in the ladies' room, towel wrapped around me, while the client dressed and prepared to leave the agency – but Amy advised him to wait for the Manager, who wanted to speak to him. The client was a big man, at least six foot five; not overweight or overly muscular, but very powerfully built and strong.

I wasn't quite sure where the pain was centred most acutely; as I sat recovering on the toilet seat, it seemed to shoot up my back in continuous flashes for some time. I was afraid to touch my anus. When I saw the blood on the towel it set me off wailing again; and when I saw more blood on the toilet paper, and more, I wailed more and more.

Amy had been on desk duty at the time and was trying to comfort me, on bended knees next to the toilet, rubbing my arm soothingly. "I'm sorry, I didn't hear you shouting for help straight away – I'm sorry, Rachael, I'm so sorry." Poor girl – she got such a fright too.

"It's not your fault," I assured her between sobs.

The bum bloke said he didn't do it on purpose. Puff told him he'd better not show his face in the agency again, ever. Then he came back to talk to me in the ladies room and asked me if I'd like to lay a charge against the client. I declined.

Lay a charge? How could I do that? I thought. Firstly, I'm a sex-worker – I do this for the money. Who would believe me? I felt sure I didn't have any rights on this score. Secondly, I was a female – females are second-rate citizens anyway, with hardly any rights at all; the majority of rules governing our planet have been made by men. So isn't it odd then how sometimes one hears reference to "bowing to Lady Justice"!

I nursed a torn anus for about ten days after the bum bloke and was continuously in the bathroom with the jar of Vaseline. If I ever had a thing about not having my bum touched before, I can assure you, I'm worse now. Anyone who suffers from confusion about which is my vagina and which is my anus is in for trouble.

In time, I came to almost loathe James. I felt I almost hated him. I was exhausted from the ongoing inquisition he put me through. Whilst I understood his jealousy and possessiveness, understood he was entitled to know some of the sexual experiences I had while earning money in the racket, I felt his constant and relentless badgering for detailed information and descriptions drove a wedge between us. Eventually I didn't want him near me, I didn't want him touching me – and moved into the spare bedroom. I had to have some space, to be on my own a bit.

James and I were two people actually in love, but caught at the same time in financial problems and the emotional trauma of my escorting. In short, two people travelling the same road, but blinded by the agony of life – lost, and getting more lost. All we could do when Grace wasn't around was fight and break each other down.

Moving into the spare bedroom didn't solve the problem either; James was in my room continuously. Quite simply, I had to leave. If I had to do escorting work with its own unique stress, and add to that the stress James caused me about it – even though it was done to help us – then I reckoned I may as well do such work for myself only. So I needed to find my own little peace place, away from him.

I pulled out one of my favourite CDs and played a particular track – Liza Minnelli's "Cabaret": I could relate pretty well to Elsie in the song, and I liked her. Yes, I'd most definitely leave James; it seemed the only solution.

> "She wasn't what you'd call a blushing flower
> As a matter of fact, she rented by the hour
> The day she died the neighbours came to snicker . . .
> When I go, I'm going
> Like Elsie . . ."

I told Grace of my decision to leave James – she'd understood from the beginning that her secretarial work for us was temporary. Grace and Rosemary both became an enormous emotional support to me during this time.

Every bit of sadness in the world became magnified. I even started feeling an unfair anger towards the beggars and hungry kids on the street when they came up to me – asking for money for food, but probably to sniff glue instead. Perhaps your mother could go and sell her body for money like I do, I thought.

Chapter Thirteen
Rachael's Migration to Greener Pastures

I would prefer to report, now, that I migrated north, settled in a little green pasture and found a pot of gold at the end of the rainbow. I'd like to add that I met a prince, and that we lived happily ever after – and that this story ends right now, right here, with this one short paragraph.

However, I've been on a crash course in life for as long as I can remember and must therefore report a somewhat different tale.

I did, indeed, migrate north. I did indeed find a pasture – and the priest and the prostitute, so to speak, lived side by side! I did indeed find my prince. And I also did indeed almost get to "go", like my friend in the song, Elsie!

But I did not find a rainbow, nor a pot of gold.

There was to be no order to this particular part of my life – not a totally new phenomenon to my existence. However, as best I can, I'll try to relate in sequence the events that followed.

James and I'd agreed, when I moved in with him at the end of March 1996, that if I ever wanted to leave I'd have to pay my own way out. So I needed money and a suitable house to escort from, which had to be fairly close to the agency: I'd still be going to Puff's, plus doing my own out bookings. My residence would also have to be too far away for James to pitch up unexpectedly and stress me out – he'd be on the phone continuously anyway, which was stressful enough.

Finding a house with James checking on my every move would prove extremely difficult, so I contacted a friend, Ivor, who I'd met in 1992 at a braai. Ivor had always had a yen to be a private detective, and I felt sure he'd know how to go about house hunting with discretion. I gave him the run-down on my present situation, advising that the rent had to be reasonable, even though three bedrooms were a must. Money was a definite concern: Mary-Lou was at boarding school and there was the upkeep of Copper.

"Not a problem," he said, "I know exactly the kind of place you'll need. Must be private, don't want any neighbours knowing what's going on. And it'll have to be walled so your animals will be safe."

Ivor and I'd remained friends since we first met – not regular visiting friends, mostly telephone pals. I knew he found me attractive – that he made obvious – but he'd been in a long-term heterosexual relationship for years, so on the odd occasion when we'd see each other, nothing sexual came of it. He'd flirt with me a bit though, and I felt quite flattered by his decidedly charming, gentlemanly attentions. Women found Ivor extremely attractive, and he was quite open with me about his numerous other female conquests. He was a tough chap, Ivor; he'd often say, "I always get what I want" – and he meant it too.

A few years younger than me, Ivor had dashing but austere good looks: neatly trimmed blond hair with blue-grey eyes, long lashes, and a lovely smile with good white teeth. Standing at about six foot one, his carriage and attitude were extremely confident, sometimes to the point of making one feel uncomfortable or threatened, and he had a hearty laugh. His body seemed in good shape, with no extra weight, not overly muscular on the shoulders or arms – more a wiry strength. Personally, I thought he'd look superb in a top hat and tails, or perhaps even dressed in riding regalia astride a white Lipizzaner; and Ivor in navy whites, I reckon, could make most women's knees wobbly.

We agreed that I'd buy the newspaper every day and contact him on his private number if I found a house I was interested in, and he'd check it out for me.

I needed money first. As far back as I can remember, I've had to struggle for everything – so it came as a pleasant shock to be given an immediate loan by an elderly lady friend of mine, who came to visit me and felt concerned about the stress I was under with James. When I told her what I needed it for, just like that she agreed to lend me money to cover the house deposit, first month's rent, electricity and furniture removal.

Then with the same easy luck I found a house in the paper; the rental and location seemed to be what I needed. My gut, by now, was telling me this was all happening too easily – but perhaps for once, I thought, I should just accept good luck. I phoned Ivor, who wasted no time in checking the place out.

"Well," he reported back, "I couldn't get inside the actual house to have a look, but the nice lady neighbour gave me a run-down on it as she's visited there before. It seems perfect, you don't need to see it, just take it – don't mess around, sort out the papers before you lose the opportunity."

So I did. The landlord, a Mr Cupido, was most friendly and helpful. What a nice chap, I thought, as I paid the deposit and rent in advance, as required.

We've all at one time or another felt that distinct intuition that guides you without words, that feeling in your gut and heart that what you're proposing isn't going to work out exactly the way you think. I've personally disregarded this inner voice on several occasions in my life, and come short. This time, things had definitely come together far too easily for me, and my little inner voice was really nagging – I should've listened to it.

I'd already told James that I was leaving. When I said I'd found a house, but wouldn't divulge the location, getting away from him for even short periods of time became almost impossible – he tracked me everywhere; the cell phone never stopped ringing.

Managing to visit Rosemary one morning, I took a quick drive with her to see my new home. The moment I stopped my little bakkie outside the house, I knew it was wrong, totally wrong – the setting, everything; but it was too late. The money had been paid.

There was no wall around the front garden; the grass was totally neglected, brown and virtually dead. I knew I could fix the garden as I love working the soil, but no front wall was a problem indeed – no privacy, no enclosed front area for my animals. Next, the garage: it was separate from the house, the roll-down door was kept closed with a broom handle, the back garage door was hanging on its hinges, and worst of all, you needed a 4x4 to even drive in, there being a mountain of builders' rubble at the entrance.

One front window of the house had a smashed pane. There was no gate to the back garden. Two poles for a washing line, but no line as such. I could easily enough buy washing line, but no gate! How would my animals be safe? However, there was one blessing: the walls around the small back garden were about six foot high. The occupants of the house were not there at the time of our visit, so Rosemary and I could only look from the outside, and that was bad enough.

If you're perhaps feeling a little sorry for me by now, friendly reader, it's appreciated, because I was feeling pretty sorry for myself. If you're not, then I won't be surprised – after all, I'd brought it on myself, hadn't I? A man's idea of a perfect house differs drastically to a woman's. We made a quick dash back to Rosemary's place, and I phoned the nice landlord from there – at least I could have the conversation without fear of James catching me while I tried to sort matters out.

"Not a problem, lady," he said reassuringly. "Don't worry, everything will be fixed by the time you move in. We've some gates in stock and everything else will be sorted out – we'll even paint the inside of the house for you."

Okay. Well, now I needed a companion for General; he was used to company of his own kind, having had James's two dogs to play with. So I got Dancer – my Heinz 57 mixed-breed stray dustbin dog, with her little heart of gold. We were thrown together. The advert in the newspaper had been for two dogs, one of which I wanted; but when I met the lady at a local park, she'd brought the wrong dog. How do you tell a joyful dog looking for a home that she's the "wrong dog"?

I called her Dancer because she literally danced and bounced all over the place, all over me, licking my face and arms. Her energy was over-powering, but her heart was full of love and joy. General was man down the moment he set eyes on her and fell in love immediately; they had a marvellous romp on the grass. That was that. Dancer came home with us, but it took me about ten days to teach her some manners and to obey simple rules – one being that she wasn't allowed to keep walking across the coffee table!

The friendly landlord seemed to be experiencing some problems and asked me to change my furniture removal dates – three times. I obliged, and was finally informed I could move into my new home in early March, and that everything was fixed. He said he'd arrange to leave the keys with the nice lady neighbour, just pop next door and collect them when you move in, he advised. And don't worry about a thing.

The removal people collected my furniture and went ahead of me in their truck to unload; I told them to get the keys from the lady next door, who I'd spoken to. James stuck around like shit under a shoe throughout the packing, trying to get the house address from the truck driver – but I'd given strict instructions that this information was not to be divulged to James at any cost.

Cats need time to settle, and James very kindly agreed to look after Chocolate and Petal Pie for me until I'd unpacked in my new home (with hindsight, this turned out to be a wise decision).

By the time General, Dancer and I left James's house to move to our own greener pastures, it was getting dark already. My little car was loaded to capacity, my two pooches perched on top of our possessions in the back, full of excitement. Next to me on the passenger seat was my adored fern, handbag and whatever else could fit in, including the torch (another wise decision). On top of all this, I'd gently settled the ornate fabric Chinese dragon that my mother had bought in Hong Kong for me on one of her holidays.

We arrived at our new home after the sun had set, and I left General and Dancer in the car while I checked things out. The removal truck was gone. The front door wouldn't open; the car headlights showed the back garage door still hanging on its hinges and there was no back garden gate.

I navigated my way through the dark jungle of the back garden to the kitchen door, which stood open, and felt the wall for a light switch. No electricity either. Back to the car I went to fetch the torch.

The kindly lady neighbour arrived then with a friend – they'd heard my car. I thank them both, today, for their help that night. She hadn't been given any keys; in fact, there weren't any keys at all! By torchlight, back to the kitchen we went, and found the electrical box – which operated on pre-paid coupons. Luckily, there was enough electricity to last till morning, and I flicked the switch. Some light, at last!

Oh God, no.

I haven't exaggerated so far, so I won't now. In my entire life, in all the places I've lived in Africa, and there've been many, I've never, ever, seen the inside of a home covered in such utter filth! There were dried faeces stuck to the carpets; the sink was leaking water into the cupboard below, all over various pots and pans, and it stank from the rot. All my furniture and possessions were packed tightly into the little lounge-cum-dining room due to the disgusting state of the rest of the house.

With the outside kitchen light on and with the torch, I checked the back garden – which would be difficult to describe. Let's just narrow it down to rubbish, rubble, rotting dog food, other rotting things I've no words for, shovels full of old dog shit, holes in the ground and over-grown grass. It was a definite health hazard to General and Dancer – I wouldn't be able to let either of them into that area until I'd cleaned the place up.

The only way to get my belongings from my car into the house was by way of the main bedroom window, which faced the street; I stood outside and passed everything to the two kindly ladies through the open window. There was no cupboard in the front bedroom, just a hole cut in the filthy carpet where one had been or should've been. The place was infested with fleas, literally jumping onto us from the carpets. Later, after my two helpers had left, I found that the front door was in fact not locked, and by moving the furniture around I made a path so that at least General and Dancer could go into the front garden for wees and poohs – with their leads on.

Next surprise: a very pregnant, starving white cat perched herself on the kitchen counter. She was affectionate, friendly and lovable, rubbing against me and purring, and seemed hungry as hell. Poor thing, she tucked into dog food quite happily, and lapped up an entire bowl of milk; then off she went into the night again.

General, Dancer and I slept on the camping mattress on the lounge floor that first night, with everything piled around us; the back door remained unlocked, but closed.

What else can one do in despair and exhaustion, except try to sleep while the fleas jumped and fed? To them this was a dream come true, like a takeaway joint come to rest in their own home! The bugs bit, and the vast quantity of spiders – little, medium and big, green, black, brown – spidered away merrily. Even the dogs looked decidedly disgruntled and uncomfortable in their surroundings. Space was at a premium as the three of us tried to fit onto the thin little mattress – neither canine nor mistress wanting to walk on the floors!

Squashed together, I gave General and Dancer some lovies, and thought of a song I remembered from my school years, which I'd loved at the time: Lynn Anderson's "Rose Garden". The words sure were appropriate:

"I beg your pardon
I never promised you a rose garden
Along with the sunshine
There's gotta be a little rain sometime . . ."

Yes, well I hadn't been looking for a rose garden, I could make that in time myself. However, I hadn't counted on this much rain either! The moral of this story, I admonished myself before I fell asleep, is that next time I really want something in life, I jolly well better find it for my self! "Umm . . ." my inner gut voice jiggled in reminder, "I told you so." And you were right – again – I thought quietly in response, but it'll be okay; I'll sort it out in the morning.

I was up early: my canine kids needed to go out in the parched front garden for their ablutions, each time with their leads on. I needed coffee, tranquillisers – and smokes! And mummy cat needed feeding, for she was perched on the kitchen counter once again, waiting.

By nine o'clock I reckoned I'd catch the nice landlord and hit the cell phone. It was a Saturday.

"Oh, lady, I am sorry," Mr Cupido said ever so sweetly. "But no worry, I'll send two men today with the keys and paint, it won't take them long to finish a new coat on the inside for you, and I'll send someone straight away to clean the carpets. We'll have the back gate on by Monday latest. Please don't worry, everything will be sorted out."

The two painters arrived with the keys and paint, trays, brushes and rollers and proceeded amongst all the upheaval and filth.

The carpet cleaner arrived, took a look round the place and refused point blank to clean the carpets of a home in this condition! As he left he advised, "And by the way, I wouldn't let your dogs in that back yard if I was you, it's a health hazard."

My stomach couldn't cope with the rotting contents of the cupboard underneath the kitchen sink – there were strange, insidious moulds and growths I feel sure microbiologists would've found interesting. One of the painters emptied the lot into black plastic garbage bags, while I heaved and held the bags open for him. On top of the sink was a jug containing a quite large piece of some kind of meat, together with a rag, soaking in some kind of solution – the stench was appalling, and the sight wasn't just revolting, it was downright frightening. I poured off the liquid and dumped it into the garbage bag as well.

After the painters left, I put General and Dancer in the car and went in search of a park for them, where they could ferret around, run and play in hygienic conditions. Thankfully, we found one a few blocks from home, with lots of tall pine trees, and from that day on I walked my two dogs there at least three times in any twenty-four-hour period.

Then followed the cherry on the top! The kindly lady neighbour popped in to see how things were going; we had a cup of coffee together and a chat, and I thanked her again for all her help the previous evening. Well, surprise,

surprise – I now learned that her husband was a church elder! Talk about the priest and the prostitute living side by side! What a mess.

Thanks, Ivor, I thought disdainfully, some checking up you did! Just as well you never became a full-time private detective, hey.

Well, there's not much use whinging about all the unexpected rain, I thought after my next-door church elder's wife had left; the only cure for a filthy house that I know of is to get to scrubbing, and I'd best get on with it pretty pronto, otherwise I'd be broke. Cleaning house was a definite priority, but a sex-worker can't afford to have an idle fanny either!

I've scrubbed and cleaned more houses in my life than I care to remember, but this one would take more than a few days to sort out – and that meant, in short, loss of income for me. Just as Bert and Mary-Lou had encouraged me many times in our lives when things were hard, so now did my two canine kids hold me up. I saw love and encouragement in their little brown eyes and enthusiasm in their licks and tail wags.

"Come on, Mum," they were saying, "you can make it!"

So out came the disinfectants, detergents, buckets, brushes and vacuum. Garden hose connected and sprinkling the parched front lawn, hi-fi set up to keep me going, I started – with the best cleaning music I've ever heard, Van Morrison's "Cleaning Windows." It has a wonderful beat, just right to get you in the mood for scrubbing backwards and forwards or pushing the vacuum endlessly, the words real catchy:

> "What's my line?
> I'm happy cleaning windows
> Take my time
> I'll see you when my love grows
> Baby, don't let it slide
> I'm a working man in my prime
> Cleaning windows . . ."

Of course, I sang, "I'm a working *girl* in my prime" as I scrubbed and scrubbed, washed and lined drawers and cupboards with paper. Remember – bucket under kitchen sink to be continually emptied until the landlord could get the plumber in, and nothing, but nothing else to be allowed in that cupboard. I went through bottles and bottles of various germ killers.

I couldn't work at the agency until the house was hygienic for the "kids" and me, and I couldn't have home appointments either until the place was in an acceptable condition for clients. For about ten days I made zero money – five cleaning days, plus another five I couldn't work anyway, due to my periods.

After a week of waiting for another carpet cleaner to arrive, I myself found someone who'd do the job, and called in a plumber as well to fix the leaking sink. That made two unexpected bills I had to foot. Apart from the colour-ful and plentiful variety of spiders, I even found ticks crawling on the walls on occasion, so I kept the house as spotless as possible at all times, vacuum-ing and cleaning daily. The back yard took me two days to clear and I had to get a man in with a truck and trailer to remove the garbage – and pay that bill as well!

James, whilst not openly gloating at the predicament I'd gotten myself into, made it quite clear his priority in life was to get me to live with him again. Extremely helpful and considerate, he brought his weed-eater over to cut the overgrown dead grass in the back yard, as well as bottles of Jeyes Fluid to disinfect the entire area. Though I appreciated his assistance, I didn't appreciate the stress that came with it.

James now considered himself entitled to Sundays as his visiting days; he reckoned he could phone me whenever he liked, and he wanted his sex as well! I hadn't had to give him very explicit directions to my house and found that a bit odd – and he then admitted to me that he'd gone through my entire bedroom before I'd moved out of his house, found my papers concerning my new place of residence and even taken a drive out to see it, all the while pretending to myself and the driver of the furniture removals truck that he hadn't a clue where I was moving to! I was right peeved.

The first Sunday, I gave in to James on the sex bit to stop his nagging, relentless pleading – like a stuck record he was. After that, no more, fin-ished. Basically, I'd had enough of men and told him so; all I wanted was peace.

Right, so now he offers to pay me for sex – men and their contingency plans! And still I refused, still he nagged and offered payment, still I refused. I thanked James for continuing to take care of my two cats until our environ-ment was suitable for them, and I meant it. But I still refused the sex.

"Okay," James said, "I can wait." His whole ambition now was to be as helpful as possible, in order to win me back.

I bought a washing line, net curtaining and a couple of small floor rugs, and after a long and exhaustive slog was finally settled adequately in my little peace place. I had to use a round, rusty old tabletop as a back gate – yes, the landlord still hadn't put one on – propped up by whatever could keep it in place and fill in the gaps. At least General and Dancer could go into the back garden at last, though still under my watchful eye.

Bert's old single bed was in my main bedroom, which faced onto the street. The back bedroom became the "visitor's room" or den of iniquity, and the third small bedroom had Mary-Lou's bed and whatever else I couldn't fit in the rest of the tiny house.

Even after all the problems and hassle, this little home of mine gave me the strangest sense of inner peace I'd ever known until then – no incessant television to disturb my bandage of tranquillity; my thoughts seemed not to race so much; my heart beat quieter and with less emotional pain.

I distinctly remember lying in the bath one day, the steamy water full of foam bubbles, eating some yoghurt while the music played softly in the background – Bert's Neil Diamond double CD – feeling blissfully content, the gentle touch of God's sun shining soft yellow-orange on the frosted glass window. Heavenly – the quiet and calmness within and enveloping my being, the bathroom warm and freshly clean.

> "Did you ever read about a frog who dreamed of bein' a king
> And then became one . . .
> 'I am,' I said
> To no one there
> And no one heard at all
> Not even the chair
> 'I am,' I cried . . ."

Being alone wasn't actually lonely though; I had the comforting peace of General and Dancer, and I was happy – getting the chance to find me inside again. I was ready to start anew.

No arguments, no incessant questioning from James; he wasn't around to drill me because I'd eaten the occasional pie or had a cup of filter coffee somewhere in town. A few words of a verse I once read came to mind: "The loneliness of being together makes me long to be on my own." How brilliantly apt, I thought, and wished I'd written it down, with the author's name.

Anyway, how was Mary-Lou doing, I wondered as I lay back in the water, studying the white foam bubbles clinging to the warmed pink of my fingers. I hoped she liked her pretty birthday flowers – I'd gone to the florist and had a beautiful selection delivered to the hostel for her precious, special fifteenth celebration. I missed her so.

I walked the dogs regularly at the park, sometimes at four or five in the morning after working at the agency. On our nocturnal jaunts, the three of us wandered amongst the tall pine trees, the moon out, casting silent, dancing shadows. Peace, utter peace; General and Dancer having a wee, ferreting around, having fun – except on the odd occasion when a massive bulldog-faced canine would appear from nowhere and scare the shit out of us. He reckoned the park belonged to him!

Hot on our heels, slathering jowls flapping, he'd ferociously chase us back to the car, me just managing to get the door closed in time. Sniffing and growling angrily around our vehicle, he'd jump up with his enormous front paws against my door, panting heavily and slobbering sticky gob streaks on the window, whilst peering intently through the glass with a decidedly vicious glare; then proceed to chase us down the road with deafening barks when we drove off! After the first time, I kept my eyes peeled for him, and carried a plastic sjambok with me just in case we didn't get back to my little Nissan fast enough.

Ivor pitched up one afternoon to see how we were doing. I opened the front door to his knock and he stepped inside the lounge.

"Hey, the place looks good – you've really done it up nicely."

"Pity you didn't see what it looked like when we moved in," I answered a bit sarcastically.

"I'll just nip out to the car – bought you some groceries," he said with a charming smile.

Ivor returned with a couple of shopping bags and put them on the kitchen counter. "I'll leave them for you to unpack," he said casually. "I couldn't buy much – you know, the missus keeps tabs on how money's spent." He grinned, crossed to the couch and plonked down.

"Want some coffee?" I asked and he nodded. While I made for both of us, I gave him a rundown on the problems with the landlord.

"Just give me all the bills for the plumber, carpets and refuse removals. I'll sort him out," he said seriously.

I kept quiet. He lit up a Camel, paused for a puff and added convincingly, "Don't worry about it, I mean it, I'm not into the private detective stuff for nothing, you know. We guys have ways of making people cough up money."

I gave him an uncertain smile.

He patted the space on the couch next to him. "Now, come and sit next to me for a bit."

I did, taking my coffee and smokes and putting them down on the carpet.

Ivor pulled me across to sit on his lap. "What you need, woman, is some decent sex," he said, grinning broadly, and then gave me a hug.

"And I bet you reckon you're just the right guy to give it to me," I answered over his shoulder, then sat back to look at him.

"Yup," he said confidently, hands now under my T-shirt, caressing my breasts.

Maybe I could do with some TLC, I thought, after all the drama and stress of the house move. Even though I was in the sex industry, one couldn't exactly term what I had satisfying sex. And the one time I'd given in to James since I'd left him, well, I couldn't say that'd been enjoyable either, what with his nagging and pleading – rather harassed sex I'd describe that as. Besides, at least I could kiss Ivor – yes, it'd be a pleasant change from the rules of the racket.

Sitting on his lap as he fondled my breasts, I could feel the hardness in his trousers. "Okay," I replied, "how long can you stay?'

"About an hour or so, can't get home too much later than that, the other half will start wondering where I've been."

"All right, I'll run the bath for you then," I said.

"I showered this morning," he countered, finishing his mug of coffee.

"Well, I'm going to have a bath – I always bath first, just a quick one. I'll be about five minutes," I answered, getting off his lap. "If you like, you can go through to the back bedroom in the meantime, pull down the covers on the double bed and make yourself comfortable. Want another coffee?"

He nodded yes thanks, stood up and went to investigate the bedroom. I quickly got the bath water going and made another mug of coffee for each of us, putting his in the visitor's room on the bedside table, together with an ashtray. Ivor was busy undressing and I gave him a hanger from the cupboard for his shirt and trousers.

"You've decorated the room very tastefully," he said, nodding his approval as he hung his clothes up, seeming quite relaxed.

"Glad you like it," I answered, pretending not to notice his near-naked physique.

The bathroom was next to the visitor's room. The house was tiny and you could speak to each other in different rooms without having to shout.

"By the way," Ivor said, "I know what you women get up to in your business, so don't try any of your tricks on me."

"Like what?" I asked innocently from the bathroom.

"Like trying to get a guy to come as quickly as possible," Ivor replied.

I didn't answer – I was soaping hurriedly, all over.

"It won't work with me," he added in a louder voice. "I like to make sure a woman feels satisfied before I come, and I can keep an erection without a problem until I'm sure she's climaxed enough, a few times if necessary."

"Good," I answered from the bathroom, "a man after my own heart – just what I need."

"You're on," he laughed.

I put on a clean G-string, nothing else, took about three condoms out of my basket and went through to Ivor, who was lying relaxed on the double bed with only his underpants on. I put the condoms and my coffee down on the bedside table.

He glanced at the little wrappers disdainfully. "Oh, no, I'm not using one of those," he said taking off his watch and putting it down next to the ashtray.

"Ivor, let's look at this logically, okay? Firstly, I'm an escort, secondly, you live with a woman that you have sex with – it's just not fair on her. And thirdly, you also sleep with other women, you've told me as much." I took the dark blue velvet scrunchie from my long hair and added, "So what's it to be, condom or no sex?"

Ivor hesitated a moment. "Yeah, I suppose you're right. Okay, I'll wear the bloody thing," he relented, then picked up a condom, tore the wrapper and put it under the pillow.

That issue resolved satisfactorily, I climbed over him onto the bed and lay down, head on the pillow. He turned towards me and we looked at each other a few moments in realisation: the time had finally come to fulfil our mutual physical attraction.

Holding his gaze, I touched his chest lightly and ran my fingers down his stomach, to his navel. Ivor remained still a few moments, then slowly leaned towards me and kissed me gently on the mouth, then kissed my nipples, sat up and took my G-string off. Umm . . . he was hard, alright. Lifting my head in his one hand, his fingers through my hair, he eased his body onto mine, looked searchingly into my eyes and tenderly teased my lips with his own. Short, playful kisses at first, then long, intense, sensual kisses – it felt good to linger in the tantalising soft wetness of his mouth and my body was drawn to the warmth of our tender foreplay; I ached to feel his hardness inside me.

Passion was building: Ivor was sweating, drops falling from his forehead onto my face, onto my neck, and he kept wiping his brow on his arm or on the pillow.

"Reckon I'd better put the condom on," he said as he reached under the pillow.

I didn't offer any assistance, just watched as he pulled it down over his penis. He had a nice body, just as I'd thought, and he had a nice pecker too. I opened my legs and we watched together as he held his penis in one hand and guided it slowly into my wetness, then lay down on me gently again. Our mouths met, slow and searching, and our bodies responded, moving instinctively together. His sweat dripped on my face, in my hair, onto the pillow.

I reached down and held his hips still, moving rhythmically beneath him, moving for me, moving so I could feel his hardness in me better, the way I liked. He wanted to move with me, but I held his hips firmly and continued my own thrusting, my pelvis moving sensually, faster now, still faster, my womb aching in his hardness, more, more. Oh, it felt good – nearly there.

"Oh, fuck," Ivor suddenly gasped as he climaxed – he was just a bit too quick for me, I hadn't expected him to come so suddenly, especially considering that he'd said he could maintain an erection without a problem until I was satisfied. He lifted his weight off my chest, leaning on his elbows, wiping his sweat on the pillow. I kept quiet, waiting for his breathing to settle.

"Sorry about that," he said, as he eased himself off me, pulled the used condom from his penis and leant back against the wall. "But I can't help it if you turn me on," he murmured with an apologetic smile.

"That's okay," I answered and lay quietly next to him.

Ivor wiped his forehead again on his arm, then lit a Camel, took a drag on the smoke and had a relaxed, satisfied drink of his coffee. I sat up, leaning across him, had a few sips of my coffee as well, then lay down against him once more – the enticing sensation of skin against warm, damp skin.

Well, I thought to myself, I guess there's more than one way of blowing your own trumpet, and my time had come! I wasn't going to mention it to him, no, won't mention a thing about it – but decent sex is what he'd said I needed and would definitely get, and quite frankly, my womb was aching from wanting and I wasn't totally satisfied, so there was only one thing left to do. See if we could entice the pecker to erection again.

Without a word, Ivor still leaning against the wall having his smoke, I deliberately put my hand between my legs and started touching myself. He kept dead quiet and watched. I know exactly where to touch myself – years of pleasurable practise – and reached orgasm quite unselfconsciously, my eyes closed, lying against his damp skin. Well, that was it – the pecker was up, Ivor's smoke was out, another condom was on, and we were on again. This time I got what I wanted, which made for a most pleasant change – so we both got it twice.

After he left, I unpacked the groceries he'd bought for us. Food for the dogs, coffee, bread, margarine, baked beans. "Thanks, Ivor, my darling," I said out loud, "everything's appreciated, even the baked beans – the kids will have to eat those though."

One thing I can't eat is baked beans; I love the taste of them, but they don't love me – I only have to read the label on the can to start feeling inflated! But General and Dancer loved them and baked beans loved them, so happy ending.

After that first visit, Ivor would just pitch up in the afternoons whenever he had time in his busy schedule: he'd drive past, and if there was no other vehicle in front of the house he'd stop by. We had passionate, sweaty, safe sex, and by the third time, he managed to maintain his erection long enough for us to climax together – and then have more.

I gave him the receipts from the bills I'd paid so he could get my money back from the landlord – which he never managed to accomplish, despite his most confident assurances. We also agreed on a short specific message for me to leave on his answering service in case I should ever need help or have some emergency, so that he'd know to contact me immediately.

The house now being in an acceptable condition for clients, it was time to earn money. I had a most unusual large ceramic bowl, with a lid, in a rustic red-brown earth finish – this I called my "honey pot". I never touched the money when clients came to the house – simply told them to pop my fee under the lid of the pot on the kitchen counter.

Working from home pricked my conscience considerably due to my religious neighbours, and I therefore started working more from the agency. I'd joke to Puff that I needed to get back before my next-door deacon awoke from his nightly slumbers.

One evening they invited me over after they'd had their early dinner. I took some wine with me, and was rather surprised when I was invited into the main bedroom to sit on the double bed with my glass of red whilst the husband and wife partook of some brandy that was kept in the built-in cupboard.

"The other church elders, who visit regularly and unexpectedly, wouldn't be too pleased if they knew," my dear priest's wife told me as we sat on the bed together. "We take a drop sometimes with certain of our guests, but it's really more for medicinal purposes," she explained as she replaced the bottle of brandy in its hiding place, making sure the pile of her husband's shirts offered not the slightest glimpse of this minor indiscretion – whereafter we retired to the lounge for coffee and rusks.

I had to giggle about the brandy though, compared to the grave indiscretions going on in my home. I reckoned God had a sense of humour and a shot of brandy would probably go unpunished, and be treated with a gentle, forgiving smile instead!

Puff scared me a bit as we chatted one night at the agency, saying that if I was caught working from home as an escort, I could be in real hot water – in the shit, to be exact. You never knew if the client was a set-up; he could be a cop.

"Well," I said, taking a sip of my whisky as we sat talking in his office, "I think I know the business pretty well by now; I'm sure I'd know if the guy is a cop."

"Then how come, after all this time, you haven't picked up that I'm an ex-policeman?" Puff answered with a smile, taking a relaxed drag on his smoke and studying my reaction closely.

Youch! That one took me by surprise, in fact knocked the wind out of my sails – though I wasn't quite sure I believed him. Perhaps he was just trying to scare me.

"I know you were in security before this, but I didn't realise – I mean, I hadn't twigged you'd been a cop." I had another sip of my drink. "You're just trying to scare me, aren't you?" I said uncertainly.

"Rachael, we know each other well enough by now for you to realise that I don't scare my girls unnecessarily," he answered, putting out his smoke in the ashtray, "and that I'm pretty protective about the women who work here." He leaned back in his chair, hands clasped behind his head, and looked me in the eyes.

"I was in the police force for some years and I'm telling you now, as an ex-cop who's seen and knows quite a lot about life, to be careful working from home. You don't have to take my advice, but you need to become more aware. You're a lot safer working from the agency, I can assure you." He was quiet a few moments. "If you get caught doing sex work from home, I'm not sure whether my contacts will be able to bale you out of the shit."

Well, I'd never been in the tronk before – behind bars. And I didn't fancy that idea at all. So, what with the neighbour being a church deacon and the danger of being arrested, I worked more and more from the agency. I'd leave home with my tog bag and basket, dressed in my leggings, jersey and takkies, when I was sure the neighbours were either sound asleep, perhaps engaged in sexual pleasures themselves, or firmly planted in front of their TV sets.

The two little faces of General and Dancer would watch me through the bedroom window, the net curtain becoming worse for wear, each time I left home; and returning in the early hours of the morning, adorned in my abominable snowman gear, I'd see my two canines peering through the glass pane at mistress returned safely, at last! Then it was exercise time amongst the tall pine trees, then back home, bath and bed.

My Muslim gentleman, Mr Ebrahim, was a regular client at home; he never quibbled about my fee, just popped the cash notes under the lid of my honey pot. Said he'd have a wall built around the front garden for me – I looked forward to that and felt certain General and Dancer would appreciate it as well. The front lawn was looking nice and green by this stage, and trimmed; there really was a phenomenal difference to the garden and house compared to what I'd had to move in to.

One night, General nearly died – some kind of poisoning. I'd taken them out into the front garden for their ablutions, without their leads on. General couldn't resist the temptation for a quick dash around the neighbourhood for a few minutes, while Dancer and I waited outside for him. Then we went inside so that I could prepare for work at the agency later – I wasn't planning to go in too early that night.

At about nine-thirty, I noticed General didn't look right, and I picked him up and put him on my lap to check him over – and he went limp, completely limp. I put him down on the carpet again to see if he could sit or stand. He just fell over on his side, his eyes confused.

Oh God, *no*! I went into terrified shock and frenzy – I couldn't bear to lose General; we'd been through so much together, he was part of my heart. His gentle brown eyes were glassy, struggling to focus, silently asking me to help him, *Now, right now, Mum, it's bad.*

I didn't know where the SPCA was in my area. The only one I knew was in the southern suburbs, and if I remembered correctly they closed at five-thirty. I phoned James – yes, there was a vet in his area, I could meet him there.

The drive normally took me about forty minutes, but this time my little car had her engine put to the test! I sat Dancer on the floor on the passenger's side and wrapped General in a blanket on the seat next to me. While I drove like a maniac, I talked to him and stroked his head. I talked to Dancer too – she knew something was wrong, she was confused as well, but she knew not to jump up onto the front seat and disturb her mate during this critical time.

General's head lolled, his tongue hung out the corner of his little mouth; he was gasping, and his eyes rolling. I was terrified I wouldn't make it in time.

The vet was magnificent. It was poison of some kind, and he gave General all the necessary injections and medication to combat the unknown substance, after which the little fellow spent the night in animal hospital. General was home safe with me once more the next day – still a bit shaky, but his gentle eyes sparkled again and his little stumpy tail wagged twenty to the dozen to see Dancer.

One month and four days after moving into our "little house of green pastures", I woke to find an envelope left on my front door step. Guess what? I now learned that I had a new landlord; the nice one hadn't been paying the bond to the bank, the house was to be sold, my lease wasn't worth the paper it was written on and I should start looking for alternative accommodation!

Well, now I had to work extra hard to earn more money in order to find a new house, pay a new deposit and rent, pay for furniture removals – and still pay back my initial loan. Fuck, I'd just about had it! I reckoned I'd earned my right to tranquillisers by this stage.

Despite all the on-going hassles though, at the age of thirty-nine, I felt the best I ever had in my life – about myself as a woman, that is, and particularly about my body. Maybe it had something to do with finding peace, or with unconditional love – which dogs give freely from their little hearts, asking only for food, kindness and love in return.

I remember only three appointments from this time – so here they are . . .

The first was a man in at least his early seventies who arrived in a very expensive 4x4: well spoken, well dressed, a true gent; he'd never had a blow-job in his life, and that was his desire, he told me during our telephone conversation – quite happy to have it with a condom. Put the fee in the honey pot, then waited with the patience of a saint while I retrieved General from down the road. He'd managed to get through the front door like greased lightning, to visit every garden in the neighbourhood and pee on a bush in each!

As always, I was bathed and ready. The gentleman declined to bath and I showed him through to the visitor's room; the dogs I always put in my bedroom. I'd furnished the den of iniquity very nicely and the linen was changed after each client. The lighting was soft, and there were always clean towels, bubbles for the bath and baby oil and body lotion for a massage.

And underneath the bed, unbeknown to the clients, lay my little cast-iron frying pan, in case I should ever need it.

The client had politely declined any assistance with undressing and when I went back into the bedroom, wearing my G-string only, I understood why – he had an artificial leg below the knee. He'd been wearing long trousers and I hadn't noticed any difficulty in his walking or movement when he'd arrived.

Anyway, if I said I'd spent more than fifteen minutes in the bedroom with this man it would be a lie; I never got round to the blow job, but that wasn't deliberate on my part – when I caressed his penis and scrotum while he lay naked on the double bed, he ejaculated after a short time. I think what he'd enjoyed and appreciated was the attention and open, gentle affection shown to his masculinity – his genitals – without it being some kind of sin or something dirty. I didn't find his prosthesis sexually off-putting in any way.

The second appointment I recall was a double booking – two guys, another girl in her early twenties from the agency and me. It was to be a seven-hour booking, which meant good money. However, and for what reason I'll never know , it turned into five hours and we were fetched earlier than planned by the driver.

Since arrival at the house, I'd noticed the young girl didn't like the guy she was with, though I personally couldn't find fault with him as a client. He'd specifically chosen this lady out of several at the agency and she'd seemed quite happy to do the booking with him. Puff had checked the two clients out first, particularly because it was to be such a long booking, and they'd paid rather a hefty sum of money.

Both men had good manners, spoke nicely, dressed smartly and had decent behaviour – and drove a pretty magic BMW. The house was scrupulously clean, the furnishings tasteful and we were treated respectfully, but whenever the one man danced with the young girl or tried to touch her in any way she pushed him aside.

After about two hours of dancing and drinks in the lounge, we all retired, two by two, to our separate bedrooms, whereupon I did my duty. Remembering my mess-ups in the very early days of my escorting – one hour one fuck! – I wasn't keen on the seven hours, seven fucks part if that was required. However, the dancing had taken up about two hours and the alcohol consumed by my client I reckoned would hopefully cut things down a bit further. Thankfully I only had to perform the procedure twice, after I'd given him a body massage.

In the meantime, unbeknown to my client and I, the other client had phoned the agency and complained that he wasn't getting what he'd paid so much money for, and wanted the fee back.

I'd needed to use the bathroom, which was down the passage near the bedroom which the other couple were using, and found it rather strange that not only was the bedroom door open, but the bedside lights were on and the two of them were quite clearly fully dressed, turned with their backs to each other, pretending to sleep.

To cut a long story short, I didn't get paid when the young lady and I arrived back at the agency around five thirty in the morning, after being collected by Henry from the clients' house in Stellenbosch – only about two nights later, when the matter had been investigated to Puff's satisfaction. Unfortunately, the young girl was fined, and fortunately I was not. It'd been a long booking and I'd done what I was supposed to do – I was battling enough at the time for financial survival, without having to face a fine as well.

The third was an agency booking as well. I would rate this, together with the bum bloke, joint third place in my worst experiences as a sex-worker.

There were some nights you'd go to work and have no physical interest in men or making a booking, even though you needed the money – it's difficult to explain this feeling. This particular evening I was in that kind of mood, having a good natter at the bar with some of the girls and one of the drivers, when I was called to the desk and told I'd been booked for an hour.

The client turned out to be a drop-dead gorgeous, one hundred and five-kilogram hunk of masculinity, in peak physical condition: a professional deep-sea diver, who I hadn't even noticed arrive at the agency. This white man left me feeling destroyed, that's the only way I can explain how I felt afterwards.

He followed none of my rules, except – and this is the only due I can give him – he did not try anal on me. I had my back towards him, closing the lounge door after we'd showered, when he suddenly grabbed me from behind, throwing me onto the bed. From that moment, I was literally fighting for my life, fighting him off, trying to breathe, trying to move. He was all over me, pinning me down – no condom – under his powerful body. Absolutely no match against his physical strength, I felt almost suffocated; despairingly helpless as his brute force seemed to crush me like an eggshell. Forget my frying pan, I couldn't even lean over the bed to get to my basket.

After that night, I spent a day and a half in bed just resting my pulverised body. I could hardly move without wincing; my legs and arms felt deeply bruised, the dull ache seemed to permeate through my being, past bone and marrow, to some lonely place inside. It was another valuable lesson for me: never turn your back to a client, not even to close the door. And never judge a book by its cover. You only learn one way: the hard way.

While I lay in bed at home with General and Dancer, my little comforters, snuggled next to me, the cell phone rang. It was a schoolteacher. He wanted to be given a hiding; said he was so tired of disciplining children and wanted some discipline himself – that was his thrill.

I'd had many phone calls from men wanting discipline, but had declined them all. Firstly, it's not my thing to beat someone with a belt or whip or whatever, let alone in order to arouse them. Some of them want to be beaten till they see blood; only then can they ejaculate. Secondly, and without meaning to be derogatory about how other people get their sexual fulfilment – different strokes for different folks, and everyone has a right to their own personal sexual desires – but I'd have fallen about the place laughing if I'd ever had to beat someone to satisfy them sexually. I just found it funny – of course, I didn't tell the client that. I just said I didn't do it.

"You don't sound too well," the teacher said into the phone. "Are you ill, have you got the 'flu?"

"Yes," I answered. I wasn't ill; my body and mind were just trying to recover from the pounding meted out by the deep-sea diver. I cut the call, switched off the cell. I needed complete peace and quiet.

There is a distinct difference between allowing a penis to be put inside my body and having one thrust inside me by brute force; even during consensual prostitution, when money is paid for my sexual favours, I still consider my body to be a gift from me to a man. I did not give my body to the deep-sea diver; he took and abused me.

I remembered my job-interview rape experience when I was seventeen – and how I'd developed mysterious but excruciating pain in my kidneys for months afterwards. Despite numerous medical tests, which showed no kidney problems, and copious medication, the pain continued unabated. My elderly boss, Mr Goldman, together with a group of his friends cured me though. After a ten-minute session of healing hands, placed on different parts of my body, humming and strange praying, I went home – and never had the pain again. It was gone, just like that.

Rapists not only injure and steal from their victims physically; they take and crush a part of the soul as well. The physical body has the ability to heal, but the damaged soul wavers, unseen, searching for completeness of self.

Nevertheless, back to work I had to go. The incident with the diver had really shaken me up, and I was feeling on edge.

Only two of us girls had our own vehicles; we were required to park at the back of the agency building so that clients had sufficient space at the front. The back parking area had no lighting; there were two enormous rubber trees with long, dangly branches, and a surrounding wall of about eight foot – so parking at the back was sometimes quite eerie, the only light coming from the street lamps out front, the shadows from the rubber trees doing a spooky dance even in a gentle breeze.

It'd been another long night; Puff had left early and Tammy was in charge. My car was the only one at the back at closing time on this particular night – or I should rather say, early morning. It'd been a quiet night business-wise, and we said weary goodbyes at the front door; Tammy and the other two girls who remained were getting a lift home with the driver, whose car was parked at the front. When it's go-home time, it's go-home time, and the driver's car left within a minute or so, at speed.

I felt uneasy as I walked down the dim driveway towards my little LDV, wearing my abominable snowman gear with my takkies on as usual, so my footsteps made no sound on the tar; tog bag in my right hand, basket in my left. Sure, I'd walked this driveway many times before, but . . . I stopped dead still. Yes, there was someone at the driver's door of my car.

I lowered my tog bag to the ground slowly, and with my right hand I quietly reached into my basket and gripped the handle of my frying pan in its plastic wrapper. My vehicle was parked facing the wall. There was no way of jumping the wall; whoever it was would have to get past me, whichever way he, she, they ran around my car.

I think my heart left my body temporarily; I don't remember breathing. I walked quietly, as if in a trance, towards the back of my bakkie's canopy. Oh, fuck – he, she, they'd seen me, the shadow had ducked. Where? Blind panic – fuck, I didn't know where, and I wasn't going to wait to find out!

Doing the only thing I could think of, I hit the back of my little car so fucking hard with my frying pan it sounded like a fucking gunshot in the stillness of the morning! The shadow started running, around my car and up the driveway towards the street. I dropped my basket.

Anger, fear, adrenaline – I don't know what drove me. I ran after the shadow, beating my little cast-iron frying pan against the wall like a fucking lunatic, clattering and banging with all my might, till I saw it make a frenzied dash across the street. No voice though, just this pathetic, warbling, irate croak coming from my throat. Oh fuck! I was finished. My nerves had had it. I looked at the white plastic packet covering the pan – that looked a bit fucked too! The frying pan still seemed to have the same shape though.

I walked back to my car, my legs like jelly, picked up my tog bag and my basket, then put them down again to open the driver's door – which seemed to take ages to accomplish; I was shaking so much it took me a while to find the right key on the key-ring. I wasn't going to waste further time trying to find my pills to calm me down – he, she, they might come back. I sat with the frying pan on my lap and lit a smoke. I'd beat the fucker – he, she, them, it – and burn them too with my smoke if they came back.

Starting the engine, I reversed shabbily, trembling and panicky, collided with the big black garbage bin, nearly knocking it over, and drove up the driveway in a series of coughs and farts, so to speak – my legs and feet were so wobbly I couldn't seem to get the natural accelerator-clutch footwork going, even though I'd been driving since eighteen.

Once on the street, with the lights and robots and buildings and normality, I felt my breathing start to ease, but I was still shaking like a leaf and drove home at a snail's pace. Was I glad to see those two little faces of my canines peering through my bedroom window! They bounded through the front door when I opened it and Dancer gave me a million licks, General jumping up and down like a bouncing ball. I gave them both a big love and let them run in the front garden while I sat on the step and had a smoke, still shaky and nervous.

General – under my watchful eye – ran around in a few neighbouring front gardens and peed on a few bushes along the way. And what's a bit of dog's pee on a bush, when you come to think about it? What's dog pee compared to a fucking car mugger? Dancer always did her business on our front lawn, within sight of me; only on our walks in the park would she run off adventurously with General.

"Sorry, kids," I said out loud, but quietly in the morning stillness when General got back from emptying his bladder, "but there's no park walk tonight. I'll have a fucking heart attack if we meet with the bulldog now!" And then added, somewhat quieter, "Sorry, Mr Deacon as well, about the language, but . . . well, that's it."

Then I got my tog bag and basket out of the car and we went inside. I double-checked every window and lock in the house. Forget the bath. Coffee, plenty of Brozam tranquillisers, my dogs and my bed were what I needed.

I was up and about by ten in the morning to take General and Dancer for their walk amongst the tall pine trees. Better have a look at the damage to the back of the car, I thought. Oh, shit. Yes, it could definitely do with some panel beating, but that'd have to wait. Come to think of it, what's wrong with having a frying pan dent in the back of your car anyway? Nothing, absolutely nothing – besides, it'd probably saved my life. So I'd keep it, no panel beating. I rather liked it: like a reminder of a dear friend, my car could wear it with pride. The frying pan was okay, apart from some scratches – I only needed to replace the white plastic packet.

Despite all the above, it was good to feel the sun on my back while I walked with the kids in the park.

From then on, either Puff, one of the girls or one of the drivers would walk with me to my car when I went home in the mornings.

Then I missed another four nights of income due to giving myself a fanny wash at the agency one evening. Feeling the need to freshen up, I stupidly put liquid hand soap from the basin in the ladies room straight onto my flannel. Almost immediately, it felt as though I was on fire! I knew they bought the stuff cheap – but holy moly, did the soap have bleach in it or what? Should've used it for cleaning my house!

Okay, so I still had the fight in me to find another place, make the bucks to move etc. We'd get through. Money was improving – the best single-day earnings I'd had was eight hundred and forty rand.

My faithful canines did quite a lot of enthusiastic people-dog hip-dancing with me as I sang and thumped along gaily with Bob Marley:

"Don't worry about a thing
'Cos every little thing
Gonna be alright
Rise up this morning
Smile with the rising sun
Three little birds . . ."

Yup, General, Dancer and me – that made three.

Chapter Fourteen
My Red Indian Man

*A*nd so he came to me, towards the end of April 1997 – my knight in his white charger – a tank of a Ford F 510 truck – thanking me for my kindness to a weary traveller.

For one night he stopped my silent, inner dying and this time there weren't any rules. His brown eyes soaked up my pain, found the tiny crack in my heart, releasing my stifled, scared love – starting with a drop, turning into a stream and then a tumultuous river. We loved unashamedly. A complete bonding of our minds and souls – a journey homeward to our essence within, as flowing water seeks the stillness and tranquillity of a mountain pool.

We soared together on the cloth of deep, purple velvet. And when he left, my knight, he lay within my heart, cocooned in his own gentleness forever, nurturing my soul for what was to come.

And when I close my eyes I can still see your slow smile – my Red Indian Man.

It was a Friday night, or rather, a Saturday morning – about two-thirty a.m. I'd been on a two-hour cell phone booking to one of the posher hotels in the city, on the foreshore. A smart business executive from Bloemfontein, about thirty-four years old, blond, overweight bordering on flabby; said he was single, with oodles of boodle, a couple of houses, couple of smart cars. Had a healthy dose of the "I love myself" attitude and thoroughly enjoyed the room service procedure, which he was obviously accustomed to.

"Ah, yes," he said, stepping back as he opened the door to the early morning knock of the waiter carrying the tray with the bottle of champagne on ice. "Over there, please," he said with a theatrical sweep of the arm, gesturing in the direction of the glass coffee table. He then made a little show of studying the bill, saying, "I trust the champagne is well chilled." With a quick and confident stroke of the pen, he signed the room-service slip, moved to the door and ushered the man out with a quieter, dismissive "Thank you".

A good bottle of champagne, it was – Here XVII – and definitely a pretty costly hotel room, considering the tasteful décor. He was easy and pleasant to converse with while we sipped on our chilled champagne, and I tried to look composed and relaxed in the high-backed, plush chair facing him; but

215

his overbearing, superior attitude reigned throughout our pre-sexual activities. Said he'd never met a lady in this business before who he could have an intelligent conversation with, and offered me a job in Bloemfontein as his assistant, at a salary of nine thousand rand per month. (Lucky me, my value was certainly on the increase!)

During what he considered to be romantic sexual moments, which commenced after about half a glass of the champagne – and which to me were simply paid time – he professed that he could fall in love with me.

I enjoyed the conversation, sweetheart, but please, don't feed me that bull-shit, I thought, as I dutifully endured the remainder of the two-hour booking. Nine thousand rand a month – and I suppose that includes a poke as and when it suits you, anyway and anywhere you like, on the desk, on the boardroom table, on the floor, in your fancy chair. Oh, give me strength – another hot-shot businessman with his fantasy to poke-'n-stroke at the office!

Anyway, nothing lost. It'd been a pleasant booking without much stress, I'd made good money and I'd had my shower before I left for home. At least he didn't want his cum in my hair and he didn't ladle me from head to toe with baby oil. Give him his due – he'd been very respectful about the use of condoms. He'd got his rocks off twice and looked as though he could use some sleep if he was to be his impressive self to the world in the morning. We said goodbye at the door, the white hotel bath-sheet wrapped around his waist.

It had been raining steadily but gently during my twenty-five-kilometre trip back to the northern suburbs, and I stopped at the petrol station about two blocks from home, pulling into a well-lit parking bay. Awareness of one's surroundings is a necessity in the racket and especially at this time of the morning. As I locked my driver's door, I noticed the white truck parked next to my little Nissan bakkie. The driver was slumped forward with his head on the steering wheel.

I'll get my smokes and if he's still like this just now, I thought, I'll have to take a look and see if he's all right. Can't just leave someone all night like that – maybe he's sick, more likely drunk – it's raining as well, better take a look.

The petrol station night attendant was used to my nocturnal smoke purchases and said hello; he gave me my cigarettes and change and I went back to my car, unlocked the passenger door and dropped my smokes on the seat.

Then I walked around to the driver's side of the white truck. The window was open and the occupant didn't make any movement – the rain running down his black leather jacket, his hair tied back in a ponytail.

I poked him in the shoulder. "Hello, are you okay?" Zero reaction. Do it harder, I thought. "Hello, hello, are you all right?"

The head lifted from the steering wheel, dazed, not sure where the voice was coming from; he turned slowly and focused.

"Hi."

"I came to get some smokes and saw you sitting here. Are you okay?" I pulled my brown hat down a bit further, to keep the rain off my face.

"I feel like hell," he said – and then came the slow smile.

"Been partying? Don't feel so good?" I asked.

"Something like that – worked late and went for a few at the pub. Where am I?"

"At a petrol station in Bellville. Where're you supposed to be?"

"Am I near the hospital turn-off?"

"Depends – which hospital?" I said.

"The big one, umm . . ."

"Tygerberg, you mean?"

"Yeah, that's it."

"Then the answer's no."

"Oh, shit, must've taken a wrong turn. Fuck." Slow smile. Hand to the eyes, rubbing.

"Well, can you drive home? It's raining and you're getting wet sitting here with the window open."

Slumps forward again on the steering; laugh, cough. "Can I drive? Can horses fly?"

He looked nice. Perhaps I should use the word "safe" instead. My gut feeling wasn't sending me any wild "this one's a bit dicey" messages. And he certainly appeared to be sufficiently inebriated, to the extent that I felt he'd probably pass out before trying any mean stuff.

"Look, I don't know you at all, and I'm not in the habit of picking up strange men at petrol stations, but if you feel you're too drunk to drive I live a few blocks from here, and I'm on my way home. If you want to sleep over till you feel better in the morning, that'll be okay," I said, then added, "There are three bedrooms and I'm not living with anyone, so it won't be a problem, but I do have two dogs."

"I don't live with anyone either," – mumbled into the steering. "You're not going to steal my money while I sleep though, are you?" Laugh. Cough.

"No, I'm not going to steal your money – but if you'd rather sit here that's your choice."

Looking up again, slow pissed smile, focusing. "Okay, well if you really don't mind. I could do with some proper kip."

"All right, I think you should leave your car here and come with me. I'll lock it for you and you can fetch it in the morning. I'll just move my stuff off the front seat – I'll be back now."

I opened the canopy of my car and put my basket in the back, unlocked

217

my passenger door and then went back to help him. He sort of fell out of the truck when I opened his door, and I put his arm around my shoulder and guided him to my vehicle, opened the door and manoeuvred him onto the tiny front seat. He didn't look too comfortable, but it probably didn't bother him, in his condition.

"I'm just going to lock your car," I said, "back in a moment."

I got back with his keys and was just about to get behind the steering when he looked up and said, "I need my books and cell."

"Books – where are they?"

"On the seat I think – a couple of books and the cell phone." Head slumped to the side again, conversation over.

So I went back to the white truck, checked the windows again, gathered together the exercise books on the seat – three of them, now a bit damp – and found the cell, luckily in a cell pouch as it was also wet.

Fuck, I thought, what the hell must the petrol attendant think? Too bad – it'll keep him busy till the end of his shift. Can't imagine what he'll tell his family tomorrow about this white woman – comes to buy smokes and drives off with some drunk in her car!

It was a short drive home without conversation, the body next to me resting, head against the window, oblivious to the world, eyes closed, asleep, gone. I left him in my car while I let General and Dancer out for a very quick wee, and then put them in my bedroom and closed the door while I got him into the house, otherwise they'd make a racket. General would go mad barking at this strange, drunk guy staggering into our spare bedroom, and the last thing I needed at this time of the morning was to wake my kind, priestly neighbours from their slumbers.

I went back to my car and, with some whispering and more prodding, woke my guest a second time and guided him, arm about my shoulders, as we stumbled up the step and through the front door. I headed him towards the spare bedroom where he collapsed on the double bed. After locking the front door, I went back to make him more comfortable – sat him up, took off his wet jacket and pulled back the duvet as best I could. He immediately lay down again, so I put his legs up on the bed and tried to take his shoes off.

He sat up himself then and said, "That's okay, I can take them off," and I let him try. With some difficulty he accomplished this, dropping his shoes and socks on the floor haphazardly, and fell back on the bed, rubbing his face.

"Would you like some coffee?" I asked.

"Yeah, I could do with some. Thanks."

I put the kettle on and thought I'd better introduce the dogs to him. They were scratching frantically on my bedroom door by this stage, and their patience wouldn't last much longer. Both of them would start barking soon if

I didn't satisfy their curiosity. Dancer, being slightly larger and heavier than General (though General was hyperactive), would literally dance all over the place with her energy and enthusiasm, and could be a shock to anyone's system.

"Here goes," I thought, as I opened my bedroom door for them to greet my stranger. They bounded to the spare bedroom and leapt onto the bed, bouncing around with great enthusiasm all over the mattress and our intoxicated guest, licking his face, pushing their noses in his neck and hair, and just having a jolly good hello sniff.

He rolled onto his stomach, covering his head with his arms. "Okay, okay, guys, hello." Then he stretched out an arm and gave General and Dancer each a rub and a pat, in turn.

"I'm sorry about the onslaught," I said, "but they get very excited."

"Don't hassle, it's all right. I like animals."

"I'll get the coffee," I said, and went back to the kitchen. General and Dancer followed after a few seconds, and I gave them their treat of chocolate – a square each – which I kept in the fridge door. When I went back with the coffee, he was fast asleep, so I left it on the bedside table, put an ashtray next to the coffee, took out a clean towel from the linen cupboard and put it on the pillow next to him. Best just leave him alone to sleep it off, I thought.

I unpacked my basket per the normal procedure, the music on softly, ran my bath for the Nymphae Soak, then lay back in the water with a smoke and my coffee on the side of the bath.

What is it about him? I asked myself. Definitely the brown eyes – even pissed, there's something about his eyes. And the smile, oh God! Not bad at all, considering where you found him. Quite a chance to take though – but the dogs will go mad if he tries anything funny. Better leave the loo light on, I thought, and the bedside light, otherwise he won't know where he's going – might land up peeing in the cupboard or something.

Even after my long soak in the tub there was still no movement from my stranger and he hadn't touched his coffee, so I left him and went to bed, General and Dancer in their usual places: General at my feet, Dancer at my side. It took me a while to fall asleep and even then, tired as I was, I was up again at five past seven in the morning. I hadn't slept properly – with him in the next room, I felt a bit odd – and quietly went to his door to see how my drunken guest was doing. He was sound asleep on his side, his hair now loose on the pillow.

I sat down next to him, shook him gently by the arm and said, "I'm just taking the dogs for a quick walk, okay?" – which I had to repeat before there was any response.

"What time is it?"

"Quarter to eight," I answered.

"Oh, God – can I just sleep a bit longer?"

"Yes, you sleep as long as you like. I thought I'd better tell you though, in case you wake up and find yourself in a locked house, and not even know where you are."

"Okay." And that was that. Back to sleep.

I picked up my purse, locked the house, General and Dancer bounced into the car and I took them to the park for their usual walk – a much shorter outing this time, ten minutes tops; I was worried about my drunken guest. Making a quick stop at the corner shop, I picked up half a dozen fresh rolls and a small tin of coffee, and was back home by eight twenty-five. He was still asleep, so I decided to let him be and just go about my ordinary chores – tidy the kitchen a bit, hand-wash my underwear, make my bed.

At about nine, his cell phone started ringing, and only after the call came through a second time did I hear him answer in a sleepy voice. I made him a cup of coffee with two sugars and took it through to the room. He was leaning on one elbow, staring out of the window with a definite night-after look.

As I walked in he said, "Do you know where my books are?"

"Yes," I nodded, putting his coffee down on the bedside table. "I'll fetch them for you." I retrieved his books from the lounge and handed them to him without a word.

"Thanks. It's work, I need a number," he said. As he started flipping through one of the books, he paused, looked up at me and said, "Sorry – I didn't mean to order you around like that, asking you to fetch my books for me."

I said it was okay, I hadn't thought about it in that way at all, and left him in peace while he made his phone call. I pottered about the kitchen and put out the garbage. When he'd finished, I heard him go to the bathroom, have a pee and flush the loo, run water into the basin and then go back to the room.

I stood in the doorway of the bedroom while he lit a smoke and had a sip of his coffee. A deep drag on the Camel – and then the slow smile, brushing his long, wavy brown hair away from his face. "You haven't told me your name yet."

"Margaret," I answered.

"Hello, Margaret, I'm Vincent." He leaned forward, holding out his hand. We shook hands and laughed a bit self-consciously. I leaned against the frame of the door.

"Okay, Vincent – how are you feeling this morning?" I asked.

"Somewhat under the weather and my mouth feels like the bottom of a birdcage. Thanks for letting me sleep over. You were taking quite a chance, doing that."

"I know, but I couldn't just leave you there at the garage, soaking wet and drunk."

"So what do you do for a living, Margaret?" he asked.

"I'm an escort," I answered, looking him straight in the eye.

No shock, no wild surprise – just the slow smile, and another drag on the smoke. "So – would Margaret be your real name, or your work name?" he said with a gently amused look on his face.

"My working name's Rachael," I answered, offering no further enlightenment.

"Now, that's what I call interesting," he said, patting the mattress, indicating that I sit next to him – which I did, a bit nervously, but without further hesitation. And we chatted, just chatted, on the same wavelength, so easy – about anything and everything, myself, him, whatever, and the dogs jumped on the bed and he played with them, had some more coffee and another smoke.

It turned out that he didn't live in Cape Town, was down on business from Natal for a few days and was staying with friends, which was why he'd got lost the previous evening in his inebriated state and taken the wrong turn-off. Vincent was seven years younger than I was.

"Crikey! I'd better be going," he said, suddenly remembering to check his watch. "I must get to the bank, and its ten fifteen already."

"Well, I think the banks close at eleven on a Saturday – I don't think you'll make it," I replied.

"I have to," he said earnestly. "Where's the nearest Nedbank from here? And I'd like your 'phone number – I'll give you a call later, if that's okay."

Things were rushed now, extremely rushed. He dressed quickly and while he washed his face, I told him he could use the blue toothbrush. I locked up the house and he said a quick goodbye to General and Dancer, giving them each a gentle tousle on the head. Then he threw on his jacket, his hair hanging loosely about his shoulders, collected his books, cell and smokes together, on with the one-way shades, and it was time to go. We made a quick dash in my car to where we'd left his truck at the garage, and on the way I gave him directions to the bank and he made a note of my telephone numbers, home and cell.

"Thanks again." And giving me a quick kiss on the cheek, he was gone.

I sat quietly in my car for a few minutes, recovering, my heart pounding. You beautiful man – my Red Indian Man, I said to myself. No, he wasn't Indian and he wasn't a Native American Indian. Maybe it was the long hair that made me think of him as that. But I bet you won't phone. I'll call you later – how many times have I heard that before?

Vincent was everything I'd always thought I wouldn't like in a man. For one thing, his hair and dress sense was different. Short-back-and-sides was the male hairstyle I'd always seemed to prefer, perhaps because that's what I'd grown up with and was used to. Office-style suit and tie I'd also seemed to be drawn to, or socks with garters so they didn't fall down when wearing safari suits or khakis. Polished shoes. Male authority. Vincent surprised and awakened buried senses within me. He seemed without need to impress, content being just himself, not more than me as woman.

I could see his slow smile, his brown eyes, hand brushing the long hair away from his face. I could never hide anything from those eyes. And suddenly I knew why I'd wanted the piece of rich, thick, sumptuous, deep, deep purple velvet – so, so soft. I'd found it in a fabric warehouse in March when I was looking for curtain material; I'd stood transfixed by its simple beauty, my hand stroking the soft velvet. I fell in love with a piece of cloth! Curtains or no curtains, I had to have it.

This is made for loving – the kind that only happens once in a lifetime, I'd thought, mesmerised. I'd bought enough to cover a double bed, taken it home like a prized possession and washed it carefully by hand. And when it was dry I'd folded the cloth, throwing in handfuls of potpourri, and stored it, wrapped in tissue paper, in my linen cupboard. Maybe one day . . .

If you come back to me, I'll love you on the deep purple velvet.

My mind was in a daze as I drove home and said hello to my two faithful bouncers, eagerly awaiting my return. I cleaned the whole house, for once vacuuming with energy, took the dogs for another walk and eventually fell asleep around five in the afternoon with the help of some Brozam. My mind was so alert and I was so keyed up – for what? To see those eyes and that slow smile again.

I was awake again by six-thirty that evening. General and Dancer needed their dinner and always looked forward to noodle night – they wolfed theirs down, and then checked each other's bowls, just to make sure not a single morsel had been forgotten! I poured myself a whisky, double on the rocks, and soaked in the bath, the cell phone next to me on top of the loo. I had shampoo on my hair when it rang.

"Hello," I answered.

"Hi, it's me. Are you busy?"

"Sorry, I didn't catch your name. Could you repeat it, please?" I answered deliberately. Let's not show too much enthusiasm here.

"Vincent," he replied. "You know."

"Oh, Vincent – sorry, I didn't recognise your voice. Yes, I am busy – if you call sitting in the bath busy. I didn't think you'd phone."

"I said I would, so here I am. Would it be all right to see you tonight – say about nine, if that's not too late?"

"I'd like that," I answered.

"Um, you don't have any appointments? I'm not messing up your time?"

"No, I'll reserve the evening just for you."

"Okay, I'll fetch you at nine – then it's your choice as to what you'd like us to do for the evening."

That's a dangerous thing to say, I thought, but said, "Okay, see you at nine."

"Whoopee!" I yelled out loud when we'd said goodbye.

General and Dancer bounced into the bathroom at the sound of my excited voice. The two dogs put their paws up on the edge of the bath, their tails wagging like mad, trying to figure out the cause of this sudden happiness radiating from Mistress in the bath, her hair full of shampoo bubbles.

"Know what, kids?" I said to them. "My Red Indian Man's coming to visit us just now. Isn't that just great! So I'd better move my backside, hey?"

Dancer always gave my wet arms plenty of licks while I bathed, and she did so now, with great enthusiasm. I gave them both healthy, happy pats on their rumps, rinsed off the shampoo, put on the conditioner, shaved legs etc. etc. in a mad, disorganised, ecstatic flurry. Oh, boy, was I nervous! I had to put the kohl pencil and mascara on really slowly – the jitters were setting in.

When I opened the door to his knock, Vincent took both my hands in his, stepped inside and gave me a long look, and then a long, slow hug. I closed the door and there followed a couple of seconds of silly self-conscious silence; then we laughed and he said, "Give us another hug – it's good to see you again." And I could feel him trembling too.

We didn't go out for dinner. Instead, we decided to get a pizza and eat it in the park while the dogs ran around and had fun. We took a couple of beers and a bottle of wine along to go with our takeaway meal – and remembered to pick up some fresh cream on the way, just in case we felt like an Irish coffee later. We strolled around the park and Vincent held my hand a bit. More than that, we were afraid to touch each other.

Under the protective strength of the pine trees, we sat together: my Red Indian Man and me, on the green wooden park bench, the light from the street lamps filtering down, the shadows of the outstretched arms of the tall pines dancing gracefully about us in the gentle evening breeze. The night was blissfully quiet. Without touching him I felt Vincent's peace, I recognised it – it was as mine: the peace of togetherness.

General and Dancer had had an extra-long walk that night, and they were happy and tired, their tummies having had a treat of pizza as well. Luckily, we weren't interrupted and chased by the enormous bulldog – perhaps he was home with his owners. When we got back to my little house at about eleven thirty, General and Dancer both fell fast asleep on my bed in no time at all. I put some music on, got the kettle going for the Irish coffee and whipped up half the container of fresh cream.

Vincent was stretched out, relaxed, on my two-seater, navy-blue couch, his feet dangling over the end. After a thoughtful silence, he said hesitantly, "May I stay over again with you tonight?"

"You sure you want to?" I answered. "You know what I do for a living."

"I'm well aware of what you do, and it doesn't bother me. I'd like to stay with you tonight – if you feel okay about it."

"In that case, shall I run a bath for you, and while I soak you in bubbles – lots of bubbles – you can have your Irish."

"Sounds perfect," he said, and smiled – his slow smile.

"All right, while I run the bath you pour the cream on the coffee – deal?" Did I sound controlled here? My mind raced – I felt so terribly and suddenly nervous, I could feel my hands shaking. I didn't think a Brozam would help in this instance and I didn't want to mess up by feeling so self-conscious, maybe make a botch and spill the Irish or something. Don't mess up, I told myself, not with Vincent, he's too special.

"You bet," Vincent replied happily, "I'll finish making the coffee." Sitting up, he put his pack of Camels from his shirt pocket onto the side table, then hung his black leather jacket over the back of the kitchen bar stool.

Hurriedly leaving the two unfinished Irishes on the kitchen counter, the whipped cream next to the glasses in a bowl with a spoon, I vanished to the bathroom, turned on the hot and cold water and poured a more than generous amount of lavender foam under the hot tap. Perhaps a bit too much bubbles, I thought, nervously swishing the water around in the tub as I squatted at the side of the bath, my back to the door.

A strange thing happened then, and I've never forgotten it. I hadn't noticed or heard him come into the bathroom, but without a sound, Vincent suddenly put both his arms around my waist, bending down behind me, and gave me a slow hug, his body against mine. Then he walked out of the bathroom again without uttering a word. I carried on topping up the water – a good couple of inches of bubbles!

He reappeared with the Irish coffees, putting them carefully on the side of the bath, and I noticed with a smile that he hadn't allowed the cream to mix with the coffee – knew his stuff obviously: pour the cream over the back of a spoon so that the dark and light layers remain separate.

I turned around, put my hand to his lips and began – slowly and without speaking – undressing him. Vincent stood still and just watched me as I unbuttoned his shirt and touched his skin, his nipples, with my fingers, and rested my hand on the rise and fall of his smooth chest – felt his heartbeat, as my own; then he raised his fingers slowly to caress my face and still my trembling, as his mouth gently sought and covered mine.

224

Our self-consciousness gone, replaced now by a shared wish to remember these gestures of our intimacy, he sensuously traced his fingers down my neck and across my shoulders, while I undid his belt and unzipped his jeans. I wanted to remember every part of his body, so naked, so innocently and beautifully aroused before me. I knelt and kissed the delicate skin below his navel, and held the warmth of his nearness to my face a while, as I imprinted him into my memory forever. I never wanted to forget him or his brown eyes, oh God – or the smell of his long, wavy hair.

I put him in the bath, knelt down by the side and washed him all over – Vincent lay back, his hair floating in the water, full of bubbles, as my fingers played with his hard nipples beneath the foam, across his chest, down his stomach, down to his exquisite aroused manliness. He closed his eyes.

My Red Indian Man, you are everything I've ever wanted and more, I thought. And my heart ached in the ecstasy of his nearness and for a moment I felt like crying.

"What music's playing now?" I asked softly.

His eyes opened slowly. "I don't know."

"Yes, you do." I kept quiet.

Eyes closed again, he answered after a few seconds' silence, "Vangelis."

I thought, why are you so perfect? But said, "Have some of your coffee before it gets cold," and lifted it gently to his mouth. "You've got a white moustache now."

He just smiled, eyes closed.

I wiped the cream from his lip with my flannel and put his coffee on the side of the bath. "I'm just going to pull the bed down for you, and then I'll have a bath."

I took the purple velvet from its tissue wrapping and shook it gently across the double bed in the spare room; it sank down, covering the sheet, nestled against the mattress and waited amidst the petals – waited for its promised loving.

I dried him, and he went through to the bedroom while I had my bath in his bubbles.

It was time.

Trembling, skin on skin, warm, hot, mouth on mouth, lips, wet, mouth and skin, his hair, my hair, our hair, bodies joined, wanting, searching, aching, finding. We did for each other, with each other, together, again, half asleep, awake again, more.

The cloth damp beneath us, I snuggled against Vincent's warm back under the duvet, in the cool of God's morning as it dawned over our Mountain, and drifted with him in his peace – loving his each new gentle breath, loving his loose hair on the pillow, loving his sleeping eyelids. Just lost in the love and tranquillity of his unconscious beauty, like that of a rose – for it knows not its own splendour, nor the emotion that fills the human heart of one whose eyes should rest upon its silent, sculpted perfection. There could never be anything or anyone that could remove my sense of completeness as I lay next to Vincent that morning.

I pulled back the duvet in the early light of the precious day, and gazed at the flawlessness of his body, at the sensuousness of his penis – yes, there is immeasurable beauty in the male human form, if one would but see it. We are so exquisitely crafted by an Unseen Hand.

My eyes traced the outline of his masculine chest, his soft nipples a delicate brown on the muscles of his breastbone, his flat belly dipping toward his light brown pubic hair. He was with me because he could love me for who I was – I felt his honesty in the ease and contentment with which he slept peacefully beside me; and I could love him without fear, without rules, without loss of my self.

I longed to touch him, and leaned across his sleeping, tranquil nearness to awaken the desire within his soul once more – to feel the way he so naturally and unselfconsciously gave of himself; my face between his legs, my mouth and tongue in the warmth of his manliness, aching to pleasure him. He stirred and offered himself willingly, and as he released his aroused passion within me, I climaxed with him in the moment of our fulfilment of life – of shared love of the joined soul.

And the purple velvet was the only witness to our loving – creased into soft folds of exhausted after love, the petals crushed beneath us.

When he left that day, I pulled the phone out and switched off the cell, took my coffee and lay on the soft folds of purple. Buried my face in them, wiped my quiet tears on them, smelled his smell in the fabric, breathed him into me. Breathed his gentle, passionate strength from the cloth and caressed it, and re-lived us, over and over. And the wetness came back in my aching for his exquisite beauty, and I touched myself because that's what he would have wanted.

Then as the sun went down, I gathered the soft velvet in my arms, took it outside and burned it. I would never allow anyone else to lie on it with me – only one man could ever love me so unconditionally on our cloth.

And as I watched the purple fabric flare, burn, and then turn to ashes, my heart quietly sent him a message: Wherever you may be, Vincent, no matter who else you may love, wherever life may take you on your journey in the quest for Nirvana – I am attached to you.

That night, when I returned to my own single bed to sleep with General and Dancer, I found a folded sheet of white paper under my pillow. It contained several banknotes, a considerable amount. On the page of white, he'd written the following:

"Take good care of yourself, Rachael Margaret. I hope the enclosed will be of help until I can get back to Cape Town to be with you again. Yours, Vincent."

I lay in the peace of the darkness with General and Dancer as my mind searched for a song for him, my beautiful lover. Lynn Anderson's recording of "You Needed Me":

> ". . . I sold my soul
> You bought it back for me
> And held me up and gave me dignity . . .
> You held my hand when it was cold
> When I was lost, you took me home
> You gave me hope when I was at the end . . ."

I never asked Vincent for a telephone number. I had no way of contacting him.

From being with James, I understood the enormous emotional turmoil that my occupation as a sex-worker could place on a relationship. I needed my beautiful lover to be free of such emotional anguish – I had to remain content in the short, but exquisitely perfect love I'd known with and in him.

Chapter Fifteen
Rachael Bites the Dust

*P*erhaps it was the intensity of being loved by Vincent, maybe it was accumulating stress wearing me down without my really noticing it; I don't know. Perhaps I didn't have inside me what it actually takes, because I became a bit unhinged, for want of a better word. My sense of justice really went up the spout – despite needing every cent I could make, I now had an agency booking where I gave a client my entire share of his money back! Here's the story.

It was a night not long after my Red Indian Man; he was still inside me as warm as toast – inside my heart that is, inside my being. It was about two-fifteen in the morning. General and Dancer were at home, on my single bed as I knew they'd be, peering out from behind the lace curtains every now and then, waiting for me to get home so we could go for a park walk in the early hours.

There were only four of us girls left that particular morning, the others having gone home already. Tammy was on desk duty; Lindy and Diane were there as well, and myself, the oldest.

A nice fellow came in and paid for an hour. Tammy asked him to choose the lady he'd like to spend the hour with, and he chose me. The clock started ticking at two-thirty, so I'd be finished by three-thirty; then it was half an hour to pay time and going home. I knew the girls were tired and bored – business had been slow that night; it was always more tiring and difficult trying to stay awake when there were no clients to keep the adrenaline flowing. It was my first and only booking that evening – which made the incident even worse.

The guy was nice-looking, well-mannered, quietly spoken, in his late forties, from a conservative country town and very shy. I could see he was keen despite his nervousness. Sometimes it takes guys weeks, even months, to pluck up the courage to go to an agency and book a lady. Even then they're still very nervous, but hopeful that things will work out the way they'd fantasised, or seen on blue movies.

I undressed my gentleman client in my normal manner, put a towel around him and took him off to shower with me, which usually worked wonders. After I'd washed his chest and stomach, I rubbed myself against his lathered back while I washed his bum and scrotum. Then I washed his penis, rhythmically moving up and down his soapy hardness with my hands. I reckoned he'd be okay once we got back to the room, as his nervousness seemed to ease – he was getting into the swing of things, washing my breasts, stomach and bum with extreme care and gentleness.

Back in the room he had a few hasty swigs of his drink before lying down on the bed as I instructed. He seemed nervous again, and when I took his towel off I noticed his penis had gone soft. I said I'd give him a massage, he should just relax. He voiced concern about the time, and I assured him there was plenty left – I always placed my watch on the table where I could easily see it. We could hear the chattering of the three girls' voices from the front desk as the reception clock quietly ticked the hour up. Sometimes they'd laugh loudly or bang on the desk, or turn the music up.

I massaged his shoulders, back, buttocks and legs with my body lotion, and then sat naked on his back while I put my hand down and between his legs and caressed his scrotum. Yup, he was getting hard again. I rubbed myself slowly and rhythmically against his skin just above his bum, and he raised his backside so that I could reach his penis. That was when the first round of banging started on the door.

"Rachael!" Bang, bang, bang. "Five minutes left!" the voice yelled. It was Lindy.

My client raised his shoulders and said, "Is that the time already, only five minutes left?"

Plenty of giggling could be heard coming from the girls.

"No," I answered, "there's plenty of time left, don't worry about it, I'm keeping an eye on my watch."

He reached for his drink on the table, had a couple of sips, then put the tall glass down again. "Sorry, it's um, it's, you know . . ."

He'd gone soft again. I assured him it was okay, he needn't worry about it, and he lay down again. I started rubbing my body and breasts up and down his back, my dark nipples lingering sensuously against the cheeks of his bum. My arms were around his waist, feeling his chest, his stomach and then down, down to his pubic hair, gently, teasingly across his penis. He turned on his side, and I lay behind him as I continued to caress his manhood, his hand reaching backwards to touch the skin of my body and breasts. His penis grew hard in my hand and I ran my tongue across his skin, down his side to his waist. As he turned towards me – his nervousness now eased, wanting full-frontal bodily contact – the second round of banging started on the door. My stomach turned anxiously.

"Rachael!" Bang, bang, bang on the door. "Five minutes to time!" It was Diane's turn. More giggles followed from the front desk, then a shriek of laughter.

I knew what was happening here. Granny was known for giving a man the one-hour he'd paid for; the girls knew I'd only walk out of the room before time if the guy was satisfied, wanted to go home early and didn't want to talk the remaining time away. None of them had been booked since my client had started with me and I knew they were tired, just wanted to go home – but still, it was my booking, my income. I was feeling a bit agitated by their behaviour; it was starting to get to me and was distressing to my client as well – which meant I had to work harder each time to ease his nervousness.

"Why do they keep banging on the door?" he asked me anxiously, taking another gulp of his drink.

"I'm sorry about that," I answered. "They just want to get home, they're tired – but they shouldn't be disturbing us, I know. I really apologise. Take no notice – I'm keeping an eye on the time for us, myself. It's okay, really."

I pushed him down gently on the bed on his back, rubbing my clitoris against his thigh, while I sucked and nibbled his nipples to hardness. He put his one hand in my hair as he pushed my head down towards his stomach, his other hand caressing my breast. His body stiffened and his legs opened as I played with his penis, and ran the tip of my tongue around the delicate skin above his pubic hair. He was hard again, and wanting – good, now I could get the condom on; he would climax quickly and my job would be completed.

"Rachael. Time's up!" yelled Tammy now, as she, third in line, banged on the hollow wooden door.

We both froze. I looked at my watch and sat up; there was definitely still time left. I was mad inside, really angry, I couldn't work in this manner – and my client, who was already nervous when he'd arrived, wasn't coping with the interruptions. I'd had enough – not of him, of the girls; I felt they were being inconsiderate. He was a nice guy. I'd just have to give him his money back, or he might complain to Puff that I hadn't done my job properly, that he hadn't been satisfied.

I sat on the side of the bed next to him. "I sincerely apologise for all the interruptions," I said, "but I can't work like this. It's not your fault. I'm going to give you my share of your money back."

Standing up, I took his clothes off the hanger and put them on the bed. "Do exactly as I say," I said, looking him in the eyes. "Put your clothes on and wait here for me. When I get back with your money, walk straight out the door and out of the agency without saying a word to anyone. Okay?"

He nodded, picking up his underpants. I tied a towel around myself and said again, "Remember – out the door when I get back, not a word to anyone."

I walked through to the reception in my towel, something I'd never done before. Tammy, Lindy and Diane were sitting at the front desk, Tammy with her feet up on the counter. They looked surprised and went quiet. I knew my pay would be waiting on the desk for me, and it was.

"Is that my money?" I asked, pointing at the notes. Tammy nodded. I leaned forward, picked up the cash, turned round without another word, and walked straight back to the mini-lounge. My client was dressed and waiting and I handed him the notes.

"Sorry it's not all of it," I said, putting the money into his hand, "but I can only give you my share back, the rest the agency keeps."

Tammy pounded into the cubicle behind me, and I stood between her and my client. She had a pretty mean temper when provoked – I'd seen her give a client the mop handle in his back when he peed all over the bed and the carpets – plus she was a karate expert. I'd no idea what could happen next, but I'd just have to stand my ground.

"What do you think you're doing, just taking your money?" she yelled at me viciously.

"You've been interrupting my booking and I can't work properly. Under the circumstances, I've decided to give this gentleman his money back," I said firmly. The man stood behind me, not knowing what to do.

"You've no right to give the client his money back," she screamed at me, waving her arms hysterically. "Do you know who I am? Don't make me mad, Rachael, I'm warning you – you know I've got a black belt." Her face was red and she was breathing heavily from anger and exasperation.

"The money I gave back to the client is my share, the agency has the rest already, and I can do as I please with my own money," I said, facing her squarely. I paused for a second, then said quietly but assertively, "Now, if you'd please step aside, Tammy, this gentleman would like to go home."

I motioned to him to go, and as he passed me I said, "Remember – not a word." Tammy moved aside as he walked past.

All hell broke loose then. Tammy did her nut – how dare I speak to her like that? How dare I give a client his money back? I'd better watch it or she'd knock my block off. I was strangely calm as I faced her – I knew I was no match for her physically, but I wasn't intending to have any fisticuffs anyway.

"If you don't mind, Tammy, I'd like to go home now myself; I think we'd all like to go home – it's been a long night. So, if you'd kindly leave, I'd like to get dressed." I turned away from her, and reached for my G-string in my basket. Tammy stormed off and continued yelling at the reception. Lindy and Diane were quiet – no more giggling.

I didn't expect anyone to walk with me to my car that morning – no one was talking, so no one offered as they usually did, but I was too tired and fed up to care much about a mugger by that stage – I reckoned I'd bust his neck this time if it happened.

After driving home slowly, I took General and Dancer for a walk in the park – the torch with me, and the sjambok as usual, in case the selfish enormous bulldog pounded across the grass to chase us back to our car. The moon hung suspended in half-light in the dark sky as we walked amongst the trees, and the street lights shone faintly on the jungle gym and swings as General and Dancer ran around sniffing at tufts of grass and under bushes.

I must be nuts, I thought, giving a client his money back – and remembered James yelling at me during one of our many arguments, "You don't even make a good whore – can't even manage to support yourself properly doing that!"

We all say things we don't mean when we're upset or angry. I knew James hadn't meant it at the time, but the truth hurts – and at this rate, he certainly had a good point! Well, I'd just have to toughen up more if we were to survive and make enough money for a deposit on another house, plus removals again. Really, I mused, a sex-worker giving a man his money back – that takes the cake!

I called the dogs and they followed me to the car, jumping onto the front seat. When we got home I put on the music first as usual, made some coffee, unpacked my basket and then relaxed in the bath – peace and quiet, what bliss! I was sure Puff would be on the phone sometime before tomorrow night though. General, Dancer and I fell into bed and I lay in the early morning quiet of their comfort, with my thoughts. There were much happier things to think about before going to sleep than the drama with Tammy – like having a holiday!

General lay at my feet in his own world of dreams, curled up, head tucked in against his chest. I scratched Dancer's tummy and she stretched out on her back as I told her all about the fun we were going to have together one day, when things would be easier, when we'd found another house and were making regular money.

Yes, a real holiday it would be! Ten whole days at the seaside somewhere – I wouldn't have to make the bed or wash dishes or cook, and the two of them would have lots and lots of fun till they flopped down to sleep, exhausted. I'd beach myself on a deckchair, put on my sunglasses, ladle myself with suntan lotion, plonk my trusty, favourite hat on my head and lie back, watching the clouds drift by. The waiter would bring me one of those blue cocktails with a cherry on a stick, a little paper umbrella poking out the top . . . Yummy, I'd drink blue cocktails till the cows came home, and General and Dancer would run on the beach, chasing sand crabs till the sun set, then romp in the evening surf and get all wet and salty, shaking their coats all over the place with joy.

And Madam Sophie and Pablo the parrot could come along as well. Pablo could sit in the palm tree and toss dates down, or nibble off a coconut or two, depending on which kind of palm happened to be there, and mumble away the day in French. Hopefully, his timing would be right by then, so he wouldn't say anything rude to upset the waiter bringing the blue cocktails!

Sophie and I could laze around some, then swim in the sea as the sun set in the coolness of the evening, like a couple of playful dolphins; then I could retire to bed and fantasise some more about My Red Indian Man.

I'd already ridden with him on his mustang, my arms about his waist, as we galloped together across the prairie. This time we'd be at the ocean though. Me at his side as he hoisted the sails of his ship in the chill evening wind – I'd see his shirt billow in the warmth of a morning breeze, run my fingers through his hair, stand beside him with a pride that swelled my heart and released my soul to fly with the eagle on the currents of love. We'd ride the white crest of the wave, together, on his ship of courage – plunge into the terrifying, gaping blackness of turbulent, uncertain seas, feel the hardship, the aching pain, soothed only by the reservoir of hope; live the excitement, hold the joy, taste the glory and bask in it, as the seal basks with her pups upon the rocks under God's sun. Ooh yes, we'd definitely be having a holiday!

Dancer's brown eyes were closed by now, and General hadn't stirred once throughout my happy pre-sleep ramblings. The early morning light filtered through the curtains; it was time to get some shut-eye. Hopefully I'd make some money during the day from a cell phone booking, I thought as I swallowed a Brozam with the last of my coffee. Maybe one day I could eventually quit the pills as well – but the proper way, with help; now certainly wasn't the right time. Pulling the duvet up under my chin, I fell asleep with my two dear canine friends as the new day started for the rest of the world.

Puff phoned at a little before twelve that day. I gave him my side of the story.

"We'll have to discuss it further in my office, Rachael. I'll be at the agency tomorrow night," he said. He didn't sound angry – Puff never jumped to conclusions without getting all the facts first, that was one of his strong points; I reckoned he was a pretty fair man, Puff.

My regular Muslim client, Mr Ebrahim, called me and arrived for his two-hour appointment at one thirty. General and Dancer were out of his way in my bedroom, the spare room readied and waiting with clean linen and fresh, cold orange juice, which he liked, on the bedside table. I'd had my usual double whisky on the rocks, with a tranquilliser to calm my nerves, before he arrived.

Though scrupulously clean, Mr Ebrahim always bathed before we went through to the spare bedroom, as did I. He knew those rules of mine by that stage. I'd run his bath, wash him in the tub, then bathe myself while he relaxed on the double bed for a few minutes and had his orange juice.

A good lover, he treated me with the utmost respect and I was genuinely fond of him – but not in love with him. His face was clean-shaven; he shaved his pubic hair as well, and his finger- and toe-nails were impeccably cut and clean. Over time, I'd relaxed my rules with him a bit; his standard of bodily hygiene gave me no reason to not allow kissing. His body was in good form and he had a nice, strong erection. Generally, sex with him was far nicer and more normal then other bookings. We kissed sensuously, and I allowed him to stimulate me between my legs with his fingers. On a few occasions, I also allowed him to perform oral sex on me. He had, however, become increasingly persistent in trying to persuade me to have intercourse without a condom, and to try anal sex. These two things I wouldn't give in on though, and he had to remain content with the relaxing of my initial rules.

I always massaged him – he preferred baby oil to body crème, and openly voiced erotic thoughts when I sat on his back against the oiled smoothness of his creamy skin. We tried various sexual positions as well, and by the time he left the den of iniquity and went home to his wife, I was as much satisfied as he was.

A wealthy and very charming man, I felt sure his wife could only be a nice, good woman. I'd no idea why he would seek sexual pleasure elsewhere, but in this game – the racket – his money was good, pretty much unstressed income for me.

Back at the agency that night, I made only one booking between ten and four in the morning. Tammy wasn't there. The following night at the agency, I was called in to Puff's office.

"Tammy's off for a few days," Puff said, after I'd finished explaining matters in detail. "I'll discuss it with her next week and get back to you."

Business was slow that night as well; a couple of the girls went home just after midnight. Puff poured himself a double Red Heart rum and coke with plenty of ice, lit up a Chesterfield and put his feet up on the reception counter, ready to answer the phone. The volume on the hi-fi was turned up, and he watched, easy and relaxed, as his remaining ladies had a bit of fun to lighten the boredom of waiting for clients. These jolly let-your-hair-down times always left the girls with sparking eyes and a healthy, happy glow and were good for morale. Puff understood our need for a bit of innocent, clean entertainment.

Our high-heeled shoes discarded haphazardly around the room, we danced in a circle, one at a time in the middle, or in lines with Cindy as leader. The numbers certainly warmed us up, got us singing together, and gave us plenty of silly giggles as we pranced about, show-acting into the imaginary microphone and raising our already short skirts. I loved these times with the girls.

Sometimes we'd get the broom or the mop out and hold it between two of us, while the others tried in turn to limbo their way underneath it. Cindy was best at this – with all her experience in varied sexual positions, she'd no problem bending her supple back into a low arch, or her knees, as she danced to the rhythm and thump of the music.

"Mustang Sally" or "In The Midnight Hour" by the Commitments were real deep-throated, pounding numbers. Then there was Whitney Houston:

> "And when the night falls
> Loneliness calls
> Oh, I wanna dance with somebody
> I wanna feel the heat with somebody
> Yeah, I wanna dance with somebody
> With somebody who loves me . . ."

"Ladies!" yelled Puff, as he leaned back to turn down the volume on the hi-fi. "Car lights, shoes on please!"

We grabbed our heels, someone would vanish with the mop or broom to the kitchen, and we'd take up our sedentary poses on the couches once again, trying to hide our flustered appearances and rapid breathing.

As the doorbell rang outside the security gate, Cindy pulled down her snug-fitting blouse over her ample bosom, checked her lipstick and whispered to me, "Hey, Granny, got any sarnies left? I'm starving after all that exercise!"

My bookings weren't enough. It was crucial I find more clients if General, Dancer and I were going to find enough money to move house.

Round about this time in my chaotic life, when I really needed the income, I had to turn down a cell phone booking. The call came through during the day.

"I want a woman with really long, red nails," the gentleman caller advised. "I want to be scratched down my back till your nails leave marks on my skin," he said. "How long are your nails?"

"Actually, they're short," I answered. "I deliberately keep them short for hygienic reasons in this business."

"Well then, can't you go and have long nails put on for me?" he asked.

"I suppose that could be done," I said, "but it'll be an additional cost over and above my normal fee." I paused a moment – I wasn't the right escort for this guy. "Apart from that," I continued, "I don't think I'm the kind of woman who could scratch your back with my nails until you're left with marks."

"But I love it, I need it," he groaned into the phone on the other end of the line. "I love the pain of it, that's how I come, how I shoot my load," my caller crooned with persuasive enthusiasm and a deep sigh of pleasure. "How much extra for the nails? But they must be red – I'll pay. What's your price?"

"Really, thank you for phoning," I answered, "but I think you should call another lady. There're plenty of sex-workers advertised in the paper that could help with your particular request, who've already got long nails. Sorry, I've got to go, goodbye." I hit the cancel button on the mobile – the only way to end calls you weren't going to do.

On a Friday early in May, around midday, I noticed what seemed to be an insect bite on my left arm when I took my jersey off before the Nymphae Soak – the size of a pinhead and black, the area around it was pink, inflamed and slightly painful. I squeezed it carefully, and the tiny black head popped out – must be a tick or a spider, I thought, as I disinfected it after my bath, covering it with a plaster. Lord knows, there'd been plenty of fleas, spiders and ticks when we'd moved in, and although I checked the dogs and cleaned the house every day, I still noticed ticks about, and the small, colourful spiders – didn't take them long at all to spin their webs and feel at home.

Well, I thought, I'd have to be careful at work that night – any sores or broken skin are areas of possible infection for a sex-worker – and took plasters and disinfectant to the agency that night in my basket. The swelling and pain had increased.

I didn't make any money that evening: business was exceptionally quiet, even though the agency doors remained open until four in the morning. Amy was on night-desk duty.

And I never did get back to be with the girls again at the agency, to make another booking; neither did I get the chance to entertain another client in my little house.

By the Sunday night I wasn't feeling well at all, and knew I shouldn't be driving a vehicle. I left a message for Puff on the Monday and he took me to a clinic in the early hours of Tuesday morning, where I had a tetanus injection and opted for an anti-biotic cream for treatment of the bite and surrounding tissue. Apparently, a penicillin injection wouldn't do the trick for the bite as it wasn't exactly clear what had bitten me. I was advised to report back to the clinic if my condition hadn't improved within three days.

I was between a rock and a hard place: even taking Inteflora tablets I always got a terrible dose of thrush from oral antibiotics. I'd already lost three days of potential earnings, business was slow and I really needed to be able to work to earn a living; thrush would put me off work for more than another week – a "thrushed" purse doesn't make for a "thrusting" purse! Then of course it would be period time again and I'd lose another five days.

Two days later I telephoned my priestly neighbours and asked if they could perhaps take me to the clinic as I felt I needed further treatment. The skin on my arm surrounding the bite had turned a liquorice-black colour and my joints had started swelling, particularly my knees; this was very painful and made it difficult to walk. My eyeballs and neck were painful, a fine blood-spot rash had broken out from my thighs down, and I'd started getting the rigors – freezing cold shakes – followed by the sweats.

Unfortunately, my neighbours weren't able to help me with a lift, so I phoned and left a message for Puff with Tammy. She was back at work, on day-desk duty – I hadn't seen her since the incident when I gave the client his money back. I then also left a message on Ivor's answering service as per our arranged emergency code – perhaps he could get me to the medical centre.

No one phoned back. In the morning I telephoned Rosemary in despera-tion; not having her own car at the time, she in turn phoned James for a lift, and they fetched me.

Admitted to hospital within three hours, in a general ward, I handed Rose-mary my switched-off cell phone and telephone book. James, thankfully, had taken General and Dancer home with him as I was more worried about them than myself, and actually didn't want to go to hospital at all. It seemed il-logical to me that a tiny insect bite could result in a condition which could prove fatal – but I don't think I was registering too well by then; I was just worried about General and Dancer.

The following day I was placed in high care on oxygen. Puff and Mrs D came to visit me that night, along with James who'd alerted them to my worsened condition – apparently Puff hadn't received my second message. I had given my house keys to James to check on matters that side and water my plants, and he brought me some yoghurt, juice and a burger as I felt in-credibly hungry. Puff and Mrs D arrived with toothpaste and a toothbrush and Mrs D, having some nursing experience herself, helped me with the oxy-gen mask and cleaned my teeth – oh, it felt wonderful having clean chops again!

The following morning a very kind young lady doctor gently advised me that I'd be moved to another hospital as I was in danger of going into res-piratory failure – they apparently didn't have the necessary equipment to save me if this happened. She remained religiously at my bedside, talking to me, holding my hand, wiping my face, giving me water to drink, even ac-companying me in the ambulance during the hospital transfer. I felt touched by her genuine concern and obvious desperate efforts to help me. Later that day, in septic shock and with pneumonia, after five excruciatingly painful arterial blood samples had been taken, I was placed in intensive care – alone, heavily sedated, on a respirator and unconscious for five days while the doc-tors tried to save my life.

James filled me in on the story after that. Apparently, he'd been told that I was critical, and to prepare for the fact that I may not pull through; he'd phoned my aunt Myrl and was also in regular telephone contact with Rosemary as to my condition.

Rosemary came to visit me in intensive care with aunt Myrl on several occasions – Rosemary posing as my aunt, aunt Myrl posing as my mother, as only family members were allowed. They both tell me they even pinched me in desperation to get some reaction out of me – nothing.

James, posing as my estranged husband, apparently sat with me for hours on end in intensive care, put my leg warmers on as he knew I hated the cold, and talked to me – no reaction.

The doctors advised all three of them that my children should be called to my bedside, and James telephoned Bert and told him to get the next flight to Cape Town. Then he fetched Mary-Lou from the boarding school.

In desperation, when James couldn't remember the third song I'd requested for my funeral (we'd discussed this on a couple of occasions when we were living together), he'd stuck my father's picture on the wall next to my bed and decided to think positively.

My aunt Myrl had phoned my mother (still living in the country outside Cape Town); apparently she'd broken her leg, which was in plaster, and her second husband was unable for some reason to bring her to the hospital to see me.

Of those five days I remember only a sensation of drowning in blackness – James says this was when medical staff regularly inserted a tube to clear the mucous from my lungs.

But you know the old saying – only the good die young! Perhaps a bang on the head with my little cast-iron frying pan would've proved more effective than the insect bite. I remember hearing Bert's voice at my bedside the morning I started to come round.

That night, Puff came to visit me in intensive care. James was sitting with me when I was advised my church minister was there to see me – and in walked Puff, complete with black Bible under his arm! That gave me a smile – he sure thought of everything! It was good to see him again.

James and Mary-Lou brought me the most delectable bowl of macaroni cheese with ham when I was transferred to a normal ward, and fed me – I've never again tasted it that good! And Bert, Rosemary and aunt Myrl visited me often. There wasn't a phone call from my mother or a note or card; I felt incredibly pained that she seemed to care so little about me – all I could think of were Meg's haunting words before her death: "I'm not really such a bad person, am I Maggs?"

Well, things actually now got worse – to say that it poured instead of just raining would be accurate! The night before I left hospital, Bert went into a sideways skid in the pouring rain, hit the concrete ramp on one of the highways, and wrote off my little car – prized frying-pan dents included! Thank

God, he was all right, apart from some pretty nasty gashes, grazes and bruising – mostly on his face, which was very swollen and looked exceptionally painful. I was eternally grateful he'd been wearing his seat belt; having Bert was more important than losing my little car. While he lay waiting for help at the scene of the accident, Bert's wallet and identity book were stolen off him. Luckily, he had his cell phone with him and phoned James, who fetched him and tended to his cuts.

No car, seriously ill and hardly able to walk, let alone work – well, that narrowed life down considerably for me; back to James I was, direct from the hospital. General and Dancer bounced all over me, so relieved – they were fine and happy; he'd taken good care of them during my illness. Bert flew back up country. Lock, stock and barrel, James forthwith packed up all my possessions, transferring everything back to his house. It wasn't the way I'd intended getting back with James, but he was thrilled to have me home again with him and nursed me back to health with extreme love and care.

Hardly able to feed or bathe myself, let alone wash my hair, I asked two of my friends, Grace and Rosemary, to do this for me at James's. Rosemary stayed over for four days to nurse me after I came out of hospital. I had repulsive, purplish bedsores, a blood clot in my right eye, my weight had dropped to fifty-two kilograms and my legs were covered in a dry rash of blood spots from my thighs to my feet. It took me six weeks to be able to walk up two stairs, one leg at a time; I was anaemic and my entire body peeled – including the palms of my hands and the soles of my feet, the skin of which James cut off with scissors!

Rosemary returned my switched-off cell and phone book; I in turn gave my phone to James, who advised all callers that I no longer "did escorting". Having no mobile phone himself, and with my complete agreement, James then took over my cell for use in his work.

There'll only ever be one Freddie Mercury, and one Queen. One afternoon during my long weeks of recovery, I crossed slowly to the hi-fi in my pyjamas, gown and fluffy slippers, put in the CD, selected the track and sat down shakily on the dining-room chair, my energy already sapped from such little exertion.

> "Are you ready for this
> Are you hangin' on the edge of your seat . . .
> And another one gone
> And another one gone
> Another one bites the dust . . ."

All that was left now, really, was to put my mind to building the business with James again, as we'd done together before I left him – as soon as I was free of having to stay in bed, and able to walk about the house normally once more.

That was what I did. Out with the files and on with life; Mary-Lou still at boarding school, coming home at weekend and for holidays.

I telephoned Ivor some weeks after coming out of hospital – he said he'd wondered what had happened to me, that he'd driven past my little house; he never got my message from his answering service when I urgently needed to go to the clinic. Our friendship then dwindled; forget the sex – it was the last thing on my mind, totally irrelevant, not remotely required. Ivor seemed disappointed in me for some reason; I distinctly remembered him telling me, before the move to my little house, that he'd never speak to me again if I ever went back to James.

I married James in early July, at a registry office in Cape Town. Towards the end of the month, my hair suddenly and rapidly started falling out by the handful, till I was almost bald. Standing at the basin in my bathroom, I stared in despairing vanity at my nightmarish image in the mirror.

> "Gimme a head with hair
> Long beautiful hair
> Shining, gleaming,
> Streaming, flaxen, waxen
> Give me down to there hair
> Shoulder length or longer hair . . ."

That was the Cowsills' hit from 1969. How much more can go wrong? I thought. The tufts of hair I had left, I had to have cut to about an inch. Being almost bald really put the lid on things. Of everything that'd happened since March 1997, this was the most difficult to accept and deal with.

One afternoon in August, while I was busy working on files at the lounge table, the cell phone rang and James answered. Sometimes clients would still call for me, having kept my number, and James would tell them I was no longer in that line of work. This time, the gentleman asked specifically to speak to me, using my real name, Margaret, which set James off wondering – I'd told him about Vincent – and he refused to leave the room while I had my conversation.

I had a strange feeling when James handed me the cell that afternoon.

It was a stilted, difficult conversation on my part. Vincent wanted to see me when he came to Cape Town – and as much as I'd have liked to see my Red Indian Man, my life had changed drastically since we'd been together. I'd no idea if he'd phoned before, because my cell had been switched off when I was in hospital, and then given to James for his use; the telephone at my little house had been disconnected.

240

Vincent was understandably confused at my odd response, though he realised I was unable to speak openly due to someone else being in the room with me. I'd nothing to hide, but would've preferred to discuss matters in private with him, to explain properly about my illness and everything. James, however, wouldn't budge; he sat in the lounge, listening to my every word.

"You've changed, Margaret," Vincent said, his voice pained.

I could only reply, "No, I haven't changed."

It was partly a lie – hardly any hair on my head, for one thing.

I never heard from him again after that, but I've no idea whether he ever phoned again as I didn't have the use of the cell, and didn't give him my new home telephone number. Maybe it was for the best. He'd just have to remain within my heart forever, my Red Indian Man.

When I was strong enough to drive a car again, I went to visit the girls one evening. I missed their chatter, their optimistic, courageous attitude towards life: relentlessly putting their lives on the line to ease the burdens in their day. And I missed their laughter, missed sharing my peanut-butter sarnies with them.

As I walked through the door of the agency, Tammy ran up to me and gave me a big hug. "God!" she said as we embraced, "Am I glad to see you, Granny! I thought you were going to die."

"What the hell happened to your hair?" asked Cindy, as she joined us and put her hand through my short, sparse dark curls.

"It doesn't look that bad," chimed in Denise kindly, to ease my wounded ego while she peered at my new hairstyle with a grin. "Anyway, she can always wear her hat, can't you, Rachael? You love your hat."

"Yeah, don't worry about it, Granny," said Tammy comfortingly, her hand on my arm. "Want a double whisky, on me, to celebrate? It's good to see you again."

I went to the bar with her as she poured a drink for us.

Cindy shouted from her seat on the couch, "Hey, Rachael, what's on the sandwiches tonight?"

"No sarnies tonight, I'm afraid, I'm just visiting to say hello," I shouted back. "I missed you lot."

"Okay, well, keep in touch," she answered with a grin, then added after a moment's thought, "Maybe you'll have time now to do your pencil fanny exercises!"

"Maybe you're right!" I replied, laughing.

Tammy looked at me as she handed me my glass of whisky. "That one! She never changes," she said, smiling, motioning for me to sit with her at the front desk.

It was good to see all the girls again, to have a natter and a laugh, and turn the music up a bit. I felt strangely pained again to leave them as I drove home, but this time I'd hung up my little frying pan for good. They'd always be with me, the girls, in my heart, and every night in my thoughts, as they sat waiting for clients to walk through the agency door so they could earn a living.

Chapter Sixteen
Imagine the Pearl

The 26th of January 1998 was my fortieth. I've always loved birthdays, but I wasn't sure how to grow old gracefully, especially with a one-inch long hairstyle of curls, mousse and gel. I had to admit, long hair suited me far better! And I'd picked up a considerable amount of weight, eleven and a half kilos to be exact, since I'd been so ill in May '97 – James had fed me plenty to ensure I regained my strength, and I'd taken quite a fancy to eating since then, quite unusual for me; seemed like my system was completely upside down.

"Coffee for the birthday girl," James said, as he put the mug down on the bedside table and gave me a kiss on the forehead. "Or should I rather say, for the birthday granny, now that you've hit the big forty!"

"Thanks," I said, sitting up, to find he'd placed several gifts next to me on the duvet. Our five canines bounced all over me and the packages – little wet noses, tails wagging like mad, barking, wanting to play their usual morning game. I just loved their enthusiasm, their never-ending joy, every day, rain or shine, and gave them all a good morning love. Yes, we now had five dogs – per special request, General had happily sired some beautiful pups with another lady's Maltese and we'd chosen a little female; she was about six months old by this time. Pa Dog ripped at my birthday present wrappings, gripping a package as best he could with his front paws and tearing the paper with his teeth in excitement.

"Quick," James said, "some of those are breakable!" Finding a spot to sit down on the bed amongst all the commotion, he asked, "Fancy breakfast in bed today?"

"That'd be great," I answered, as I retrieved and unwrapped my presents from General's clutches. There were presents from each of the five dogs, presents from James as well – I was really spoiled: four different ceramic piggy ornaments for the coffee table, a beautiful tall clear glass vase, Cadburys Brazil Nut Chocolates, bath crystals and a new CD.

"How about fried eggs on toast?" James asked amid the excitement and crinkled shredded paper. "Eggs, shall we say, fried in Granny's frying pan?"

I smiled, nodding. "Thanks, that'll be nice – with chutney, please."

The day brought flowers from James, and even flowers from my mother, delivered to our front door. A wonderful, scrumptious chocolate cake, baked and iced by James, was devoured to almost the last crumb as we shared it with our canines on the double bed. Bert and Madam Sophie phoned as well, as did Rosemary and Tammy, Grace and aunt Myrl; my mother drove in from the country to spend a few hours with us at lunchtime, and gave me some new wind chimes for my collection. It was nice to see her again; I appreciated the effort she made to see me on my fortieth. Her leg was well healed; that wasn't the real reason she'd been unable to visit me in intensive care in May 1997 – apparently she and her husband, who'd been decorated for bravery after the Second World War, had flown to England two days later to have tea with the Queen Mother at St James' Palace. This second marriage of my mother's had since ended and she lived alone now. I didn't ask questions in that regard – she seemed quite happy and content.

In the afternoon, the most magnificent bunch of forty large, deep red roses arrived from Bert, with his love. What a sight they were! I was speechless – as James would say, "For once!" – and my heart quietly sent Bert a message: "You've been and still are my greatest, most loyal friend – I love you, my boy."

Stepping out onto our front lawn, I held my roses up to our Mountain, for her to admire the sight of the forty perfect buds, tied together with shiny red ribbon. She smiled at me dreamily.

"Thank you for my children," I said to her. She acknowledged this quietly, waiting.

"Sophie says I've got another forty years to go." I paused.

She sensed I hadn't finished and remained patient, her long back straight and strong; ever encouraging, ever nurturing – a grey, sentry-like timeless presence of sand and granite cupping the shores of the peninsula which lay before her.

"But I'm tired right now," I continued to her silent strength. "I'm not sure if I can do another forty without a proper holiday. And I need to find the will to quit the pills, as well."

"It'll come," was her answer, carried on the gentle breeze. The sun danced gracefully on her great back, and as I turned to go inside the house, hugging my roses, she said, ". . . Margaret, before you go – do you still remember your pearl?"

"Yes," I sighed, as I stood in the doorway.

I stood in the peaceful silence and remembered the wisdom of "the pearl of life" – the words our Mountain had comfortingly whispered on the breeze to me on the night of "Granny's First", as she towered above the twinkling lights in the sleeping bay at her feet. It seemed so long ago. She was right: I needed to be reminded again of such wisdom.

"*The tears that fall are those that form the pearl in your heart, to sustain you on life's long journey . . . For now, be gentle on yourself; and remain patient.*"

And I just loved her – our beautiful Table Mountain.

James and I sat outside in the garden, later, having birthday sundowners. General was perched on my lap as usual, the other four dogs lying quietly on the still-warm brick paving.

"Cheers," he said, touching his glass to mine.

John Lennon played on the hi-fi – and the words of James's favourite song echoed gently on the idyllic Cape evening air:

"Imagine all the people
Living life in peace . . .
You may say I'm a dreamer
But I'm not the only one . . ."

Afterword

$\mathcal{B}$y the end of 1999, I was in severe depression and addiction to tranquillisers. In May 2000, a suicide attempt required paramedic assistance, hospitalisation and forty stitches. Dr Cohen referred me to a psychiatrist colleague; by September, at home but under medical supervision, I had quit my nine-year tranquilliser addiction. Simultaneously, I required six months of antidepressant medication. I remain, in 2003, tranquilliser- and antidepressant-free.

Mary-Lou now works with thoroughbred horses. Her training for this career closest to her heart was largely covered by the money her father, Terry, had left for her in a trust fund after his death. Bert now pursues a future sailing the oceans; James's business continues to flourish, just reward for his years of steadfast work; and I am a housewife, with our five dogs as my faithful companions.

The issue of decriminalising / legalising prostitution may well be put to the South African Constitutional Court in the near future – although at present, it is considered something of a hot potato! Decriminalising prostitution would mean that anyone involved in sex work – be it on the supply or receiving side – would not be committing a criminal offence. Legalisation means that, once decriminalised, a legal framework could be introduced to regulate the industry. For various reasons, I am of the firm opinion that although there will always be negative aspects to this oldest of professions – which will never be stamped out – the time has come to work with it instead of against it.

Amy and Christina have since found other occupations. Cindy met and fell in love with her very own "prince" (who hopefully has a strong back!) – she too has left the sex-work industry. Tammy continues, though in a managerial position, giving emotional support and guidance to the girls whose lives take a path through the escort agency doors.

To all the "working girls" out there, from Granny Rachael – take care, go safe, and remember: each and every day belongs to you as well.

Acknowledgements

First and foremost, I wish to express my sincere gratitude to Dr Annari van der Merwe, head of Kwela Books in Cape Town, for the enormous opportunity she has given me in publishing my work. To publish a story on a controversial, sensitive subject takes courage and strength of character – may this blessing that you have bestowed upon me return to you a hundredfold.

My grateful thanks also go to the young editor from England, James Woodhouse, who first saw the potential in my story – heartfelt good wishes to you on your successful (I have no doubt of that) journey in the publishing world.

To my final editor, Ms Henrietta Rose-Innes – we have travelled our own road together, through these pages, to what I consider is a successful conclusion of this work. Your efforts, dedicated commitment and talents have been of great value and are very much appreciated. Thank you.

To "James", "Bert" and "Mary-Lou", Aunt Tessa, my late Uncle Ron and Aunty Joan, and my good friends, who have stood by me and continuously encouraged me to pursue the possibility of having this story published, my thanks. I am eternally blessed that all of you touched my life so magnanimously. Despite my fears and lack of self-confidence, you have relentlessly had faith in me and my writing abilities, when I have had little in myself – you have been the soldiers of my soul.